DO ASK, *DO* TELL

DO ASK, DO TELL

Queer Life, Love and Culture Laid Bare

STU OAKLEY AND LOTTE JEFFS

BLUEBIRD

First published 2025 by Bluebird
an imprint of Pan Macmillan
The Smithson, 6 Briset Street, London EC1M 5NR
EU representative: Macmillan Publishers Ireland Ltd, 1st Floor,
The Liffey Trust Centre, 117–126 Sheriff Street Upper,
Dublin 1, D01 YC43
Associated companies throughout the world
www.panmacmillan.com

ISBN 978-1-0350-4207-4

'PADAM PADAM'
Words and Music by Peter John Rees Rycroft and Ina Wroldsen
WARNER CHAPPELL MUSIC LTD (PRS)

Pan Macmillan does not have any control over, or any responsibility for,
any author or third-party websites referred to in or on this book.

1 3 5 7 9 8 6 4 2

A CIP catalogue record for this book is available from the British Library.

Typeset in Questa by Palimpsest Book Production Ltd, Falkirk, Stirlingshire
Printed and bound by CPI Group (UK) Ltd, Croydon, CR0 4YY

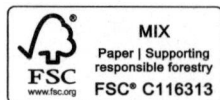

MIX
Paper | Supporting
responsible forestry
FSC
www.fsc.org FSC® C116313

Visit **www.panmacmillan.com/bluebird** to read more about all our books
and to buy them. You will also find features, author interviews and
news of any author events, and you can sign up for e-newsletters
so that you're always first to hear about our new releases.

For my queer and trans friends. I love you.
– Lotte

This book is for me. Throughout writing this book I've learned I need to be a lot nicer to myself so I'm starting here. Well done me, I'm proud of you.
– Stu

*Real knowledge is to know
the extent of one's ignorance.*

Confucius

*Padam, padam
I hear it and I know
Padam, padam*

Kylie Minogue

Contents

Introduction 1

1 Just a Phase? The Spectrum of Sexuality 11
2 The Male Gaze Gays 23
3 Lesbi Friends 37
4 The Gender 'Agenda' 52
5 Transformative: The Power of Understanding 65
6 Stone Butch Seeks High Femme 82
7 Serving Body 97
8 Fundamentally Frivolous?
   Understanding Camp and Drag 113
9 No One Is Alone: Our Queer Minds 128
10 The Portrait in the Attic: Ageing Disgracefully 145
11 Undetectable, But Does the Stigma of HIV Live On? 158
12 Just Like a Prayer: Queering Religion 174
13 What's Your Pleasure? 189
14 Three's a Crowd?: The Possibilities of Polyamory 210
15 YOLO: Why the Party Never Dies 226
16 Is That All There Is? 241

Glossary 247
Resources 253
Acknowledgements 257
Endnotes 259

Introduction

We're three spicy margaritas deep at a mutual friend's birthday party in Soho and feeling a happy loosening after a long week. We're gabbing, on a velvet banquette in a corner of the bar. It's been a while since we saw each other so we've got a lot to cover; our jobs, our kids, our respective spouses whose names both start with J and were born on the same day (weird), reality TV, upcoming trips, our mums, our pets, Botox, Ozempic, lesbian haircuts, Pedro Pascal – you know, the usual. Hours pass. It's 10pm and we're both thinking of the next day – the ballet classes, football matches and trampolining parties we've got to schlep the kids to. But there's word of a drag show and there's no way we're missing that. Shortly after refreshing our drinks and messaging J & J not to wait up, a glamorous queen with a blonde bouffant and wearing a sparkling gold dress takes to the small stage. We push our way through the throng for a spot at the front.

It's only then that we look around us. Wow. Everyone here is extremely (stereotypically) good-looking, white, cis, gay, male and in their early forties. We've known these guys for a while, and we love them, but they are all essentially the same type of person. It doesn't help that at least 80 per cent of them are called Andrew. They work in media, mainly, they're middle-class, able-bodied, neurotypical. They shop at Little Waitrose, think Mykonos is over, wear tight-fitting T-shirts, have a PT and will drop £100 on dinner without even checking the bill. They're single, child-free and always up for a good time.

We're like them in lots of ways, but we're also not. As a he/him with body and mental health issues, a husband of almost 20 years and with three kids under 10, and a she/they with a wife, a daughter and a penchant for a 9pm bedtime, sometimes our 'otherness' in such spaces creeps up on us. We ignore this feeling, most of the time, pushing it out of our minds with another cocktail. Maybe Drew, Andy and Andrew *are* different after all, plus they're gay so they must be, you know, like all of us queers, outsiders in some way ... right?

A spotlight finds the drag queen, and a hush falls over the crowd. The pianist plays the unmistakable opening notes of a Peggy Lee classic, and she starts to sing, asking herself, us, everyone in the room if that's all there is. At the chorus, we look at each other. We're both thinking the same thing.

It's a hot July night when we emerge from our basement shindig. Drunk queers are careening down Old Compton Street and we have last trains to catch, but something's happened. And we need to discuss it.

Is this all there is? No! God, no! Our little gay microcosm represents a single pixel in the spectrum of queerness. There's so much we don't know and that we want to know. There are gay people out there who are not called Andrew! What are we missing out on by settling for our lives and our friends being what they've always been?

It has become so much more common to broadcast opinions than ask questions. Whether you're at a drinks party, on a first date or posting on social media, there's a sense that you have to have it all worked out and be totally convinced by your own hot take on an issue.

Perhaps it's time to start saying 'I don't know', or even just 'I'd like to know more'. But delving into the unknown is daunting and it makes us vulnerable because it's hard to admit that we might be wrong or misinformed. These kinds of realizations are scary –

sometimes our deeply held beliefs have defined our sense of selves and the way we live our lives. It shakes our very foundations to challenge them, as though, if we loosen our tightly held ideas about people and the world, it all might just unravel – and then what?

Well ... then we learn, then we change, then we build up new, informed ideas, opinions and ways of understanding other people. We listen, we empathize, we ask more and better questions.

Do Ask, Do Tell is our attempt to understand queerness in a deeper way. To push against the limits of our own lived experiences and get out of our gay comfort zones. For the title we took inspiration from the US military policy 'Don't Ask, Don't Tell', which aimed to silence LGBTQ+ people within service in the early 90s by prohibiting discussion of queer sexuality, and which was ultimately ended by the Obama administration. We feel that with so much misunderstanding from outside the community, and from within, we need to break any silence, and more importantly we need to listen. To face the rising tide of prejudice and other challenges of the next decade and thrive, we are going to need to understand each other better.

We'd like this book to answer some questions for our straight and cis friends. Maybe you've got queer besties, an LGBTQIA+ child or family member, or perhaps some feelings about your own gender or sexuality are stirring somewhere within yourself.

Because even as queer people we too can be in danger of just assuming we know it all. That we are automatically well versed in our collective queer plight and we 'get it' – but do any of us? Do we really know what is happening in our LGBTQ+ neighbour's garden? It's time to get curtain twitching, people.

Knowing our limits

The beauty of being queer is that there is no one-size-fits-all. But this also means we are potentially limited by our own siloed experiences, which perhaps don't take into account the rich tapestry of LGBTQ+ life and the intersectionality within our community. Let's all challenge ourselves on the areas of queerness that we've thus far ignored, and attempt to fill in some gaps and address our deep-seated issues. For example, I (Stu) often feel like 'a basic vanilla gay' and the world of nightlife, which forms such a pillar of queerdom, yet is completely alien to me. Does this make me a bad gay? And what about queerness and ageing? While we're both heading into our forties, do we really know what will happen when we become OAQs (old age queers)?

As children of the 1980s and 90s, our own education about HIV has mainly been via traumatic film and television stories. What is PrEP and what does it mean to have HIV today? We need to find out. And on the subject of chasms in our knowledge, as a cis gay man, does Stu really 'get' lesbians and what it means to be sapphic? Come to think of it, why do some queer women hate the word lesbian? And does the word sapphic mean something different, or is it just a sexier synonym?

As boring married people (not to each other, mind), are we too judgemental about casual sex? What are our preconceived notions of what it means to be a trans sex worker? What exactly is polyamory and is it queer even if one of the partners involved is straight? Oh, we're on a roll now. What about being queer and religious? How can people reconcile their faith with their sexuality?

These questions are just the tip of the great pink iceberg we want to uncover. Ageing, HIV, drag, open relationships, religion, racism, body dysmorphia, hedonism: we're going there – literally and metaphorically, as we hit the frontline of queer experiences and head so far outside of our own comfort zones along the way that we'll need more than a pair of ruby slippers to get us home. We'll go from sticky dancefloors to churches, sexual health clinics, old people's homes and gay saunas.

Checking our privilege

We do want to be clear that although we are both cisgendered (neither of us is transgender; it is often shortened to 'cis'), a gay man and a gender queer lesbian, we are white, able-bodied, neuro-typical, middle-class and London-based. Our queerness is the limit of our intersectionality. Lotte, as an AFAB person (assigned female at birth – deux points to you if you already knew that one – Stu didn't; he thought it was a typo for *Ab Fab!*), perhaps has the upper hand when it comes to marginalized identities, but essentially, living in the Global North, we are both privileged in so many ways.

Neither of us have experienced any real issues while 'coming out' or have had any major problems with our families due to our queerness. We recognize that all these factors may further limit our experiences of the entire global queer spectrum. Therefore, part of our mission with *Do Ask, Do Tell* is to ensure we represent and listen to a diverse array of queer people. We are all too aware of the white, rich, stereotypically 'good-looking', non-disabled gays that for far too long have been the poster children for the LGBTQ+ community.

But can we ever really understand the hardships and joys inherent in communities outside our own skin colour and abilities? There are so many experiences that need to be lived in order to be truly understood, although we believe that shouldn't stop us exploring our ignorance and asking the questions that many of us simply don't even think to ask, potentially for fear of upsetting or offending.

The magic for us when writing our first book, *The Queer Parent*, was that we not only explored our own experiences of what it means to become, and be, an LGBTQ+ family, but we broadened our under-standing to learn about families outside our limited knowledge. By the end of writing the book we felt so inspired, enriched and enlightened by the queer people we spoke to, and this is what most excites us about this book.

We, your intrepid queer explorers, want to explode our own biases and delve into the deep ocean of LGBTQ+ life, love and culture, with you as our fellow passenger in our queer little submarine. And while we may sound a bit average compared to some of the fabulous characters we'll meet along the way, we do want to share with you the experiences we have lived and breathed because we hope you'll relate. We promise we are fun, and flawed, too!

For example, we'll get into the ups and downs of Stu's mental health and ask why, statistically, queer people are not OK and live with more mental health problems than the rest of the population. Lotte takes a look at her lifelong relationships with gay men as she unpicks the nuances of gay maleness. Stu's body dysmorphia opens up questions of the serious body issues that are rife within the LGBTQ+ community. And Lotte explores the butch and femme push and pull she's often felt as she lifts the lid on the labels that can box us in.

OUR VIEW: Using the Term 'Queer'

Before we continue, a note about the use of the word 'queer' throughout this book. We truly understand that this is not a term everybody is comfortable with, particularly if it was shouted at you in the playground by bullies. While Gen Z are claiming the term 'queer' to express a whole spectrum of the LGBTQIA+ experience, older generations remember it as a slur. Although, interestingly, on the flip side, we've also spoken to people who feel the same about the words 'gay' and 'lesbian', having experienced these as attacks, too. For us, it's a useful short-hand that encompasses the many gender and sexual identities we include in the book. We feel comfortable that we have wrenched the word back from homophobes and can redefine it as something wholly positive and inclusive. If it evokes unpleasant memories or doesn't sit well with you, we totally understand, but we hope you can find a way to accept its use within these pages.

We know it's going to be impossible for us to cover everything within our word count, but believe us, we'll try. If you read this book and think, *well, what about me, what about my unique queer lived experience?!* We see you. We want *Do Ask, Do Tell* to be an ongoing dialogue, so tell us! You can find out how to get in touch with us on page 259.

We also know that we're going to be covering a big range of terms and words, not all of which we were familiar with ourselves before starting this project. We've explained what these mean as we go along, but we've also included a handy glossary that you can flip to at the back, on page 248.

Why and who?

The landscape of queer politics, and issues arising from the relentless 'culture wars', are both constantly changing. As a community it feels like we are always taking one step forward and two steps back. At the time of writing our trans siblings are still continuously having to fight for their very existence and we don't see this coming to a happy fairy-tale ending any time soon. LGBTQ+ rights seem to be very much up for debate, and homophobic attacks are sadly on the rise. We have a long way to go to achieve widespread equality and a queer life full of security and freedom, both at home and internationally. We anticipate that whenever you pick up this book we will sadly still be facing prejudice from some, or even many, corners of the UK and beyond. Although if you are dusting off this book and reading it in 2094, and living life in queer utopia, please get into your glittery Time Machine, come back and tell us that things do, in fact, improve.

This ongoing prejudice means we need to improve our understanding of each other because, as history has taught us, we are stronger when we're united. There is power in holding hands, being able to look each other in the eye and feel that you know that person a little more than you did before. We like to think that all the different letters in the ubiquitous LGBTQIA+ acronym would have each other's backs when needed and know that we have their backs too.

This book is for the queers who want to know more about their fellow queers, but we hope that cis straight people will also find our own exploration of the LGBTQ+ experience insightful for their continued allyship. The whole point of the book is to hold up our hands and say 'we don't understand – tell us', which we hope will reassure our non-queer readers. It's OK to not know. It's OK to be curious and to want to learn.

One of the first people we spoke to after coming up with the idea for this book was Glyn Fussell, the man behind the legendary LGBTQ+ night Sink The Pink and the Mighty Hoopla festival. 'Queerness is a lens that enables you to look into the cracks and be in the mess,' he tells us. 'I don't think you deal with anything in the binary. Nothing is straightforward. You're constantly looking at the kinks of society, and that never stops. And I think that's why people refuse or are fearful of queerness, because it feels quite dangerous and scary. It's a Pandora's box. I feel queer euphoria because my eyes, my brain, my senses, my life has been opened so greatly to the world as it should be seen.'

Ahh – queer euphoria. The promised land! We wonder where we'll find ours. Will it be in a place of worship, a nightclub, a gym? What more queer joy is there for us to uncover on this yellow brick road of discovery? Because we already love being gay. We wouldn't change it for the world. Oh, the parties! The beauty! The humour! The culture! Drag! Pop! Camp! Lesbians! Why would anyone be straight (sorry, Huns!)?

We've always seen our sexuality as a kind of magic power. We're not just 'proud', we're really pleased we were born this way. We love how queers talk about sex and challenge norms with open relationships, and new ways of gender non-dependent parenting. We love that we care about dress codes, that we have friends who are two decades older or younger than us, that we will be the first to join a protest and be the last to leave a dancefloor.

So, are you ready to join us on this adventure as we lay bare queer life, love and culture, ask big questions and learn big truths? We hope so. Because one thing's for sure, our way of being gay is not all there is.

Two Become One

In order to tackle the sheer breadth of material we want to cover, we have each written different chapters in this book. It's meant that we've been on our own journeys and have chosen to write about things that either push us out of our comfort zones or resonate deeply as themes within our own lives. We've been on some adventures together, and where we have set off on a chapter alone, it's been fun coming back and sharing our experiences and learnings with each other. You'll see who has written what at the top of each chapter, and hopefully you'll get to know us and our different voices along the way!

Chapter 1

Just a Phase?
The Spectrum of Sexuality

Lotte

When I came out in the late 1990s you were either gay or straight, and if you were a lesbian you were either butch or femme. Bisexuals often got short shrift from the gay community and were pressured to pick a side.

Today, Gen Z embraces the wild spectrum of sexuality with far more nuance and creativity, finding a language to represent identities that exist in between the limited binaries we grew up with. Now, there are no 'sides' to pick, just a happily amorphous queer space that welcomes anyone – 'he', 'she' or the gender-neutral 'they' – who exists outside heteronormativity. Stu and I want in.

So, what's the difference between being 'queer' and being gay or lesbian? Well, for me, it's a more open-ended identity. It can be a way of saying: 'I exist outside labels. My gender may not fit pre-existing boxes in the same way that my sexuality might not.' It also leaves space to evolve as a person. To not be a lesbian who finds themselves attracted to a man and then feels that they have somehow let the side down, but to be a person attracted to another person and on a long and winding journey of 'becoming'. Queer is less finite and allows for a certain ambiguity that I'm increasingly drawn to. Queer leaves space for me to explore my identity without having to book a one-way ticket to Lesbos. As I approach forty-two, I've realized that my gender identity and sexuality are less fixed than I made them out to be earlier in my life, when I was so keen to make sure that my 'coming out' wasn't dismissed as a phase, that I neglected to enjoy the possibility that sexuality is in itself a series of phases that ebb and flow throughout a life.

How many of these sexualities have you heard of?

Androgynosexual: Attraction to androgynous or genderqueer individuals.

Asexuality: The official definition is 'lack of sexual attraction or interest in sexual activity', but this is quite limiting and asexual, or 'ace', as it's known, experiences are many and varied.

Aromantic: Having little to no romantic attraction to others, regardless of their sexual orientation.

Demisexuality: Experiencing sexual attraction only after a deep emotional bond is formed.

Graysexuality: Experiencing sexual attraction rarely, on a limited basis, or under specific circumstances.

Heterosexuality: Attraction to people of the opposite sex.

Homosexuality: Attraction to those of the same sex.

Lithsexuality: Experiencing attraction but not desiring reciprocation or a relationship.

Pansexuality: Attraction to people regardless of their gender or gender identity.

Polysexuality: Attraction to multiple genders, but not necessarily all.

Pomosexuality: Rejecting or being indifferent to categorizations of sexual orientation.

Sapiosexuality: Attraction based on intelligence. Although it's worth noting that this term has also been deemed problematic due to its ableist connotations.

Skoliosexuality: Attraction to non-binary and genderqueer individuals.

How do you know for sure how to label your sexuality?

New ways of defining sexualities are constantly coming to light and being integrated into popular language as the way we think about attraction, gender and sexual preferences evolves. I remember when my daughter's eighteen-year-old babysitter told me she was demisexual a year or so ago, having to fight my elder millennial instinct to be cynical and dismissive and instead try to listen with an open mind as she explained to me what that meant for her.

So often we default to negativity when confronted with some-thing new that seems, at least at first, to threaten our own life experience or view of the world. I think my initial eye-roll about this young cis woman, who incidentally had a boyfriend, labelling themselves proudly as 'demisexual' (something I'd never even heard of) and therefore 'queer', was rooted in my experiences as a forty-something lesbian. I had fought for the right to marry, to start a family, to have LGBTQ+ issues discussed at schools, and here was someone, ostensibly 'straight', pushing her way into my community because it's cool to be different.

I'm not proud of this reaction but I think it's important that I'm honest about it, as it goes to show that even the most open-minded LGBTQ+ people can struggle with some of the ways in which our community is evolving. I am pleased that I was able to control my facial expression sufficiently (Botox helps) to not give away my feelings and instead stay silent long enough to listen and slowly let the barriers fall that I'd erected around my opinions and experience.

By the end of the conversation, I was convinced not only that 'demi' was a valid sexuality, but that describing themselves as such had been a positive thing for our young friend. She had found a community and a way of expressing her difference and, essentially, if someone else is happy in their identity, how dare anyone try to pick that apart? I realized that I couldn't just appropriate this word queer for myself and not embrace the pantheon of new sexual identities that exists within it.

The way we think about and talk about sexuality has radically opened up over the past decade or so. Now there is an entire lexicon that didn't exist back when I first came out. If it had, I might not have been so quick to hang my Kangol hat on 'lesbian' and might have been through a biromantic demisexual phase or two first.

Is it 'just a phase'?

I understand why the term 'phase' has such a bad rep in the queer world; no one wants to have their gender or sexuality negated by someone who believes it is a detour on the journey back to cis heteronormativity. But what if that journey leads to somewhere else entirely, somewhere even queerer, and we give ourselves permission to take a few detours and try on different identities along the way?

I spoke to the psychotherapist Chance Czyzselska (they/them) about giving ourselves the space to explore our ever-changing selves throughout our lives and what it might mean to have fun with that, rather than worrying that to change is to somehow betray the person you had said you were.

I first knew Chance when they were known as Jane and edited the lesbian magazine *Diva*. I thought they were incredibly cool and someone I really looked up to in the media world, when I was a hungry young graduate looking for my big break in magazines. A number of years have passed since we last saw each other, Chance has retrained as a psychotherapist, moved to the coast and left journalism behind – although they still write and they most recently authored the book *Queering Psychotherapy*. It's so good to see Chance's familiar face pop up on my laptop screen. I'm reminded of that feeling of wanting to impress them when they were my boss. I wish I'd had more queer women and non-binary leaders throughout my career (though I'd inevitably have had a crush on all of them).

Chance and I chat for a while, and I get used to the shape their new name makes. It's not a hard adjustment but it is a conscious one. At least at first.

'I'm totally down with phases. I think phases are great. Whether that's a few years or a few months or even weeks,' Chance says. They then mention an idea explored in their book: that consistency is a cis myth. 'It is also, perhaps, bigger than that,' they add. 'It's a white, cis, heteronormative, patriarchal myth – this idea that we have to be just one thing. You know, there are so many ways in which white supremacist thinking manifests in what appears to be normal common sense. Viewed from that perspective, a changing identity can, for some people, seem like instability, or a difficulty of pinning somebody down, and we need to pin someone down because then we can control them, or then we can give them rules about how to live their life. There's this need for a map of how life should unfold, how being a human should unfold.'

We agree this is reductive and so limiting. We can and should be able to be whatever and go wherever we want in terms of our identity and sexuality. Chance recalls something a queer theorist called MJ Barker once said: 'We are all queered by life.' I like this idea. It's so true – whether we're talking about ageing, illness, becoming disabled, falling in love, grieving or parenting – these things push us outside the boundaries and binaries we may have once erected around ourselves.

Let's meet . . . MJ Barker

I do some digging and discover that MJ Barker is a 'writer, zine-maker, collaborator, contemplative practitioner, creative mentor' and someone I simply must track down for a chat ASAP! I'm desperate to interrogate my own changing ideas about sexuality.

Does a growing awareness of more 'niche' sexualities help us or does it simply encourage us to fit into even more boxes?

For me, trying to move away from binaries means always trying to reframe questions like this from 'is a thing good or bad?' to 'what does it open up and what does it close down?'

In terms of opening up, all the terms that have come into existence for different forms of asexuality/aromanticism, bi/pan sexuality, lesbian/gay identities, kink practices, non-monogamous set-ups, trans genders and sexualities and more, help people to realize that there is a lot more to sexuality than gender-of-attraction. Hopefully this means that people will be less likely to keep trying to make themselves – and others – fit into relationships and sexual scripts that don't fulfil them, or which actively hurt them. Additionally, this awareness means that people are more likely to be able to find like-minded communities – particularly with the proliferation of sexual communities online, so they feel less alone and more supported.

In terms of closing down, the risk is that each new community quickly develops rules and hierarchies about what a 'proper' person under that label is like, and what they should do. This can easily lead to people feeling they have to conform to new rigid norms, or feeling ostracized yet again from a community where they had hoped to find belonging. This can exacerbate shame and a sense of failure of never being queer enough (or trans enough, kinky enough, etc., etc.).

What's the difference between a kink or a preference and a mode of behaving, e.g., poly and asexuality?

Here we might delineate sexual attraction/desire (how we experience our sexuality), sexual expression/behaviour (how we act on our sexuality) and sexual identity (how we identify or name our sexuality). It's possible for these three things to be aligned – particularly if we're in a very supportive environment that doesn't police or punish diverse sexualities. For example, we might experience sexual attraction to more than one gender, we might enjoy sex with people of more than one gender, and we might identify as bi or pansexual. It's also very common for these things to be out of alignment, which is why research tends to find – for example – that up to two-thirds of people are attracted to more than one gender, but that a much lower percentage of people are sexual with people of more than one gender, and an even lower percentage actually identify as bi or pansexual.

Any aspect of sexuality can be an attraction/desire, an expression/behaviour and/or an identity. For example, this includes being kinky, being on the asexual (ace) or aromantic (aro) spectrum and enjoying multiple sexual and/or romantic partners. However, because of the emphasis in dominant culture on gender-of-attraction as defining our sexuality, we often see only sexual orientation as a sexual identity, and may see these other features as 'just' a preference/behaviour or an attraction/desire.

It would be great if we could move to a multidimensional model of sexuality that recognizes all these aspects of our sexuality as equally valid. It would also be great if, in enabling people to identify with them, we also emphasized that they are all fluid and can change over time, so that people didn't feel fixed in any identity. Some aspects of our sexuality may stay the same across our life, or long periods of it, while others may change radically over time.

Why are bisexuals so overlooked?

One sexuality that has been consistently overlooked and sidelined both within and outside of the queer community is bisexuality. I must admit I've only recently discovered that two of my newish 'straight' female friends are actually bisexual. I totally made assumptions about their heterosexuality based on the fact that I'd only known them to have boyfriends, but I wish I'd been more open and curious in my early conversations with them. I wonder if there's a sense that because I'm so loudly and proudly queer I take ownership of this space and quite like being 'the gay one' in a friendship group. Also, in the spirit of radical honesty, I have to admit to thinking that now there are these newer and hyper-specific terms to describe sexuality, there's something a bit prosaic about identifying as bi. Does 'pansexual' not have a bit more glamour about it? Does 'fluid' have a bit more zeitgeisty sex appeal?

If it was possible to press 'delete' on certain thoughts, I would be seriously activating that button right now.

Whatever has been going on in the depths of my psyche with this, I want to be a better bisexual ally and find out more. But before I do, it's worth setting out what the differences between bi, pan and fluid sexualities actually are. The fact is these terms can be used interchangeably, but often bisexuality refers to attraction to two or more genders, while pansexuality involves attraction to individuals regardless of their gender, emphasizing a more inclusive approach that transcends traditional gender binaries. Fluid sexuality is a broader term that encompasses a range of attractions that may change over time, allowing you to experience shifts in sexual preferences without being confined to specific categories. But language can mean different things to different people, so I wouldn't get too tied up on exact definitions and instead accept that all these identities can exist as the same, as different, or as something else entirely. Maybe it's time to queer our idea of dictionary definitions for hard-to-contain feelings?

Lewis Oakley is a bisexual activist who previously presented a show on Virgin Radio and he is a father to a teenager and two toddlers. I ask him what he thinks is at the root of the erasure of bisexuality.

'We have this thing in society where men and women are defined by their attraction towards men,' he tells me over a video call. 'So if you are a bisexual man, you're clearly gay. If you're a bisexual woman, you're clearly straight and looking for attention or to titillate a man. That's the horrible way that many people view it.'

Lewis tells me about reckoning with his sexuality as a young teenager. Because he was attracted to women, he mistook his attraction to men as 'wanting to be friends' or 'wanting to be like' the men he admired. It was only once he was at university and hanging out with gay friends and in LGBTQ+ spaces that he pursued this side of himself and realized it was of equal importance. He remembers being told that 'everyone decides in the end'. Meaning that once you find yourself in a committed relationship with someone of either gender, that relationship defines your sexuality and you are no longer bi. This is where bi-invisibility comes from. 'You just don't see it in the same way. But it's why, for me, especially now I'm in a long-term relationship with a woman and we have children together, it's so important for me to keep talking about being bi.'

I've always wondered if one person in a relationship identifies as queer in some way and the other as cis and straight (which is the case for Lewis and his partner), is it by default a queer relationship?

Lewis says, 'Yes, as a couple we are part of the LGBTQ+ community. There is someone in the relationship who is queer, so I definitely see it that way.'

He says he understands where this lack of empathy from the gay male community comes from. Many gay people do identify as bisexual on the way out of the closet, knowing that they *aren't* actually bisexual, but it is a way of coming out.

'This does two things. It creates this wider stigma in society about bisexuality being a phase on the way out to being gay. And then the other part, which I really have no tolerance for, is gay men who have done this and used "bisexuality" as an identity to hide behind, then they start thinking that every other bi person they meet must be doing the same.'

He points to statistics that show that bisexual people do worse in every measure of success. In a Stonewall survey[1] 59 per cent of bi people reported experiencing depression. And 26 per cent of bi people reported self-harming compared with 11 per cent of gay and lesbian people.

I go back to MJ Baker, who is bisexual, to ask if the LGBTQ+ community has got better at welcoming and understanding bisexuality in recent years.

MJ says, 'There certainly isn't the degree of profound biphobia in lesbian and gay [LG] communities that there was when I started engaging in bi activism. At that point – in the late 90s and early 2000s – we often still had to argue with organizations and societies to even add the "B" to LG, I was often asked to debate the existence of bisexuality, and I remember people in the crowd on Pride marches going silent when the bi group walked past, or singing "making your mind up"!'

MJ tells me that they agree with Lewis, that biphobia has not been completely eradicated. 'It is still common for bi folks to be lumped in with LG people in research, rather than teased apart – which can mean that any funding based on that research goes to predominantly LG groups and spaces rather than bi ones, even in areas where it is bi people who have the greatest need (such as mental health struggles).'

I wonder if asexuality is today where bisexuality was twenty years ago, when it was often delegitimized. I have to admit I struggle to understand asexuality's place within the queer community, because if being asexual means you don't want to have sex with anyone, are you just as 'not gay' as you are 'not straight'?

I feel instinctively like this isn't what I should really think. But I need someone to set me on the straight and narrow about it, or, more accurately, the queer and expansive.

The amazing activist Yasmin Benoit and others have done great work in improving asexual representation across all forms of media. Yasmin is especially vocal on being a Black asexual woman. In a piece she wrote for *Glamour* magazine in 2021, she said: 'Women like me will continue to be dismissed as unlovable, ugly, frigid and boring. This is especially true for Black women, who are so hyper-sexualized, that to be a Black asexual woman seems entirely contradictory to people.'

You might know what asexuality means (see page 12), but do you really understand why it is part of the LGBTQ+ community?

It's a question for which there's no definitive 'right' answer. I found lots of interesting research exploring this, but the conclusions are varied and essentially it depends on how wide-ranging your definition of queerness is.

Angela Chen, a journalist and asexual activist who's written a book on the subject: *Ace: What Asexuality Reveals About Desire, Society, and the Meaning of Sex,* said in a podcast: 'We don't want to take resources away from people who are trans or people who are homeless. It doesn't seem like this competitive thing to us. We're not saying we're the most oppressed, but we feel like we are in many ways outside of heteronormative, straight culture, and we want to build coalitions and we want to be part of [queerness].'

You might find it hard to relate to the idea of being asexual now, but it could well be something you explore later in life. Maybe it is a phase, maybe it isn't, but that shouldn't be the marker of its validity, or of its truth, or of its queerness.

I feel more strongly than ever now that sexuality is, by its very nature, an evolving, mutable force. It is so individual and specific, and yet also, so universal. I have a feeling that our current understanding of human sexuality is just the tip of the iceberg. Beneath the surface is fascinating unchartered territory. I just wonder if by mapping it, naming it and conquering it we do a disservice to its nebulous heart.

Chapter 2

The Male ~~Gaze~~ Gays

Lotte

I can get quite emotional, in a good way, thinking about my first experiences of being out on the gay scene as an eighteen-year-old lesbian among other lesbians. Because there was a gift we gave each other when our eyes met across a dancefloor. The possibility of sex, yes, but something else. Validation. To desire and be desired in return. To say 'she' when it was a story. To say *her* hot breath on my neck, *her* hands, *her* house. Maybe we'd slam into the toilets together. Or we'd come up out of the club for air, finding some doorway in Soho Square to kiss in, in the shadows.

It was the year 2000. I was eighteen and *out* in every sense, a veteran lesbian by then, having confirmed my sexuality sometime before my GCSEs. London's Soho was my playground. I started kissing strangers on dancefloors, circa Madonna's 'Ray of Light'.

That rush! I was young, hot and enjoying the heady cocktail of excitement and safety that comes from finding your people. Being gay was the best thing in my life. In many ways, it still is.

I might have been kissing girls, but my emotional connections were with gay men, boys – let's face it – at that time. I had a gang of them around me, and we'd go everywhere together, spend hours on the phone (these were the days of the landline) and plan our fabulous futures. Maybe we'd even have children together one day – wouldn't that be fun?!

I was *one of them* – the only difference was the gender of the people we pulled when we went out together. As I've gotten older, and become a parent (with an anonymous donor, not one of my many gay male mates), the differences in our life experiences have become more extreme. I used to be able to pass as a twink (a fresh-faced young gay boy, see page 26) myself. But while my friends evolved into twunks (hunky grown-up twinks), I didn't. After years of fertility treatment, my 'female' body has changed with age in ways theirs haven't. But despite the differences in our lifestyles and appearance today, these men are still my best friends.

Last summer I went to Ibiza with one of my oldest friends, Joe, a gay man, and a group of sixteen gay male friends, for his fortieth birthday. Crashing through waves as Formentera disappeared behind us, I lay on the stern of a boat and watched the sky slip on a softer evening blue. It was still so warm. Salt water splashed my bare chest. Joe was careering around looking for the last bottle of prosecco. The others lounged sleepy and sun-drunk on the deck. Andy, one of our university friends (I told you all gay men of a certain type are called Andrew!), joined me and we were silent for a while, enjoying the sobering slap of the wind. We were almost back on the island, where another night of gay revelry awaited. 'We're so lucky,' Andy said, lying back on his towel. I stretched out my arm so our hands touched. Lucky to be here. Lucky to be queer.

This little trip down memory lane might go some way to explain why I, Lotte, am writing a chapter about the evolution of what it means to be a gay man, and not Stu – an actual gay man. I have more gay male friends, have been out to more gay clubs and I am more comfortable around gay men than he is, for reasons I'll let him get into with you later in this chapter.

With gay men I've always loved the dynamic of us both being

queer. Our experiences of sex, life and relationships are different, but also so equally 'other' compared to cis heteronormativity. There is a fundamental difference baked into our queerness; and still a lot that we can learn from each other, particularly when it comes to who we have sex with and how. I enjoy this interplay of distance and intimacy between myself and gay men, and I think it puts me in a good place to investigate gay maleness.

So, where to start with the gays? I guess one thing I've always wanted to dig into a bit more is why gay men, who have historically been so ostracized and prejudiced against by heterosexual society, seem to have woven ways of excluding people based on looks and behaviour deep into the roots of their own community.

Is this what happens when men create an all-male microcosm without women to subjugate? A hierarchy of masculinity emerges where a sense of power and value can come from fitting into a particular tribe, and anyone who doesn't adhere to the rules of belonging is othered even from their own otherness. Have I been complicit in this in my own appropriation of gay male culture?

Why is gay male culture so tribal?

If you're a gay man reading this, do you have a diverse friendship group or do all/most of your fellow gay friends look like you, have jobs like you, earn the same kind of money as you, share the same kind of ambitions and desires as you? Do you like to mix up your social life going to different kinds of events, including more queer, non-binary or lesbian-centred nights? Or do you go to the same place every time because you know what you're getting?

Join the club

I wonder how many of these niche gay male identities you've heard of, or perhaps identify with yourself.

Bears

These are typically men who are larger in size, have facial and body hair, and embrace a more 'rugged', unshaven appearance. The bear community is said to have emerged in the 1980s as a reaction against the skinny, hairless pretty boy image of gay masculinity. Within the bear world there are further subsections of identity, including, but not limited to: cubs, which are typically younger or less hairy men; daddy bears, who are older, more mature bears within the community; and otters, who are generally slimmer and a bit less hairy.

Twinks

There is no single agreed origin for this term. Some think it's an evolution of 'twank', which was 1920s British slang for a client of gay male prostitutes (incidentally – what a great word!). Or it could be traced to the 1910s' use of 'twinkle toes', a euphemism for a gay man. Some also suggest it relates to the Twinkie – a cream-filled sweet treat that was created in the US in 1930. However the term came to be, it is now used to refer to young, slim (interesting how integral body shape is to these identities – Stu has more to say on this later) and hairless white boys who are relatively new to the gay scene. Of course, there are even more hyper-specific sub-categories within twink, such as 'twunk' – a hunky or perhaps more muscular twink.

Gay Geeks

Finally, one of the few gay micro communities that doesn't have body image or sex at the heart of how it identifies itself. Gay geeks are video-gamers, comic-book lovers, sci-fi and fantasy aficionados, or gay men with a passion for quirkier pursuits, such as Dungeons & Dragons.

Muscle Marys / Muscle Boys

Muscle Marys is one of those archaic gay terms that has stuck around because it's a fun way of blending ideas of femininity and masculinity and reclaiming the way 'Mary' has historically been used to demean gay men. Essentially, this refers to gay guys who live in the gym and are extremely 'built'. Steroids can play a huge part in building this kind of muscly body. One 2002 study found that 13.5 per cent of gay gym-goers in London were actively using anabolic androgenic steroids, or the synthetic versions of testosterone. Surprisingly, there are no more recent stats available but one can only imagine how this figure has risen in the decades since.

Daddies

Not all daddies are bears, not all daddies are actual daddies (though some are). Some actual daddies (hi Stu!) aren't gay daddies (because they aren't old enough). These are good-looking, older, 'silver-fox' gay men who might also be a bit of a father figure, have an appealing degree of financial security and a penchant for younger men.

Leather Queens

Gay men who are into leather and BDSM (a variety of often-erotic practices or roleplaying involving bondage, discipline, dominance and submission, sadomasochism, etc.). It might have its focus in the bedroom, but this identity extends from sexual practice to social life, clubbing and friendship groups.

While I appreciate it's nice to 'find your people', particularly if you feel excluded from mainstream heteronormative society, there's something about the above list of identities that is a bit depressing to me in its separatism. OK, sure, at Pride we see bears march with twinks and geeks and leather queens, but there's very much a sense that all these communities are together but apart. I'm reminded of what Chance and MJ Barker talked about in terms of the impact of white supremacy and patriarchy in our chapter on sexuality, even if our privilege stops us from recognizing this. For them, true queerness is a joyful rejection of all the systems of power that oppress us.

It's time to phone a friend. I need to get to the bottom (no pun intended) of Stu's distrust of his fellow gays. I know he's intimidated by my group of gay male friends – he's told me – and that upsets me because my friends would love him, and if he got to know them he'd see that they are just as riddled with anxiety, as complicated, silly and kind-hearted as he is.

I put this to him and he doesn't disagree. So come on then, let's get the origin story from Stu himself.

'I've never found myself within a "community" of queer friends, or indeed a group of gays. In my late teens I spent a lot of time with my best friend at the time, Tommy, who was also gay. We'd hit up the Brighton gay clubs together – and I document these disastrous years in Chapter 15.

'At university I knew no gay people and it took another ten years or so before I found another gay male friend in my life, my beloved mate Ollie. But even with Ollie, our common connection is more our job and "straight" friendship group, rather than being two gays out against the world. I'm always slightly envious of the friendships he has at his gay rugby club, but not envious enough to make the effort to join. Because honestly, Lotte's right, I find gay men, especially in groups, quite intimidating. I can never quite get past seeing them as gay "mean girls". And I'm not sure what came first, this intimidation or the fact that I've never found myself in a friendship group. Perhaps if I had more gay friendships when I was young I too would have found myself in a gay harem cruising around Ibiza in a boat with Lotte in tow.

'I think this intimidation has largely manifested itself out of my deep-rooted insecurities in both my body image and my camp-ness, things I discuss in depth later in this book, and again I wonder how different things might have been had I felt confident in my own skin, and able to be included in a gay friendship group. Part of me does long for a gang of queers, who look after each other, play together, cry together and, most importantly, a group that doesn't intimidate anyone outside their bubble.'

I'm pleased Stu's opened up and given me this context. But my challenge to him is that these guys don't intend to be intimidating, they are actually extremely sweet and friendly and they would have loads in common. Maybe he should get to know them more, rather than expect them to change the way they look or act to make him feel better. Oooh – are we having our first argument and it's only Chapter 2?!

It's a shame that Stu has missed out on a lifetime of gay friend-ships with people who could have validated him, lifted him up and made him realize what a brilliant man he is. I hope it's not too late.

Let's meet . . . Okechukwu Nzelu

Okechukwu Nzelu is an author and creative writing teacher at Lancaster University who has graciously offered to share his experience of being a Black gay man today.

I am a cisgender homosexual man. I don't know why I went for homosexual instead of gay. I'm very comfortable with the term queer. But I think it depends on context when it comes down to labels. I suppose I was trying to narrow it down. Because I think that if I were to just call myself queer, which I'm fine with doing in certain contexts, I think that elides certain differences.

It's kind of like the term BAME (Black Asian and Minority Ethnic). If I were anything other than Black and identified as

BAME that would be accurate, but it's only part of the picture, because I think there are different levels of privilege, or rather structural disadvantage, within BAME, just as there are within queer.

And even though there is a political reality, or political realities – plural – that unite lots of different identities and desires and orientations under the queer umbrella term, we don't all experience the world the same way.

I think for a cis gay man, even a cis gay Black man, it's very, very different from being a trans man or trans woman.

I became increasingly conscious of myself as a Black gay man as I got older. I went to Cambridge University, which is a fantastic institution in a lot of ways, but as a place, it is not as diverse as the world I was used to in Manchester.

I suspect I had a lot of shame about being gay. I had a very conservative upbringing and, years and years of therapy later, I can stand on the other side of that and look at it now. When you don't have role models who are from the same background as you, you absorb some of that homophobia, and part of you is always going to want to reject any models that you're given.

Coming into mainstream gay male culture, those niches or subcultures like bears, twinks, daddies, etc., didn't resonate, because I never looked like any of those categories. They are very white-oriented. The idea of a twink is very, very white. Even when I was that twink [twenties] age, I would have never identified that way.

I've experienced racism in lots of different ways and contexts, but I think one of the most shocking ways I've experienced it has been on the gay scene. I've been called the 'N word' on dating apps. It was very cruel, it was deliberate. I think it was someone I'd rejected politely. There's also a lot of fetishization, which I think people do not have the vocabulary to understand and to get to grips with.

If somebody fetishizes you and imposes their ideas of what they think Black people are like, that is not by mutual consent. That is someone's ignorance. My experience has sometimes been of white gay men who I grew up with just not understanding that we move through the world in very different ways. And not being sensitive to that.

One of the most frustrating things about being in the community of gay men is that a lot of the loudest, most prominent voices are wealthy, white gay men who think that because they feel powerful, all the problems in the world to do with homophobia and what gay men have gone through and go through today have been solved.

So is there a difference between being queer and being a gay man?

Is it semantics or cultural, or does it really manifest in a different lived experience? I called up Glyn Fussell, who we met in the introduction and who is a legend in queer nightlife, now doing great work raising money for LGBTQ+ charities when they need support the most with his trust, Pink Noise.

Glyn says, 'I think that you can understand your sexuality and not understand your culture. And I think that there's a real difference there. Because I know a lot of gay men that just attach their identity to their sexuality – to being a gay man, and that is an act of sexuality. That is them having sex with a man. There is nothing else. They don't know about our history. What I also love about being queer is it feels like we're part of this new force, this new way of thinking, and I see these amazing kids that are discovering and being able to come into their queerness from a really early age when you should be able to play and in a way that feels quite fearless. It makes me so hopeful for what is to come.'

So, for Glyn, identifying as queer is more political than being a gay man. But that's not to say that if you're more comfortable with the word gay than you are queer (as many of my gay male friends are) you're any less politically aware or culturally engaged. It's different for everyone.

When I told some of my gay male friends about Glyn's perspective, they slightly took issue with the idea that 'gay' is quite basic while queer is this evolved, sophisticated, enlightened utopia. My words, not Glyn's. I suppose all LGBTQ+ people are highly attuned to anything that makes us feel less than or left out, and I think the implication that there's a better or a cooler way to be gay and to party probably puts certain people's backs up. I know that's not what Glyn means, but I can see it from my gay male friends' point of view, too, and it worries me that there's yet another 'them' and 'us' emerging within our ranks – the basic gay versus the quirky queer. I think discussing this can help us all understand each other better.

And yes, some gay men are anti the word queer, not just because it's been used as a slur but because they feel it represents a culture they don't necessarily want to feel part of.

I met with an older gay man, who wanted to remain anonymous. He shared his views on this subject and I think they probably resonate with many and go to show the differences within our diverse LGBTQ+ community. He tells me:

'I think you have to earn that word "queer". I don't really understand why these straight people are coming along and going, *Oh, well, um, I'm a goth and so therefore I'm queer.* To me, what it means at the moment is political ideologies – some of which I agree with, some of which I don't. I don't want to feel that my sexuality requires me to sign up 100 per cent to a political ideology. I'm just a man who fucks men. I'd rather be a "f*ggot". Keep your politics separate. *Queer* feels like being sucked into a cult.'

I wanted to bring in my friend Tom Rasmussen (they/them) here. Tom is an incredible singer/songwriter. We'll hear more from them throughout the book, but their views on the word 'queer' are such a stark counterpoint to our anonymous interviewee that I had to share them. For Tom, queerness is a radical act, a protest. It is all politics. We were discussing Tom's exploration of their gender identity in performance when they told me: 'It's definitely mainly political. I'm quite bored of my identity. I'm much more interested in the idea of collective and shared struggles across identity markers.'

Tom believes the political part of queerness can be fun as well. 'I think queerness, polyamory, marriage, drag, transness, all these things – they're like commitments to hope and politics, and commitments to a better life. That comes through asking questions, going through hard realizations, being in a lot of pain in some ways, feeling really, really hopeless. But understanding that by asking another question there might be more hope, there might be more life, more love, more ways to keep the Tories out!'

Tom quotes the theorist José Esteban Muñoz, who said, '*Queer is always the horizon and never the shore*'.

Maybe being a gay man is to arrive in a fixed place, explore your sexuality under the cover of steam from a sauna, on a dance-floor, via a gay dating app or even at your local gay men's choir/football team/board game group, but remain unchanged or challenged by that experience. Perhaps being queer is about allowing sexual or gender-based exploration to change you, and for that evolution to be ongoing. Of course, what one person thinks of as queer and another as gay is impossible to police, and nor does it need to be. There's space for all these definitions, understandings and experiences, and with an open mind there's no limit to where such discussions could take us.

Gay as in happy?

It's interesting that I've been pretty down on gay male culture in this chapter when these are my people, my home! This is where I feel happiest! I am so grateful for all the gay men in my life and all the gay and/or queer men in the world generally – because how drab and unfun would life be without them? But it's often the way when you start looking closer at something you've just lived with or taken for granted for years. You notice a stain on the carpet, then suddenly you notice how terrible the whole carpet is, and before you know it you're redecorating the entire house.

Is embracing 'queer' the answer, or is it just painting over the problems in a glossy new colour?

I'm interested in the trans gay male perspective because I think transness is inherently queer and trans men challenge the community to reckon with their own ideas of masculinity, gender, culture and, well, dicks.

So what are some of the issues that trans gay men face?

Let's meet . . . Harry Nicholas

Harry Nicholas (he/they) is a trans masc writer and author of the brilliant memoir, A Trans Man Walks Into a Gay Bar.

Gay male culture quite specifically seems to want men to pick their team in terms of how they identify even within that umbrella of 'gay man'. What's your view of all this micro-segmentation of identity?

It's quite nice and affirming for me to register within these tribes because I didn't for a long time. No one would have seen me as an otter or whatever. But also, it can be really limiting. What I find fascinating is, on Grindr specifically, you can be a 'femme' man, but as soon as you say, 'gender non-conforming', suddenly that changes things, even though you're exactly the same person. If you're gender non-conforming, suddenly it's like, why are you on this app? You're not a man.

For the most part I think gay society is moving away from this way of thinking now. Ten years ago I'd get a fair bit of questioning about why I'm on an app like Grindr. But now, with more awareness and more openness about gender and sexuality, I hardly ever get questions like that any more. Gay men seem much more open to exploring and know that having sex with a particular type of body doesn't change their sexuality or who they are as a person. It feels really refreshing.

Which comes back to the differentiation between gay and queer, I think. And there perhaps being more openness to those grey areas within queerness?
Yes, and there's always been some disrespect towards femme gay men within our culture. The hierarchy thing is really interesting because I'm not femme, but some people would say that I have a female body. Obviously, there are the gold star gays [men who have never had sex with a vagina], but then as a trans masculine person, if you're grading people on how gay they are based on whether they have or haven't come in contact with a vagina or a vulva, then you're basically saying that I'm right at the bottom.

I just think the whole notion of that is quite disgusting and very outdated. But it is still used by some people to prove their gayness or eligibility.

Why are 'straight-acting' gays considered so sexy?

When I was in my early twenties the term 'straight-acting' was tossed around as the ultimate compliment. Looking back, I can see how and why we believed there was a 'right' way to be gay.

Take Will, from *Will and Grace*. He was rich, he was white, he didn't seem to have much sex, or really 'rub his sexuality in people's faces' (a term I recall hearing often). Meanwhile, his camp best friend Jack was the butt of the joke, he wasn't seen as aspirational at all. Coming out was about proving that *despite* being gay you were happy and successful. You weren't *that kind* of gay man, you know – camp or femme – you wanted nothing more than to pass as heterosexual.

It seems to me that shame is at the source of this. We have been so conditioned to see heterosexuality as the ideal, and everything else a deviation from that. If we could just *get* a hot masc boyf, or, even better, *be* the hot masc boyf, then maybe society will be more accepting of us. How sad. I really hope this 'straight-acting' thing is tossed into the attic along with the *Will and Grace* videos to gather dust so that today's twenty-year-old queers don't prize the performance of heterosexuality in the same way.

I wonder if gay men and their friends, like me, would really benefit from thinking more critically about the way we are participating in and defining the future of gay male culture. Who are we excluding, what binaries and biases have been appropriated from white, Western, heterosexual power structures and how might we be more radical and liberated in asserting maleness, queerness and desire today?

Chapter 3

Lesbi Friends

Stu

It's the edge of Friday night, I've put on some slap, and I am ready for a rare evening out. I'm meeting Lotte at the *DIVA* awards in Covent Garden. *DIVA* is one of the most iconic British lesbian publications, and their annual awards are an excuse for the great and the good of the lesbian world to get together. Lotte's asked me to be her plus one, as she's being honoured as one of the top 100 power lesbians of the year. I'm keen to quiz her on what constitutes a 'power lesbian', as I assume it's quite different to a power bottom.

I arrive at the swanky central London venue ahead of Lotte, another rarity, as she is always super punctual and I never am. I have two choices. I can wait outside watching in the shadows as glamorous people descend on the five-star hotel, or I can be a brave boy and head in alone to face the 'powerful' lesbians at the prosecco reception. I decide to throw myself headfirst into the proverbial lesbian lion's den with all the gusto of a gladiator going to face the roaring crowds of the Colosseum. Because what am I really expecting? If I close my eyes and conjure up a room of lesbians, what stereotypical images play through my mind? A group of fierce-looking women in power suits? Beefy butches in dunga-rees? A gang of Sporty Spice lookalikes in their smartest athleisure outfits? This is probably a good place to start asking why my go-to image of a lesbian is so reductively retro.

Because what I *am* faced with is a room of wildly different and diverse women and non-binary people. There are some proud butches and some stylish power suits, for sure, but it would be impossible to identify a single lesbian 'type'.

I take a glass of prosecco and think of how many times during my forty years on this planet I've been in a room with more than a couple of lesbians. You see, I can count the number of lesbians I know on one hand. Two fingers for two really close friends, three fingers for close acquaintances. And yes, I did just throw a finger reference into the opening of this chapter. Sorry. You see that's the type of gay I've traditionally been in life, always the first to make a camp joke at the expense of lesbians.

So, Lotte (and Sarah, my one other lesbian friend), for that I apologize. Perhaps this is the moment I can take a good hard look at exactly what my preconceived notions of lesbians are and try to atone for all the bad jokes I've made based on a stereotypical version of them over the years.

What's misogyny got to do with it?

With so few lesbian influences in my life, perhaps I have been led by the stereotypes I was confronted with in the late 1990s, when I first started engaging with LGBTQ+ culture. Namely, all lesbians love cats, hate men and move in together after a second date. These were the kind of reductive assumptions I grew up with, and the truth is I've not done the work to update my references, knowledge or understanding of this community in the years since. I don't have any statistics to prove it, but I'd guess that I'm far from the only gay man over thirty in this position. And it's time I – it's time *we* – did something about it.

Old-fashioned lesbian stereotypes seem, to me, misogynistic

in their origins. In a patriarchal society, women who don't need men are threatening, and must be othered and undermined, something that doesn't necessarily happen on a conscious level. So how did I, a boy who always felt more like one of the girls, still end up letting these kinds of views go unchallenged? It might seem obvious, but our gender, and how this influences the way we move through the world, creates a fundamental difference between gay men and gay women, despite us both being *other*, and both being queer. We experience life and the world very differently.

Helen Scott, the author of *Live, Laugh, Lesbian*, a guide to navigating life as a lesbian in the twenty-first century, joins me on a Zoom call from her home in Hebden Bridge. After she enlightens me about the queer hub that exists in her Yorkshire market town (it has the highest number of lesbians per head in the UK, with crochet and quiz nights galore, apparently!), she tells me that it's rare to find a straight man who can just be normal around lesbians, as so often lesbians are reduced to sexual objects for a man's pleasure. It makes me see how exhausting it must be to carry all the shit a lesbian has to carry: to not only have to deal with all the challenges that being queer can bring, but also all the other monumental heaps of crap that women face daily: the risk of unwanted sexual attention or even assault, workplace discrimination, the pay gap, unequal distribution of labour in the home and being generally objectified. These are parts of life that I, as a cis gay man, can't truly understand, no matter how much I might see myself as an ally and equal to the females in my life.

So 'dip me in chocolate and throw me to the lesbians', as the Pride favourite T-shirt slogan goes.

Lesbian culture: What are gay men like me missing?

The morning after the *DIVA* awards, while Lotte rustles up some breakfast, I try to select a perfect Saturday morning playlist. I decide to mark my metaphoric arrival in the Isle of Lesbos (a place I'm now determined to explore in full) by playing the most famous, surely, lesbian icon of them all, and someone I've never listened to – k.d. lang. Four songs in to the Spotify playlist and I think I'm already sold, she's great! But soon enough Lotte comes running into the living room, a look of utter disgust on her face. 'k.d. lang?!' She screams at me. 'Are you kidding?!' She stares at me incredulously. 'Yes, she's an icon, but if you want to understand the lesbian renaissance that's happening *right now*, listening to k.d. lang is like trying to understand lesbian romance by watching Beth kiss Margaret in that 1994 episode of *Brookside*.' She gives me a familiar look which I know to mean that a rant is on its way, so I turn off the music and let her say her piece.

'Today lesbian culture is having a major moment. In many ways it *is* the culture in a way gay maleness has been for a while now, and I'm so here for it. Because, yes, there were years when listening to k.d. lang and clinging on for some sad sack in a soap to have a scandalous sapphic snog, in between flicking to the sexy bits in a Sarah Waters' novel, were the limits of our lez representation. Now, you've got Romy filling stadiums with her emotional lesbian dance bangers. You've got Reneé Rapp bringing her girlfriend on stage at Coachella. JoJo Siwa declaring she invented gay pop (girl, please!), Chappell Roan being Chappell Roan, Kristen Stewart in her sexy dyke era – making movies that celebrate lesbian love. Not to mention lesbian dating shows on the BBC no less and countless queer female characters on TV. There are even lesbian mum polar bears in *Peppa Pig*! Our national women's football team features a number of out lesbians, our favourite TV and radio presenters are too. One of the most popular artists of our age, Billie Eilish, is out there saying, 'I've been in love with girls for my whole life' and riding a truck into a pile of knickers in a Charli XCX video. Oh, and you can't move for lesbian love stories in your local bookshop (as you know, Stu, my first novel *This Love* is one of them!). Lesbians are taking the zeitgeist by its collar, throwing it down on the bed and making sweet love to it. So, friend, I appreciate your efforts to embrace lesbian culture, but get with the programme. Lesbians are (finally) cool!'

OK, I nod nervously as I watch Lotte step down from her lesbian pop culture soap box, my hands shaking slightly as I reach to quickly change the music.

If I really think about where my preconceived ideas of lesbian culture come from, one TV show has a lot to answer for. When I was thirteen, the US sitcom *Will and Grace* hit our screens in the UK. It was incredibly formative for me as a young gay teen. Here were two attractive, successful, affluent and funny gay guys on TV. In a world with so little representation, suddenly we had two role models, even if, perhaps problematically, one was sanitized and straight-acting, and one was the camp butt of the jokes. And that wasn't the only issue. Looking back now, so many of the jokes were tinged with attacks on our own community, especially lesbians. 'Billie Jean King!' yells Jack as he holds a script in his hand, in one episode, 'There are lezzies in this! Please let them be played by men. No one will know the difference,' he exclaims to rapturous audience applause. In another, Jack addresses a group of people ahead of a presentation he is about to make. 'Before we begin, I would ask that you refrain from the taking of flash photography as the lesbians may attack you.' For the sake of honesty, I'll admit, I did originally titter at the last one until Lotte reminds me that 'the insinuation that lesbians are aggressive is not cool'. She's right and, with no fully fleshed-out lesbian characters within the show, these jokes just become incredibly mean.

'It doesn't feel like lesbians are in on the joke,' says Lotte. 'They were being laughed at, not with.' So, is *Will and Grace* partly to blame for encouraging a generation of gay men to make bad lesbian jokes? We could ask the same about an equally formative show, *Queer as Folk*, a drama from Russell T Davies that took the world by storm when it aired on Channel 4 in 1999. In her essay in *The New Queer Aesthetic on Television*, edited by James R Keller and Leslie Stratyner, Rebecca Beirne highlights that even in that show 'lesbians are present, but they are routinely situated as the converse of "queer" and are subjected to a great deal of misogynist and lesbiphobic dialogue.' *The L Word*, probably the most well-known lesbian show on TV, did not have a large gay cis male following (I'm going to watch it, Lotte, I promise!).

Back at mine, later that weekend, I decide to settle on Billie Eilish's album *Hit Me Hard and Soft* as background music for more of my lesbian cultural research. And as I listen to the coolest Gen Z icon singing 'I could eat that girl for lunch, yeah she dances on my tongue', I see where Lotte was coming from – lesbians are fucking cool. I need to fully reboot everything I thought I knew about them.

Is there such a thing as a lesbian twink?

So, what are the lesbian tribes[1] I need to know about and are these categories actually helpful? The answer, according to Helen Scott, is that they are. She points out that straight people don't have labels in the same way. 'They don't need to define themselves in a society that accepts them for who they are. As a minority, it's helpful for us to define the type of person that we are to easily connect with other people like us.' I get it. I mean, us gays also love to tick boxes and lean into stereotypes that define our particular flavour of queerness. After all, feeling that we belong to a clique can help us find, then further explore, our identities.

'Because we are othered,' adds Helen, 'it's important for us to be able to identify with somebody who is the same as us because we need to feel that sense of belonging and understanding. So, labels are important, not for everyone, but definitely for when you first discover you feel something other than straight or cis. They can also be super helpful for learning about the community as a whole.'

Let's Go, Lesbians! Choose Your Lesbian Fighter
Cottage Core Lesbian

A lesbian who lives a very cozy life, maybe in the country-side, and her wardrobe perhaps has a flourish of Laura Ashley about it. She has a vegetable patch to maintain, and I'm also envisioning some jam-making. Think the WI, without the conservatism.

Golden Retriever Lesbian

According to Helen, this is someone who tends to be more on the masc spectrum, but they've probably got longish hair, they wear beanies and they're just so happy to be here. Just living life, out with their mates and loving their girlfriend. They want to please whoever they are with.

Black Cat Lesbian

Apparently a Golden Retriever's girlfriend is likely to be a 'black cat lesbian'.[2] This is a lesbian who, according to *PinkNews*, 'shares tendencies with the elusive black cat. This lesbian is femme, mysteriously sexy and can sometimes be a bit of a mean girl – if you get on the wrong side of her.' The social media star Rosie Turner adds, 'You're probably going to find your black cat lesbian on the sofa watching a murder docu-mentary, painting their claws or reading horoscopes under a blanket.'

Lipstick Lesbian

Lotte helps me out with this one, explaining that the term is typically associated with a lesbian who embraces their glamorous, feminine side and wears, you guessed it – lipstick! Although this term has been around for decades and was popularized in classified ads where a 'lipstick lesbian' might be 'looking for love', it was used again in the early noughties with the release of the TV sensation *The L Word*. The show featured feminine lesbians in LA living, laughing and loving (as the iconic theme tune went) in relationships with other (mainly) femme lesbians. It spawned an era of queer women embracing their femininity. According to Lotte the term's pretty outdated now, and women would use the term 'femme' instead.

Baby Dyke

A baby dyke is probably most closely aligned with a gay twink (go back to Chapter 2 for education on this one . . .). While it references the historically derogatory term dyke, it's considered affectionate when used by lesbians to describe someone who is still exploring or learning about their new-found lesbian status. Cue lots of older lesbians flocking round to share their lesbian wisdom.

Power Lesbian

Now, my LBF (lez best friend) is officially the UK's 99th most powerful lesbian, so I'm confident I know what this one's all about – it refers to successful, high-powered lesbians in business or politics who tend to project a strong, confident and professional demeanour. Like a CEO who can run a Fortune 500 company by day and host a flawlessly curated dinner party by night.

> **Boi**
>
> A lesbian boi is what we used to call a tomboy. She's boyish, handsome and favours a beanie and baggy jeans. She's mastered the art of the 'soft butch smirk', can rock a white vest and blue jeans better than Troye Sivan, but is possibly a bit of a heartbreaker.

Do lesbians secretly love lesbian stereotypes?

The night I stayed at Lotte's I did sleep with two cats on my bed, noticed a wardrobe full of power suits, *and* I even spied the strap of a pair of khaki dungarees spilling out of the laundry basket. 'Of course there's truth in these stereotypes,' Lotte laughs when I put this to her. 'And lesbians will be the first to take the piss of ourselves. The problem comes when people think these dykey signifiers are the limit of us or that these tropes apply to all lesbians, many of whom do not fit into any stereotype at all.'

Lotte tells me about in-joke lez stereotypes, like how you can tell a lesbian by their fingernails, a lesbian manicure – short for her pleasure, I guess! She says it's true, often, that lesbians move in together pretty quickly after meeting, probably because of the intensity and emotional honesty that women are more prone to than men. And then – now this is a new one on me – there's the lesbian obsession with, of all things, a carabiner (yes, that clip you use when camping or rock climbing!). In her blog 'Lesbians and Key Rings: a cultural love story', writer Christina Cauterucci says, 'look to the waistbands of any modern-day gaggle of queer women and you're liable to find a critical mass of jingling metal attached. The belt-side key ring is one of the most enduring sartorial symbols of lesbian culture, one of the few stereotypes of our kind that's both inoffensive and true.' The lesbian pop star Romy even sells neon branded ones at her gigs as a little wink to her lesbian fans. I'll never look at a branch of Mountain Warehouse in the same way again.

And while we're on the subject of stereotypes, let's talk about cats. Where does the idea that all lezzers love cats come from? Rachel Corbman, who curated an exhibition called 'The Wide World of Lesbian Cats', said to *Dazed* magazine that 'Cats are connected with deviant forms of femininity like witches, spinsters, and lesbians. So, when you see cats come up, the pejorative assumptions are kind of reclaimed in a way, like in the way that "dyke" is reclaimed from being a slur against lesbians.'

Is lesbian a dirty word?

So, we have all these different descriptions and types of lesbians, but what about the word itself? I definitely get the vibe that a lot of . . . um, lesbians . . . are not exactly fond of the word. In fact, I noticed a while ago that whenever I would use the word around Lotte her mouth would slightly twitch at the corners and her eyes would narrow slightly. On BBC's *I Kissed a Girl*, the lesbian dating reality show, they also raised this very point with the contestant Georgia, explaining, 'It is a word that has been taken and made negative. Growing up, it was used in a way that suggested something was wrong with you.'

Having had similar experiences myself at school with the word 'gay', I can understand these viewpoints. I try to think of the times I identify myself or say the words 'I'm gay'. Maybe I don't? I personally have never felt the need to identify myself out loud. My voice, my mannerisms and my fabulous style (ha!) do that for me. Do I hold back from using 'gay' because of the way the word was previously twisted, and still is?

It's fascinating how language is so circular and personal to whatever has been used against you as an insult. Andrew Haigh covers this beautifully in his gorgeous queer film, *All of Us Strangers*. Andrew Scott's character tells Paul Mescal's character that he 'can't get used to calling myself queer, it was always such an insult.'

To which Paul Mescal's character, who is younger, responds, 'But it's probably why I hate the term gay now. "Gay" meant lame and shit, "those trainers are gay", "that haircut's gay", "your school bag's gay".' From this point of view, I totally get it. But what is clear is that not everyone feels the same.

I ask Lotte, what is it about 'that' word? She says, 'I think, for me, "lesbian" just isn't a nice-sounding word. Like *scrape*, or *moist* – the onomatopoeia is a bit off-key. I also don't love how it's used as a noun; "She is *a* lesbian", rather than an adjective; "she is queer". Personally, lesbian is too specific an identity for me. There was a time when I really liked that, needed it even to prove how not straight I was. Now, in my forties, I feel more fluid and open-minded about my sexuality and gender identity. So lesbian feels like it doesn't offer enough space within it to be everything I might want to be.'

Increasingly, I've heard the word 'sapphic' be used – sometimes interchangeably with the word 'lesbian'.[3] It comes from the Ancient Greek poet Sappho, who lived on the Isle of Lesbos, and it refers to romantic, or sexual, love between women. It's always been strongly believed that Sappho loved other women, and that's also where the word lesbian comes from because she was a 'Lesbian', aka from Lesbos. It's often been used as a bit of an academic way to describe books, art and culture written by and/or for queer women, but now it seems to be breaking into the mainstream.

Maryann Wright is the founder of Sappho Events, an organization that creates sober and inclusive events for queer women, trans and non-binary people. She shared some interesting thoughts with me on the word 'lesbian', and why she chose not to use it for her business. 'There are older women in the community who are fierce lesbians,' she tells me. 'They would never consider using the word queer, because that was a derogatory term that was yelled at them when they were younger. But for me personally I use queer and set up Sappho Events as our name because I see Sappho as our beautiful gay godmother, and because I find lesbian as a term, shocking. Perhaps it's because somewhere in my Catholic child-hood brain a lesbian is such a bad thing to be. Queer softens the edges for me and opens the idea of sexuality as a spectrum.'

Lotte sends out a bat signal (or should that be *cat* signal?) to some of her lesbian friends, asking for their opinion on the word. Kate in Cornwall comes back to tell us that when she first came out she would have used the term 'gay woman' over lesbian. 'I was uncomfortable with the word,' she explains. 'Even now, sometimes I might say lesbian in a weird voice, but I'm proud really to say I'm a lesbian because it represents who I am. I think it is being cham-pioned again and given new life, and I feel it truly represents who I am: a cis woman attracted to cis women – if that's the right terminology. I hope there's a way for the word lesbian to be used without hurting anyone or being complicated, so we can support our trans sisters while still having our own identities. The word resonates with me because of its history, as complicated as that may be. I hope it can have a fresh start.'

I also hear from the journalist and presenter Hattie Collins, who has just turned fifty. 'I am a recent convert to the word lesbian,' she tells me. 'There's so much to be proud of in it. In recent years, though, the word has become vilified for various reasons. More recently, I feel it's because of the opinions some lesbian people have expressed about trans people, which has created a connection between being a lesbian and being possibly transphobic. But I've noticed, particularly with the younger gener-ation (who typically favoured the more inclusive "queer"), that currently there's this real celebration of the words lesbian and dyke. It feels very inclusive and wonderful, with anyone under the queer umbrella – female, non-binary, trans male – able to identify with these words. I have no issue with people who don't want to use the word, and I totally understand why it's not comfortable for everyone or why it doesn't describe some people's identity or sexuality. But for me, it's a word worth celebrating, and I'm much more proud to use it now.'

'I'd say [part of] my pride in being a lesbian comes from the rise in discussions around fluidity,' adds Jacqs (they/them), a twenty-two-year-old lesbian who came calling to Lotte's war cry. 'I'm proud to specifically say I'm a lesbian rather than using terms like sapphic or queer. There's nothing wrong with those terms for others, but for me, it's important to hold on to the word "lesbian". Bi women can relate to lesbians, but they can also relate to straight people. Lesbians don't have that same privilege. It's not fair to expect lesbian experiences to be grouped under the term "sapphic". Some things are specifically lesbian things, and that's OK. As for how my other identities intersect with being a lesbian, being Black is definitely a part of that. I experience racism and colourism within the community, especially from light-skinned or mixed-race people. The background I come from is also homophobic and lesbophobic, so I feel more myself outside of home. It feels like a rebellion to say, "Yes, I am Black, yes, I am dark-skinned, and yes, I am a lesbian." I'm allowed to be all of those things at once.'

'Being Black also influences how I present as a lesbian,' adds Jacqs.[4] 'The Black community has created many different aesthetics, and I might align with certain aesthetics that non-Black people don't. People often expect LGBT people to be white, so they might not recognize me as a lesbian because I don't fit that stereotype. For example, when it comes to expressing masculinity, non-Black people may use hairstyles like the shag or mullet, but I can't do that with my hair. It looks very different. I sometimes use extensions to express masculinity through loc styles, which is a unique way for me to express my lesbian identity as a Black woman.'

If you're interested in Black lesbian masculinity, read on, as we explore 'studs' in Chapter 4.

Helen, Hattie, Jacqs, Maryann, Kate and Lotte have different views of the word lesbian, and it's clear some definitions are more trans-inclusive than others. Like many words in our evolving queer dictionary, there's not one definition that can be 'right', but it's inspiring to hear that more and more women are reclaiming 'lesbian'. 'I am a woman who loves women and I'm over the stigma of the word lesbian,' says Helen. 'People need to hear the word. They need to say it to remove this stigma.'

Maryann sums it up: 'Language is just such an evolving thing, and just when you think you're done, it's never done.'

Gays and Lesbians. Time to unite?

So, as I jet off home from my time spent enjoying the nooks and crannies of Lesbos, I think back to why I've never felt a super-close kinship to a lesbian before Lotte walked into my life a few years ago. And even if it's not 'beef' necessarily, then perhaps there is some sort of historical gay/lesbian divide that's somehow subconsciously always held me back? Are we two different groups linked by some aspects of our sexuality and identity, but worlds apart in terms of our lived experiences? In a *HuffPost* article titled 'Gay men, lesbians and the ocean between us', the journalist Tyler Curry says, 'Gay men and lesbians feel isolated from one another because we are two completely different animals who are forced to share the same cage.'

And the journalist Michael Musto portrays it more poetically than I ever could in his *OUT* article headlined 'Why Don't Gays and Lesbians Get Along Better?'. He aligns our relationship to one another as 'a string of villages that rarely connect, even on the battlefield.' The article was written over a decade ago, and while on the one hand there's a huge change in the popularity of cool lesbian culture among gay men, and straights for that matter, the divide between us does still exist in many areas. I also feel it would be a mistake to assume that the misogyny that underpins the othering of lesbians by straight men doesn't rear its head from gay men too. But with the fluidity of labels and the very idea of queerness continuing to evolve, I wonder whether this so-called divide between us will continue to shrink in the generations to come? Here's hoping.

Looking back to my night at the *DIVA* awards and being in that room full of 'power' lesbians, I realize I've been to a few gay men's magazine awards and, honestly, I never come out of them feeling good about myself. To me, and, yes, maybe this is my own insecurities talking, but it feels like a gay version of *The Hunger Games*, with each man trying to outdo the other in terms of how loud, funny or fabulous they are. Spears and swords have been swapped for loud suits and heels. But there was a really sisterly vibe to the lesbian celebration, women and non-binary people of all types – black cats, Labradors, baby dykes and Sandi Toksvig seemed to be genuinely rooting for each other in what felt like a really non-judgemental way. Maybe that's the thing us gay men could learn from our lesbian friends; a sisterly bond. I think I'd definitely benefit from attracting some more lesbians into my life. Perhaps adding a carabiner or two to my keyring is a good place to start.[5]

Chapter 4

The Gender 'Agenda'

Lotte

It's quite easy to exaggerate when you're fearful of something. *The turbulence was horrific! The spider was enormous! Everyone was staring at me!* I've said all these things at one time or another, in an effort to justify my anxieties and force someone to empathize with my perspective. Even if the spider was perfectly average-sized, I need to make it seem enormous or I feel a bit silly for being scared of it.

I believe this might be at the root of the sweeping statements and wild exaggerations we so often hear about trans people and gender identities. 'Children as young as five are being encouraged to transition' is one such statement I've heard people share casually in conversation. Or the bonkers theory that originated among parents in the US and then became a nonsense story in the UK that kids are identifying as animals and teachers are putting litter trays in classrooms. I was astounded that this rumour made it to the parents at Stu's kids' swimming class, and I quickly pointed him towards the episode of the Jon Ronson podcast *Things Fell Apart*, which debunks this conspiracy while placing it in the context of the wider culture war. In the programme Ronson concludes, 'The litter box story is a reminder that we can all fall for moral panics and that the stronger a person's conviction, the more likely they'll succumb to untruths.'

When you feel personally attacked, like someone is coming for you and your precious identity or way of life, it can seem like you're surrounded, and so you react negatively. You think in absolutes, so an individual one-off experience becomes representative of a far greater problem. Specifics don't matter, generalizations and unfounded statements express your feelings better than the truth does.

But why is it that gender has become the fulcrum of this in society? What is it about identifying as male, female, non-binary or something else entirely that creates such fear and hysteria among certain people?

Why does gender evoke such divisiveness?

I remember when I first discovered Judith Butler's *Gender Trouble* as an English Literature student. It was so brilliant and Earth-shattering for me to consider gender as a performance, which is one of the central arguments of the book. I wrote lots of very earnest essays about it and read texts from Shakespeare, to Dickens to Philip Roth through this lens. I felt like I had been given access to this deeper way of understanding the world, and it really was foundational to my thinking and writing in later life.

In *Gender Trouble*, Butler challenges the notion that gender is a fixed, natural aspect of one's identity, arguing instead that it is performative, shaped by societal norms and expectations. This idea, though radical to some (fabulous to me), sheds light on the constructed nature of gender norms, debunking the notion that they are inherent to biological sex. And this freaks out lots of people, from far-right Trump-supporting men to radical lesbian feminists.

What's the difference between biological sex and gender?

Biological sex refers to the physical and physiological characteristics that are typically associated with being male or female. These characteristics include chromosomes, reproductive organs, hormones and secondary sexual characteristics like body hair and breast development.

Gender refers to social, cultural and psychological characteristics, behaviours and identities. Gender is not necessarily determined by biological sex; rather, it is influenced by societal norms, expectations and personal identity.

Some lesbian women and gay men feel that by accepting that gender is something a person can choose, it negates the work they have done fighting for their rights as homosexual men or women. More on this later . . .

In their latest groundbreaking work, *Who's Afraid of Gender?*, Butler delves into how gender has become a battleground for authoritarian regimes and exclusionary feminist movements. They illuminate how the anti-gender movement perpetuates anxieties and fuels nationalism, demonizing efforts for equality.

The attacks on 'gender ideology' have gained momentum recently, fuelled by right-wing organizations, the media and online forums. These groups peddle unfounded claims, ranging from the fear of indoctrination in classrooms (remember the cat litter trays?!) to the erosion of traditional family values (bleurgh!). Butler explores how the reactionary anti-gender movement capitalizes on economic insecurity, social inequality and pandemic-induced anxieties, scapegoating gender and critical theories for societal ills. By portraying gender as a destructive force, these people seek to maintain power structures and uphold conservative ideologies. How boring of them!

Where have all the they/thems come from?

According to the 2021 UK census, 30,000 (0.06 per cent) of British people identified as non-binary out of the 45.7 million people who answered the gender identity question. If you feel that more people are identifying as non-binary today than ten years ago, you're probably right. I am actually surprised that more of my queer friends haven't embraced this new lexicon of identity and come out as NB (or 'enby', as the slang goes) – I guess by the time you're in your forties you feel pretty much 'done' in terms of your evolution of self. And even though there's now a word to describe a way that you've maybe always felt, you're not going to claim it because, well, you've got this far as a gay man or a lesbian, so why rock the boat?

But what does non-binary even mean?

The idea that there are only two genders is sometimes called a 'gender binary', because binary means 'having two parts' (male and female). So 'non-binary' is one term people use to describe genders that don't fall into one of these two categories, male or female.

Personally, I decided to rock the boat a bit in 2021 and I brought a few people into the internal conversations I was having about my own gender identity. First discovering the term non-binary and then finding out more about what it meant, what it could express about the way you see yourself and want to be seen by others, felt like I'd been handed this amazing gift. But I was scared to open it. I didn't want to have to 'come out' as something all over again. It was cringey enough the first time round! The other thing stopping me from identifying as non-binary was a cynical millennial fear that people would think I was jumping on a bandwagon and trying to be cool. Was I too old, at forty, to be non-binary? Had I been aware of this term when I was in my twenties I might well have embraced it then. I don't know what that would have meant for me, but I think I might have felt freer to explore my sexuality, my femininity, my androgyny, my masculinity, if I had non-binary as my anchor of selfhood.

I'm going to admit to one of my own unconscious biases about non-binary people, and that's that there is a particular way to look. I think I've conflated it with androgynous in the past, and recently when I met a quite masculine-presenting AMAB (assigned male at birth) poet who identified as non-binary I really found it hard to compute. But I'm glad I did acknowledge and work through these feelings, as it was a reminder that gender identity and presentation are connected but different things. Oh, and on the subject of *mea culpas*, I'm always messing up pronouns, calling theys *he* or *she* and then apologizing and somehow making it worse. Just because we're queer or even non-binary people ourselves, we still make mistakes.

Roll up, roll up, it's time for a pronoun showdown!

How many of these have you heard of? Award yourself ten points for having used the pronoun, five points for having heard of it, two points for knowing it existed and minus ten points for any eye-rolls.

I wondered if there were particular nuances between each of the pronouns listed below, but according to my research they are all different ways of asserting that your gender identity exists outside the binary in some respect.

- They/Them/Theirs
- Ze/Hir/Hirs
- Xe/Xem/Xyrs
- E/Em/Eirs
- Ve/Ver/Vis
- Per/Pers (this one is derived from 'person')

- Zie/Zir/Zirs
- Fa/Fae/Faer (this is based on the word 'fae', from folklore, often associated with non-binary or gender-diverse identities and favoured by those who feel a connection with mythology).

Should you bother putting your pronouns on your email signature?

Some people don't like having to write *John Smith (he/him)* because perhaps they think it's pretty damn obvious that he, John (duh), is male. And look, that's fine. No one's forcing you to declare your pronouns, John. But the nice thing about doing it is that it normalizes it for people who are trans or non-binary if pronouns aren't clear from their name alone. It's an easy way of demonstrating your allyship and is a great example of how being respectful of diversity is additive. It takes nothing from you but it might give a lot to someone else.

I will say, though, that if your pronouns are E/Em/Eirs it might be a lot to ask of people to get this right and integrate it seamlessly into their vocabulary. With the best will in the world, it's just a grammatical quagmire! Could we all just agree on they/them and shelve the zies and the xems for now? Does that make me a terrible enby? A terrible ally? Sorry! Maybe my dominant identity is grumpy elder millennial after all!

What is a TERF and what do gender-critical people believe?

TERF stands for Trans-Exclusionary Radical Feminist. It describes people or groups within feminist movements who hold beliefs that exclude transgender women from their understanding of womanhood and feminism. These are often called 'gender-critical' beliefs.

According to an op ed in *The Observer*,[1] 'gender-critical' beliefs refer to the view that someone's sex – whether they are male or female – is biological and immutable and cannot be conflated with someone's gender identity, whether they identify as a man or a woman. The belief that the patriarchal oppression of women is grounded partly in their biological sex, not just the social expression of gender, and that women therefore have the right to certain single-sex spaces and to organize on the basis of biological sex if they so wish, represents a long-standing strand of feminist thinking.' The article goes on to assert that 'as a society, we need to resolve the question of how to protect the privacy, dignity and rights of trans women while also respecting the privacy, dignity and rights of those born female.'

But don't be fooled – the beliefs shared in this newspaper opinion piece are not neutral. It continues, 'For centuries, patriarchal societies have tried to limit the free expression of women. For centuries, women have fought back against attempts to curb their fundamental human rights. It should not need stating that gender-critical feminists have the same free-speech rights as all other citizens. In a democracy, there is no debate to be had about women's freedom of speech.'

Stu and I believe that trans women are women and trans men are men, and so while discussions and a sharing of experience can be productive, there is no 'debate' to be had.

What does intersex mean?

Like many people reading this, I've always sort of known what the 'I' in LGBTQIA+ stands for, and the term 'intersex' has tripped off my tongue sometimes when talking about our community. Approximately 1.7 per cent of the global population is intersex, and up to 1.1 million people in the UK alone. But honestly, I'm not sure I've ever really understood what it means beyond having ambiguous sex organs. Nor have I ever knowingly met an intersex person to ask them more about it. Even if I had, would I have asked? I guess it depends on the context, but 'tell me about your genitals' probably wouldn't have been my opening gambit.

So, let's get into it. Intersex is a term used to describe a range of physical, genetic, hormonal or chromosomal variations that result in an individual's reproductive or sexual anatomy not fitting typical definitions of male or female. Intersex people may be born with variations in their sex characteristics that make it difficult for doctors to classify them as strictly male or female.

OK, so what's the difference between being intersex and transgender?

The word intersex refers to variations in physical sex characteristics, while the term transgender is used to describe someone whose gender identity differs from the sex assigned to them at birth. The existence of intersex people really challenges the already shaky foundations of 'gender-critical' beliefs.

An intersex person might relate more strongly to a particular gender or be non-binary. They might also identify as trans because the gender they were assigned at birth does not align with the person they know themselves to be. In fact, the existence of intersex people, albeit a small demographic (intersex is a natural biological variation, and it occurs in approximately 1 in 2,000 live births)[1] helps us recognize how distinct gender identity can be from biology, specifically genitalia.

What are some of the greatest challenges that intersex people may face?

The sad fact is that a great many intersex folk undergo unnecessary and often irreversible medical interventions at a young age, which can have physical and psychological consequences. These treatments might have been performed without their informed consent or that of their parents, who are often pressured by medical professionals to 'normalize' their child's anatomy. This can lead to lifelong consequences because the individual wasn't able to make their own decisions.

Who better to ask about the intersex experience than Anick Soni, a writer and researcher who identifies as intersex, bisexual, disabled and queer. Anick was kind enough to educate me on some intersex basics and open up to me about life and love.

'I found out about the term 'intersex' and then kind of grew into that word when I was around twenty-one. Before that, I just knew I had something called hypospadias and something called androgen insensitivity syndrome, but I didn't exactly know that counted as intersex.

'The procedures were to do with "helping me to fit in when I grew up". They were more cosmetic than fixing anything dangerous or life-threatening. But the medical opinion at the time was, we need to do these kinds of procedures so that this child can have a healthy psychological development.

'When you're born with hypospadias, it means that there's a hole alongside the shaft of the penis or in the scrotum itself. So there's a difference in the actual development of the penis. So I had various different procedures before the age of five, which were not necessarily medically needed. But my parents were just told there was a problem with my genitalia and this is what we can do to fix it. They didn't understand that the operations were a choice.

'I had a lot of anger towards my parents for agreeing to put me through the treatment I had as a child. There are still lots of issues to work through, but I think what changed for me was learning that they didn't know much, and they didn't have access to the same information that I do now. They thought their child was seriously ill, so they did what the doctor said. It took me a long time to get over that.

'For me, discovering the intersex community was more like finding an answer to a question that I never knew I was asking. My work now as an activist is all around trying to understand that my body wasn't an issue and I wasn't born into a "wrong" body. It was more I didn't have the support I needed to be able to deal with what was going on.

'The core aims of the intersex movement as a whole have always been focused on more research and consent, trying to understand that our body isn't a problem, and where there are medical needs you should address them, but if things are cosmetic or they could be delayed, they should be, and provide a range of psychosocial support instead.

'No one actually sits down with intersex people who are not trans to try and decide if they want to have the procedures. So, you've got trans children fighting for procedures to change their bodies, whereas people like me are given access to those procedures because our bodies are seen as a problem that's physical and not psychological.

'The main issue with this is it has led to quite a significant number of people within the intersex community being quite transphobic, which I was surprised about. Many of the people who don't like the idea of intersex being queered or being expanded beyond the medical realm, they tend to also have very interesting views on gender.

'And there are some people, particularly those who are a bit older, I've noticed, through my intersex community work – they feel like trans children shouldn't be given access to hormone treatments or medical surgeries without them fully understanding it. But then at the same time, when I speak to them, they don't ever seem to think it's appropriate for anyone to change their bodies. And the more I've dug into that, it seems to be a trauma response. It's a way of saying, *well, I didn't get this choice to have these procedures. Why are these trans people choosing to ruin something when they have perfectly fine bodies?*

'I've never felt like anything other than male, but I've questioned what it means to be masculine and what it means to be a boy, in ways I don't think generally people do if they aren't queer in the first place.

'Personally, I grew up thinking of my body as such a medical problem that when I found out some people include intersex within a wider queer community I was confused. Being intersex has nothing to do with who I'm attracted to, that's my sexuality, this is to do with my body. But then, my first degree was in law, and at that time I was learning about SOGIESC, which is sexual orientation, gender identity and expression, and then sex characteristics. So that's how the law organizes all of this stuff nowadays, within a human rights context and a medical context as well. And so intersex does fit in when you use it in that term.

'For me, because I'm also queer as well as intersex (not necessarily because of it), I've never had an issue with being included as part of the LGBTQ+ community. But when I speak to people who don't like to be included, they often point to the fact that intersex has got nothing to do with sexuality and that it should be kept separate because it's a medical thing, which could be, in their words, maybe fixed or not, but it's a physical problem. Older intersex people maybe grew up in a time where being queer was criminal and was seen as deviant and wrong in the first place. And if they are intersex but see themselves as straight, according to whatever gender or sex they were assigned to at birth, that can also have an impact on how they view it. Some people don't like the fact that it's mixed in with transness.

'But of course, some people are intersex and trans. They identify with a gender different to the one they were assigned at birth, which may have been harder to "define" at birth but nevertheless they would have been socialized as either a girl or boy in spite of this. So the trans and intersex little intersection becomes more complicated because we don't really know what our lives would have been like without these interventions. So who knows what impact it would have had on our sexual identity?

'Intersex shows up differently for each person. So the best way to be an ally is to have conversations and to ask what it means to the person saying it. And, you know, that's why language is also so important. Because there are people I know who hate the word intersex. And they have the same variation as me, and there are some people who love it and will only use that and hate the medical terms.

'So it's about being able to have conversations, reflect the language that's being used by the person using it and not necessarily asking that person a lot of these questions we've covered today – you're writing a book, but in reality, you don't need to know all this as soon as you find out someone's intersex.

'There are a number of very vocal intersex people on social media. Listen to them and share those voices. Just don't expect them to be spokespeople for an entire group of people.'

After speaking to Anick, in some ways I feel even more confused about why intersex is necessarily part of the LGBTQ+ spectrum. Some intersex people are queer, some are trans, and these identities are already covered within the acronym LGBTQIA+. I never thought I'd hear myself say this but *think of the straights!* For intersex people who identify as being male or female and heterosexual, is it fair for them to be forced into a rainbow wedge?

What we can agree on is that understanding more about what it means to be intersex is important. It's also clear that for some intersex people, the struggle they face in being heard, being respected and being challenged on their identity is akin to that of the wider queer and specifically trans community. So it makes sense that we welcome our intersex siblings with open arms and support them however we can. If that means an imperfect place in the alphabet soup of LGBTQIA+, which tries and endlessly fails to act as a shorthand for our diverse community, then maybe, in one of my favourite ever shoulder shrugs of an expression, *it is what it is.*

Here's what I still don't know: what gender actually is, beyond a social construct, beyond a performance, beyond an idea that makes some people feel like the very foundations of reality will come crashing down if we so much as question it. I also don't know for sure if I'm non-binary or if it's more that I've not found a performance of womanhood that suits me. Did the feeling come before the word for me, or did the word give rise to the feeling? Who bloody knows! But as we discovered when exploring sexuality in the first chapter, maybe it's OK not to be sure and to instead explore.

Chapter 5

Transformative:
The Power of Understanding

Stu

When I first started looking at transitioning as a theme for this book, my ignorance on the subject was almost immediately exposed. I was told by a contact that some of my questions were problematic for the trans community. They also highlighted that my language wasn't very inclusive. Me? Surely not! So, after my cis, white, privileged gay self took the time to pick my pearls off the floor, broken and scattered from how tightly I clutched them after being accused of such a heinous act of un-wokeness, I took the time to realize that I had indeed been lazy in my trans education. Perhaps because we as a 'community' identify as queer, we potentially think we know it all and end up just wearing ally badges so proudly without doing the proper work. We assume we are all in it together. Is posting the slogan 'I just want to say if you are trans and reading this, I love you' on Trans Visibility Day enough?

What does it mean to transition?

The subtitle of transgender role model (and actual model) Munroe Bergdorf's book *Transitional* is 'In One Way or Another, We All Transition'. Indeed, all transitioning means is 'the process, or period of changing from one state to another.'

Over the past year, we've talked a lot about 'transitioning' in our house. Our youngest was about to transition from nursery to his first year at school. The word was bandied around between my husband, myself and the teachers while we worked out the best way to essentially get him from Place A to Place B. The act of becoming a parent is also a transition: figuring out new daily routines, how the world now sees you and, perhaps, a whole new set of priorities. Getting into a new car is a transition. So is becoming a teenager. Transitions are all around us, and while lots of us know how to get into a new car, the experience of being transgender is deep, complex and something that many cis people can't even begin to imagine the challenges involved.

But to Munroe's point, the very nature of transition, and the daily transitions we all make, could be a way to connect on a human level and perhaps start to understand the changes one may decide to make as a transgender person.

So how do we, as cis people (those whose gender identity matches their assigned sex at birth), acknowledge and respect someone's outward transition?

I firstly make an important note that the word 'outward' is used a lot in relation to transitioning. So I think it's vital, from my current (and maybe basic) understanding, for us to acknowledge that there may be no such thing as an internal transition for a trans person when it comes to their gender. That person might feel they have always been the gender they are, it just wasn't the one that was assigned at birth.

Not everyone transitions in the same way. It's different, and again, so personal. Further on in this chapter I take a look at the surgical processes someone could explore during a transition. The key word here being 'could'. There is no one defined path, and certainly no 'right' path.

And while the outward aspect of transitioning is key for those who don't connect their gender identity to their biological sex, the inside elements can also be vitally important for some, with hormone treatment helping how they feel, and supporting them further in being comfortable and, hopefully, happy in their own skin.

So, what is important for cis people to understand about transitioning? I spoke to Flora Parkin, a trans woman who we'll meet again in Chapter 6. She shared some practical things we can do to help acknowledge and understand our trans siblings, and explained how cis-gender people can respect them and be effective allies.

Understand the importance of access to healthcare:

'The importance of this is fundamental and doesn't get enough attention or respect – up to ten-year wait times to access NHS services would not be acceptable in any other context, and it leads to serious, fundamental consequences for trans people.

'NHS and private healthcare providers need to respect non-binary identities and gender diversity in their provision of trans healthcare. We need to move beyond psychiatric diagnoses, medical gatekeeping by cis people, and the requirement to demonstrate binary gender to access healthcare, and that is about respect.'

Realize how much money it costs to transition:

'From changing your wardrobe to paying for hormones and surgeries if you want them, to delaying other parts of your life, to the bureaucracy around name changes and more. It's expensive, regardless of whether you surgically transition.'

Respect the time and energy that's put in:

'Emotionally, psychologically, socially and physically, transition takes time and energy, and that can take its toll, or simply need to be prioritized over other things sometimes.'

Understand what's appropriate – and what's not – to ask:

'What is or isn't appropriate to ask a trans person during their transition varies, and it also hinges on the relationship you may have with the trans person, the context in which you're chatting, and the tone of the question. What a trans person might be happy to talk about with a close friend will be different from what they'll want to discuss with a colleague, a family member or a stranger on the street. There aren't clear boundaries, but politeness, respect and awareness of your relationship with the trans person in question are key considerations that apply in any situation.'

And understand that it's fun!

'There's often a tone when talking about transition that emphasizes the hardship and struggle, but transitioning can also be a laugh, it brings great joy, and is one hell of a ride.'

Trans terminology

When Lotte and I first discovered the term 'deadname', it felt cold and unnecessarily harsh to us, perhaps because as parents we are sentimental about our own children's names. But as we've talked to more and more trans people about the term, we get why the harshness is needed. Assuming that everyone knows what words like this mean and why they exist is holding us back from true understanding, so here's a guide to the term 'deadname' and other transitional terms:

Deadname: A 'deadname' is the birth name of a person who has transitioned and has decided to choose a new name. Not everyone decides to take a new name, but for those that do, being referred to by your deadname (aka 'deadnaming') is considered disrespectful and harmful if done intentionally or repeatedly by those who know they have transitioned. Nor does everyone use the term. 'I don't use [the word] deadname personally,' Flora told me. 'Most of my friends who've changed names simply refer to "their old name" or "my birth name", but phrases always reflect the language of the times. "Deadname" is a phrase that resonates and provides a finality and clarity to some people that they find important and can act as a clear communicator that a prior name is not to be used.'

Cisgender/cis: A person whose gender identity matches the sex they were assigned at birth.

Gender identity: An internal, psychological identification with a gender. How they feel inside, and how they align to a specific gender.

Gender dysphoria: The psychological distress or discomfort experienced by people when their gender identity doesn't align with their assigned sex at birth. This feeling often arises from a mismatch between one's internal sense of self and how their body looks or how society perceives and treats them based on their assigned gender.

Gender-affirming care: Medical and psychological support that helps to align physical traits with their gender identity. This may include hormone replacement therapy (HRT), surgeries (more on this later), or other treatments.

Assigned sex at birth (AFAB/AMAB): Refers to the designation of 'male' or 'female' that's given to an individual at birth, often based on physical anatomy. AFAB stands for 'assigned female at birth' and AMAB stands for 'assigned male at birth'.

Passing: The ability of a transgender person to be perceived or recognized as the gender with which they identify, rather than the sex they were assigned at birth. 'Passing' can be a sensitive topic, as not all trans people are able to pass, and societal pressure to do so can be harmful. Bear this in mind if you ever find yourself saying things like, 'Oh, I had no idea' or, 'You'd never know', as this can obviously be harmful to some, even if that wasn't your intention.

Stealth: When a transgender person chooses not to disclose their transgender status and lives as their affirmed gender without others knowing they are trans. In her article on Them,[1] Nat Vikitsreth talks about her reasons for being stealth. 'Being stealth gave me the protection I needed to survive the violence of systemic oppression. There is no shame in living stealth, especially when your intersecting identities make you a visible target for transphobia. Your survival is valid. Your transness is valid. Stealth is a strategy, not an identity, as we trans folks are so much more than our methods of survival in a hostile, fear-stricken world.'

Let's meet . . . Thea

Thea Bardot is the CEO of a travel recruitment company and identifies as a trans non-binary femme. I first met Thea over a year ago at a work event. Thea has been sharing her transition online via her social media.

How would you define who you were back in May when we met compared to now, and what terminology should people use when talking about you in the past?

This is a really tricky question, so bear with me . . . Our name is such an integral part of who we are and how we want the world to see us. When a gender-expansive individual takes ownership of their identity and has the courage to come out as trans, non-binary or gender non-conforming in any way, it is a significant act of empowerment, often after years of self-reflection and feelings of impotence around their situation.

Choosing their name and their pronouns is the embodiment of this process. It is a signal to the wider world, the removal of ambiguity – *this is who I am, this is how I want you to see me.* Transition is all about progress, moving forward, evolving into the person you are, so that you can feel a sense of peace in the world. Referring back to someone's deadname is a reminder of the past, who that person was and everything that went with that. Allyship and advocacy is about embracing the individual for who they are, understanding that they have often fought many battles (both within themselves and with others) to arrive at their most authentic version, then supporting them in that journey.

But most of all, that person was very much still an absolute ICON (I remember what I was wearing that day we met, and they left no crumbs) and I am so grateful to them for the space they took up and the work they did to allow me to step into my final evolution (yes, I'm referencing Pokémon) to become the ME you see today as Thea. That person will always be a part of me too, but the name is very much gone as I begin this new journey. I have to stress, though, this journey is not binary for everyone and all identities under the trans umbrella are valid, as are all ways of expressing them.

How easy was the name transition? Do people often mis-identify you by name, either intentionally or otherwise? How does that feel when it happens?

On the whole, people were actually amazing, so supportive and kind. I had a name-change party at an LGBTQ+ bar with my friends where they signed my deed polls and I began the process of then changing my name on official documents like bank cards, bills, etc.

However, I had one big traumatic experience being dead-named and misgendered on stage at an event, which was like a stab to the heart in front of hundreds of people. It's the same every time this happens, and honestly, it may seem obvious, but we use our names a LOT and when it pops up unexpectedly it can be hard to deal with – my biggest nemesis right now is e-newsletters! I've done most of the 'big-ticket' items and just have my passport and phone bill left on the to-do list. It's worth noting that some trans people just never get around to these things as they cost money and there is so much admin involved (not as sexy as it all sounds). As such, don't expect everyone to have documents that match their identity.

What have been the key moments for you within your transition?

I have just undergone life-changing surgery, which I have been charting on my social media. My hope is that by being open about everything that I have been through people can begin to understand that transition is not a phase, for me it is an endless dedication to the realization of the most authentic version of myself. I've also been on hormone replacement therapy for over a year now, so there are physical changes, as well as hormonal ones, that have made me see the world differently and made others see me differently. I had to learn all over again that I can't control how others view me and that what they do has no bearing on who I am. From an AUDHD [co-occurrence of ADHD and Autism] perspective – yay for intersectionality – leading up to the surgery and post surgery I've stopped masking. I project different energy now, as well as a different aesthetic. I definitely struggled with people not reacting to me in the same way that they reacted to the 'safe' character I'd created. I'm now at peace with the fact that some people struggle to make eye contact, or the way in which their body language has changed. Now I am comfortable just letting people see me as me, but it's taken a while for that to happen. It's also important to stress that [while I have] it's not the responsibility of trans people to share their struggles 24–7 to educate others. We deserve the right to privacy too, should we choose that.

Do you feel cis people have a fascination with trans people's genitalia? Are there a lot of misconceptions about trans surgery out there?
It's like anything, we find it hard to empathize with someone if the journey they are on is at odds with our view of the world. So, for example, for a cis person, they don't need to undergo surgery to align themselves with the authentic versions of who they are – they are born that way, and as such the idea of taking steps to change their gender makes no sense. I also think that the media (and social media) has boiled transition down to hormones and body parts. While it is a part of our journey, trans people are so much more than that. We dedicate our lives to understanding and finding our true selves – this doesn't tend to be a journey that cis people go on – though I would argue that the world would benefit from everyone having as deep an understanding of themselves as our community does!

What are the next steps for you in your transition? Will there come a point where you feel you've reached the end of the journey? Or have you already?

Another problematic question, which is the equivalent of have you had 'the surgery'. It's not anyone's place to ask; if someone offers the info, great. It's a bit like asking someone who has given birth what their plans are for growing their family – people often ask, but it's not really anyone else's business.

Transition is an evolution, not a checklist.

I get that. And thank you for flagging where things I've asked are problematic. On the whole, what do you think cis-LGBTQ+ people could do to be better allies?

Listen and learn – and try not to judge trans and non-binary people by cis standards; we are not cis people who are transitioning, we are trans people who are looking for inner peace.

MY HAND IS UP! WHAT IS TRANS NON-BINARY?

If we were in a school this would be the moment I would put my hand up and ask a question, or at the very least think about it silently. Well, this is a form of school and we do want to ask the questions and not remain silent, so my hand is well and truly raised. I introduced Thea as trans non-binary, but what does trans non-binary actually mean? Do the terms not cancel each other out?

To transition is about changing your gender, right? But being non-binary is about not aligning yourself with one binary gender or another. So, if you are non-binary, how are you also trans, if trans denotes transitioning between two binaries? My head literally hurts. We ask psychotherapist Chance Czyzselska (they/them), who we spoke to in Chapter 1.

'Some non-binary people don't identify as trans, and some, like me, do. We maybe use trans as a way of making it clear we are not cis. Because I don't wholly identify with the gender I was assigned at birth, I consider myself trans, and I also personally feel trans opens up a vast landscape of gendered possibilities, like it offers less fixed/rigid possibilities/expectations and more movement. I also think that gender is relational, so we may feel that certain aspects of our gender expression are more pronounced with some people and less with others.'

I'm learning that we sometimes place ourselves in such binary ways of thinking that we can get our heads in a muddle. I also ask Thea to clarify to me her own view on her identification. 'Trans non-binary to me means that I categorically don't align with my gender assigned at birth 100 per cent, but I also don't fully identify as male or female and see myself existing somewhere in between. It's really important to understand that there is no real set definition for these labels, and they mean different things to different people. Many in the community reject traditional labels so they don't get asked to explain themselves or their gender.'

What is involved with the physical transition?

The physical change as part of someone's transition is, of course, a huge part of the process – for them. I'm keen to emphasize the 'for them' part here because, like anyone else, trans people don't have an obligation to share a single detail of their journey with the rest of us. Thea has chosen to share many of the details of her physical transition online, including discussion about her daily diliation. I had to google this word as I wasn't quite sure what that meant in this context. I know now that it's the process following vaginoplasty that helps maintain the depth of the new vaginal canal.

I'm truly glad I got time to speak to Thea. For me, there has always been a push and pull of knowing the facts and being educated, mixed with not wanting to ask questions or pry into the experience of changing your physicality. The answer is, of course, and always will be, education. But, importantly, it's down to cis people to do their own research and move on. So, it's time for a bit of a biology lesson as I roll up my sleeves and find out what various surgical procedures there are on offer for trans people, so we can then let that be that. You or I never have to ask or question again. Get ready, kids, a few big words coming your way . . .

A MEDICAL EDUCATION

From a genital point of view, for trans women, surgery options include orchidectomy (removal of the testes), penectomy (removal of the penis), vaginoplasty (construction of a vagina), vulvoplasty (construction of a vulva) and clitoroplasty (construction of a clitoris) . . .

For trans men, options include phalloplasty (the creation of a penis/phallus using tissue) and metoidioplasty (creation of a mini phallus by using a testosterone-enlarged clitoris). Although I will note that it's the NHS that use the term 'mini' (what size queens! Don't they know it's what you do with it that counts?).

Other trans male surgeries could include scrotoplasty (construction of a scrotum using the labia majora), testicular implants, hysterectomy (removal of the womb) and salpingo-oophorectomy (removal of the ovaries and fallopian tubes . . . and points for you if you can pronounce this).

I also learn that in addition to surgery focused on the genital reassignment, there are also a number of surgical procedures that trans people can explore to support their outwards transition. These include breast implants for trans-feminine people and breast removal and reconstruction for trans-masculine people. Another thing I discover is about a procedure called nipple dermal implants and tattoos, which allows for the creation of silicone nipples that can be added to an implant under the skin. For trans women, another popular treatment is FFS, aka facial feminization surgery. But all these procedures come at a cost, as not everything is available on the NHS.

And, of course, there are trans people who never have 'bottom surgery' (the term used for having genital gender-affirming surgery). When Lotte and I met Eddy, a trans man who is a sex worker (and who we chat to later), he is proud to be 'a man with a pussy' and he uses his pussy in his work, in real life and online. Don't assume that all trans people want, or feel the need, to have surgery on their genitals. The spectrum of trans people is as varied as queer people in general, so no assumptions need to be made.

After my biological fact-finding mission, I feel the need to grab a coffee to recalibrate my brain, which is buzzing with lots of '-plasty' and '-tomy'-ending words. As I walk to my kitchen, I notice a book popping out of my kids' bookcase. The title – It's My Body – screams out to me so perfectly in this moment. It's a book by Louise Spilsbury that we got our kids to help them learn about body privacy, and the description on the book jacket reads:

'It's My Body *explains to children about body privacy and why private parts should be kept private. Children will learn that their body belongs to them. They'll discover what is inappropriate and be encouraged to speak up if they are uncomfortable with how other people treat them. The book looks at respecting each other's boundaries.'*

Respecting each other's boundaries – something I don't think we do enough with trans people. So let's take a lesson from how we would expect our children to act and let these words soak in. And in the opposite of *this* book's title, when it comes to trans surgery and genitals (in fact, anyone's genitals, come to think of it), it's probably best not to ask. You see, there is a balance between wanting to be informed, educated and supportive, but also respectful and never wanting to cross a line.

Does my love of dick make me transphobic?

I've already mentioned Eddy in this chapter, and you will get to meet him properly later in the book, but when Lotte and I first had a coffee with him in Soho, I was immediately smitten. The guy was hot, and let me tell you I've been flinging fire emojis at his Insta ever since. He has gorgeous blue eyes, a chiselled physique and a damn good set of thighs. Eddy is a sex worker and proud owner of a no-holds-barred X and OnlyFans account, so I couldn't help but have a little browse. I then found myself faced with questions that I hadn't really been anticipating, as Eddy's videos and images feature him playing with his vagina and enjoying penetration.

You see, and I'm just going to say it, I love dick. I love them. Love the shape, the feel, the look and, well, they turn me on. It's a large (fnarr fnarr) part of my sexual attraction to someone. Therefore, if I was in a relationship with a trans man that didn't have a dick, would I be able to be sexual with them? Or do my sexual desires lead me down a path of exclusion?

These questions got me thinking about how our sexualities and personal desires can be weaponized against our community from within to further create a divide between us and our trans siblings. I don't think my love of dick makes me transphobic. Or does it? One of the reasons that we have these different labels of sexuality is that it enables us to align with the one that most represents our desire (or lack of). I'm confused and worried about what my feelings may mean to a part of the community I care deeply about.

I decide to confide my worries with my friend Freddy McConnell, a journalist and trans man. 'Stu, firstly we're talking about it as if this is a real problem. It's not. It's been constructed by groups like the LGB Alliance (a trans-exclusionary group) to make people afraid of trans people. The idea that preference is transphobic is in itself a weapon that is being used against trans people to paint us as unreasonable and coercive. We are not out here saying "you must want to sleep with us", and honestly, we don't want to sleep with people who are going to make judgements about us before they've even met us. The fact that you are now thinking, "well, I only like dick, so does that make me transphobic?" No, it doesn't make you transphobic. And the fact that you are worrying about whether it makes you transphobic, means that, on some level, far-right groups have succeeded in making cis people fearful.

'In terms of preference, it's OK to feel that way about dick, but if you then jump to: *that means I'll never explore sexual relations with a trans person*, that's when you slip into transphobia because you're writing off an entire group on the basis of a very reductive and often inaccurate assumption. That's when it becomes akin to any other kind of broad preference in that there is a high probability it is actually informed by prejudice and unconscious bias. Even though it might very much feel like a preference, it is actually rooted in the prejudices that pervade our society.'

I put these points to my new crush Eddy. 'For me,' he tells me, 'it often comes down to an ingrained association of men with penises. That association is hard to break. When someone says they're into men, most people picture a penis. That's just not the association I have, nor the association my boyfriend has, and not the association many trans people and allies have. I believe that most people's sexualities are not based on genitals. As a sex worker whose clients are 99 per cent cis gay men, I know this firsthand; their attraction to me, and sexual desire for me, and enjoyment of my pussy, makes them no less gay. Of course, some people's desire is dependent on genitals, and I realize this is where your head is at, and when that's the case I do not believe it to be transphobic, as long as it's conveyed respectfully and not from a place of prejudice. However sometimes the association is so strong, many people assume they're into dicks, but really they're just into men, and they never considered that the dick might not be as important as they realized, and that a pussy can bring fun and pleasure in new ways. Desires also don't have to be one or the other: you can love dick and love pussy; you can love dick, and still have an amazing and fulfilling sexual experience with someone who doesn't have one.'

I ask Eddy if that is not the difference between being gay and being pansexual? 'For me, my vagina is not feminine,' he tells me. 'Someone is pansexual if they are attracted to the person rather than their body, so the gender and sex are irrelevant. If a gay man finds me hot, he is still gay; it doesn't make him pansexual. I'm a man – a complete man – and my vagina doesn't change that. It's problematic to make this jump, as it implies that trans men are not men.'

Chatting to the guys makes me feel better about the feelings I'd been having. But this isn't about me slapping myself on the back for not being a massive transphobe. I also very much recognize, or at least hope I recognize, the difference between preference and prejudice, and what a fine line there is in between. It's important for us to accept that all of us have deeply personal sexual feelings, that range from simple to complex, and that weave between our gender binaries, non-binaries, and sexualities. It's one of the reasons we have such a wonderful array of sexualities, that Lotte details in our opening chapter. We can't dismiss how we feel, but I think all of us can benefit from sitting back and questioning how those feelings could be built on foundations of bias, rather than our true attraction.

So what more can we do to be better allies?

I can, and will, do better, and there is so much more that can be said, read and done. If you haven't already, do take the time to read books such as Shon Faye's *The Transgender Issue* or Harry Nicholas' superb *A Trans Man Walks Into a Gay Bar* to help you recognize any conscious or unconscious bias you may have towards trans people.

Just as it's reductive to say 'I don't see colour' when talking about race, likewise I think it's wrong to ignore what makes a trans person, trans. I've also learned that you shouldn't assume anything, because each and every trans person is different. Their transition is completely unique to them, so we need to use our own emotional intelligence to gauge each situation. For now, I'm going to leave you with the words of the great queer daddy of us all, Armistead Maupin, author of the iconic book series *Tales of the City*. His words, taken from a Channel 4 News interview, sum up how I feel perfectly, especially after my own journey of discovery about transitions:

'I was in an interview with a journalist some years back, who told me that the trans issue was "a complicated one" and that "a lot of people differ on that subject". And I said, well, "who differs on it?", as I don't understand anybody who can't grasp the concept that they are human beings, and they deserve the rights that the rest of us have. LGBT has got a T in there for a reason. They started our movement, this is not the time to desert them. People have a right to live their lives in this free culture, and if that means living a life as a trans person because that's what makes sense to them, it doesn't matter that it doesn't make sense to you, it makes sense to them, it is their right to live that out. Leave them alone, just leave us alone. I say "us" because I include myself with my trans brothers and sisters, we're in this battle together.'

Chapter 6

Stone Butch Seeks High Femme

Lotte

Ever since Stu started unpicking lesbian stereotypes and now wears his 'lesbian ally' badge with pride, even *daring* to befriend other queer women and non-binary people (trying not to be too jealous that he went to see Kristen Stewart in *Love Lies Bleeding* without me!), I've been thinking about where lesbian culture intersects with gender, or at least the 'performance' of it and how the ideas of butch and femme play out across the queer community.

Where better to begin a butch adventure than in IKEA on a grey Wednesday morning in March (Wednesday, I'm told, is officially 'lesbian day'). I'm meeting Ella Braidwood, a journalist and proud butch lesbian, and I'm interested to chat to her because she's only just turned thirty and, in my mind, 'butch' is an identity favoured by elder millennial, Gen X and Baby Boomer dykes, not whipper-snappers like Ella. Did I just unironically use the term *whippersnapper* to refer to a thirty-year-old? Yes, I did. Imagine it delivered with a flick of the hair and a withering look (and hold on to your feather boas because we'll be getting into camp later, too).

I want to understand more about what it means to be 'butch' and 'femme', how these queer identities are evolving (or not) and I also want to interrogate some of my own biases about the categories as I question whether or not I fit into them.

Who's afraid of the big bad butch?

I'll admit that I have carried with me some preconceived ideas of what it means to be a butch lesbian, and I'm sorry to say that they aren't all that positive. Firstly, I've been a little judgemental about the butch look: short hair, plaid shirts, baggy jeans. It's always struck me as a little anachronistic, style-wise. As a reformed fashion gay myself, this was something I may have once been snobbish about as I swooshed about in my designer clothes (I was the deputy editor of *ELLE* – it came with the territory). However, on reflection, I think much of the negativity I associate with butchness comes from the years I spent trying to prove that I wasn't one of them, for reasons rooted, I suppose, in shame.

When I came out in the early 2000s, butch lesbians were the stereotype, they were what you would find if you looked up a picture of a lesbian in an encyclopaedia. It was what people expected from a queer woman, and that instantly made me want to push against it. It felt important to me back then to demonstrate that I was a lesbian, but *not that kind.* I had shoulder-length hair, I wore makeup, I cared about fashion, I was femme-ish. Or so I thought. In fact, my ex-girlfriend and I were members of a network called Lipstick Ladies. Cringe! We looked unfavourably on butch women; they were too obviously gay to be attractive to us.

I guess this was my equivalent of the 'straight-acting' gay guy, endlessly trying to prove *it's different for me.* It was the 'too much'-ness of butch women that scared me or made me feel ashamed. Butch lesbians weren't trying to pass, they refracted the male gaze and were out and proud. Because I didn't have that confidence myself, my instinct was to be disparaging of it in others. I hope by now you've realized how much more open-minded I am about queerness and how my understanding of myself and my community has evolved? As I've said throughout this book, I feel it's important to admit to our past biases and consider why we held them as we continue to challenge ourselves at every turn.

Ella meets me in the foyer of IKEA. Being a Wednesday, it is buzzing with dykes of all ages and identities cradling display cushions and packs of tealights in their arms, walking around with tiny pencils studiously making notes of flatpack locations, pushing trolleys overflowing with bath mats and spatulas and picture frames, their biceps throbbing under the weight of a Billy bookcase, droplets of sweat forming on their furrowed brows, leather jackets flung over shoulders as they run their fingers through their barber-shop quiffs and . . . OK, stop. My butch fantasy is getting out of hand. The reality is, Ella and I are the most obviously queer duo in IKEA that day. We go directly to the cafe for some veggie balls and loganberry jam.

It's a bit embarrassing because we are wearing the same top. Vintage Adidas with the stripes on the arms. Hers is black. Mine is white. I still don't consider myself butch but I appear to have inadvertently adopted the dress code. This isn't the first time that I'm confronted with the reality that the way I see myself doesn't necessarily correspond with how I present to others. I like to think of myself as a non-binary nymph, frolicking through fields of androgyny – femme but in a masc way, masc but in a femme way – gender fluid and stylish enough to transcend lesbian tropes . . . but, maybe I'm just . . . butch?

As we tuck into our strange Swedish meal, I ask Ella why this term is so important to her.

'There is a lot of stigma around butchness, because it means being a woman and presenting in a very unfeminine way. It has a sting to it. That's why it's been important for me to use it, basically. I want to try to combat some of that internal shame put on me by wider society. I think butch does mean different things to different people. For me personally, I'd say it's a female masculinity. I identify as a woman and that is part of my identity, but the way I feel is inherently masculine.'

OK, so let's be basic for a moment – does this mean she's handy with a power drill and putting together flatpack furniture? Because it's my worst nightmare and the last time I assembled a chest of drawers they were upside down (does that make me femme?). Ella laughs. Meeting in IKEA was a bit of a joke, a nod to the butch stereotype, but like many stereotypes, there's often something uncomfortably accurate about them. True to form, my butch friend admits, she's in her element with a complex instruction manual and a PAX wardrobe or two.

We agree that the negative side of the butch stereotype, the side less rooted in truth, is 'this idea that if you are butch you're rough, aggressive, unlovable, maybe a bit toxic. An angry man-hating lesbian', as Ella puts it.

I tell Ella about my nagging sense that identifying as butch means you're likely a bit uncool, or disinterested in fashion trends. Was this an opinion she had come across prior to embracing a butch identity? 'Not really,' she answers. 'But I grew up in Cumbria, it's not the fashion centre of the world. Walking gear is big there.'

Hey, stud

While the term butch is more often used to describe white lesbians, the term stud is specifically rooted in Black culture. Not all Black masculine lesbians might say they are a stud – but a stud lesbian will be a Black woman, as it is a racially specific term. I spoke to Shan Haywood, who is a Black lesbian and identifies as a 'stud'. She lives in Birmingham.

Identifying as a stud is about more than what you wear. It's a whole way of being and I have struggled with some of the stigma and more negative connotations attached to that terminology, not because of what it means to me, it's what people wrongly assume it means that is the problem. A lot of studs think you have to act like a man, and you have to carry some of that toxic masculinity.

We get tarnished with being players and not really somebody you marry. We're not romanticized much. There's also an assumption that we are probably good-looking. Yeah, I mean, I'm not mad at that part.

But really a stud can be quite gentlemanly and very giving in relationships. We do try to fit into that stereotype of a male within a male/female dynamic. I'm happy to take on a gendered role, but don't take my femininity away from me at the same time.

I'm talking, really, to fellow studs when I say that, because I've been told I'm not masculine enough to be in the stud category. Whereas if it was a simple tick-box exercise: I wear masculine clothes, I'm masculine-presenting, I'm a Black woman – I'm a stud. I know I'm a stud, but some other studs would challenge me for being too nice. Or even because of my job, which is ridiculous. I work in recruitment, but a true 'stud job' is being in security. Bar security, basically. Or some form of labour work, like a builder. It's hard to be a female in those areas, though. So that's why I don't do it. I'm more than capable of it, but I would rather not.

Stud-on-stud relationships are a bit of a taboo. Look, it's all a spectrum and everything's fluid, but it's just not the done thing. There's a lot of competition among the stud community along the lines of who's got the coolest haircut, or who's got the fittest girlfriend, and who's got the best hat on, or who's got the best clothes, who's got the coolest tattoos. So because there's so much competition, there's no room for romance, I guess.

Dating a stud will give you that sense of security. It's just how we carry ourselves. I think there's a level of confidence that comes with being a stud. Then, because we mirror straight relationships so heavily – the femmes get that aspect of being wined and dined, like the really old-school, stereotypical 'what a woman wants' vibe. But equally, if you get the right kind of stud, you have the masculinity, but you also have the feminine side of it as well, where you're still with a woman, you're still talking to a woman, you still have that nurture and care.

Studs get treated worse than straight Black women, we're even lower in the pecking order because men in general don't look at us with any value because we haven't got anything to offer them. So, we're kind of cast to the side, we don't really matter to them, to any man really, not just Black men. I think studs are a threat to cis straight men. Especially some Black men. I was walking down the street with my partner the other day and a Black guy just stared into my soul. I looked extra stud that day because I'd just got my hair cut (and it was sharper than his!). It wasn't anger or disdain, it just looked like confusion.

Soft butch is the micro tribe that Ella identifies with 'hugely', within the butch category. She describes it as being quite silly, playful and sensitive.

I ask her to describe a butch lesbian 'uniform'. 'It's flexible,' she tells me. 'Today I'm in all black. I'd say it's my Berlin butch look. Black chinos, vintage black Adidas jumper. An archetypal look is blue jeans, white t-shirts, plaid shirts, belt, maybe Doc Martens. I quite often wear trainers, leather jackets . . .'

It's quite remarkable that the aesthetic has been maintained over the years. In the photos I've seen of butch lesbians in the 1950s, they were wearing the same gear. I suppose all of those clothing items have become such signifiers, they stand for something, are a shorthand of belonging.

It's much easier to spot a butch out in the wild than it is a femme (we'll be getting into this identity next, sit tight). And there is something quite nice about the silent semaphore of queerness. Maybe it's a haircut, maybe it's a key chain, or yes – a leather jacket worn just so. When you lock eyes with someone also in the uniform, a huge amount of knowledge passes between you in a second. I know that you know. There's a very specific lingering glance that lesbians exchange, sometimes a nod – rarely a smile. Ella says, 'I've had a fellow butch lesbian who worked in John Lewis obviously clock me. She gave me a free bag.'

We finish up lunch and start a slow meander through the labyrinthine aisle of north Greenwich IKEA. 'Is it also a misconception that all butch people are attracted to femme people?' I wonder aloud. 'Or is there some truth in it?' Ella pops a miniature IKEA bag keyring she wants to buy for her girlfriend into her basket and tells me that, yes, there is that dynamic. 'I am attracted to femme people. I think there is a butch/femme dynamic that has obviously been a thing for centuries. But the important thing to say is that if you are butch, you don't have to be with a femme person, you can be attracted to all different types of people, all different types of genders. But that dynamic works for a reason, right? There's this push and pull . . . and, well, a sexual tension!'

Hmm – there's a tick against my own butch checklist – I've always fancied girls who are more traditionally feminine than me.

Ella adds, 'I think sometimes you can overthink things, but the butch/femme dynamic for me – it's just fun, and it's part of my dating life, for sure. For me to feel truly accepted by someone I'm dating, and that actually the butch part of me is something that they're attracted to, is really nice.'

We've heard from Ella about the term soft butch. And we've met a stud. But what are some of the other categories of butch?

BUTCH LINGO

Stem: A Black lesbian who identifies as a mix between a stud and a femme.

Stone: A butch lesbian who is not comfortable with receiving sexual touch or penetration but may still engage in sexual activity with their partner.

Chapstick: A more androgynous or gender-neutral-presenting lesbian, often rejecting traditional feminine norms but not fully embracing a masculine presentation.

Diesel dyke: This term historically referred to a butch lesbian who worked in traditionally masculine occupations, such as truck driving or construction, but it's now considered somewhat dated and may carry negative connotations.

Hard butch: Butch lesbians who embrace a more stereotypically masculine presentation and demeanour, often eschewing elements of femininity entirely.

Futch: A blend of 'femme' and 'butch', futch lesbians embrace both masculine and feminine aspects of their identity and presentation, often fluctuating between the two depending on the situation or their mood.

What does it mean to be 'femme'?

Maybe I'm a chapstick lesbian or a futch, but I can't say I really want to align myself with any of these identities. Neither sounds particularly glamorous, let's face it. I might have gravitated towards one such label when I was younger, but probably in the same way I had horoscope books telling me that I was a typical Gemini. It's a pre-existing identity you can slip on like a dinner jacket. Are you creative and brilliant because you're a Gemini? Are you a 'butch' because you're a masc lesbian? Or are we all just deeply complicated and contradictory humans looking for certainty in a world of unknowns? I can also see that aligning oneself with a queer identity that comes with a whole cultural history and community can create an important sense of belonging. This can be hugely validating.

I met Alex (they/them), a twenty-four-year-old Swede, at a party. They are wearing a lace bodice, a ruched skirt and asymmetric pinstripe shirt and have a bleach-blonde crop of hair. For Alex, coming to London was a chance to 'really find out – what is my expression, what do I want to do, what do I stand for, what do I live for'.

Their first year in the city was about exploring their femininity through fashion and self-identification. Alex says, 'It was important for me to explore how can I present as feminine and feel safe and feel comfortable in that. Now, a year later, I've come into a stage where I'm going back to masculinity and reclaiming that. For me, it's about feeling confident and sexual in my masculinity, and feeling that I'm allowed to be sexual and I'm allowed to have urges and desires.'

For Alex, their embracing of femininity was political. 'I believe we need to free ourselves of expectations of how to perform gender. For me, I needed to dive deep into my femininity in order to redefine what masculine means to me. I was inspired to revisit what I take for granted, having been raised as a male. The expectation for gender to be played out in a certain way is something we need to work actively to unlearn. To many, playing a role and being theatrical is associated with femininity, yet it is when I perform my masculinity that I am my most theatrical.'

Personally, I've always been put off by how binaried the butch and femme identities are. Each is defined in opposition to the other. And there's something that feels very icky about that dynamic to me in its closeness to old-fashioned male/female heteronormativity. But after speaking to Roxy Bourdillon, editor of *DIVA* magazine, my mind is really opened to the way that binaries can be queered. By the end of our chat about identifying as 'femme',

I realize that it's maybe more interesting to see how binaries can work for us rather than against us. According to Roxy, it's about reframing what these butch/femme dynamics can mean within a queer context rather than associating them with heteronormativity – as you'll discover in this fascinating chat we had over Zoom one morning in February.

Let's meet . . . Roxy Bourdillon

Roxy Bourdillon is editor of DIVA *magazine (the UK's only newsstand lesbian magazine) and author of the memoir* What a Girl Wants *about her journey to understand her sexuality.*

I am a cis woman. I use she/her pronouns, and I am a lesbian. I'm also very comfortable with words like gay and queer. I am a passionate, committed femme.

I was always super, super girly. I always loved clothes and was obsessed with fashion. Being so traditionally feminine in my appearance is part of why it took me a long time to come out.

Did you feel like you somehow weren't gay enough because of your appearance?
When I was thirteen, overnight I developed and got a very curvaceous figure. And then not only was I perceived by the world as being straight, which is the default, I was really, unceasingly perceived as a man-eater. This was just because of my body, and the way women's bodies and different body shapes are treated in society.

How did you come through that and into your power as a queer person?
It was complicated, not only by the world seeing me like that, but by being quite a people-pleaser, which I think is something a lot of women and assigned female at birth (AFAB) people

and queer people generally can relate to – wanting to keep other people happy.

When I finally did come out, in my twenties, I had a year of trying to dress like a lesbian. I did give it a go. I did my best terrible impersonation of what I thought a lesbian could look like.

In terms of when I've been dating, I've mostly been presenting femme, but I did see a difference in being in gay bars when I went through my 'lesbian drag' phase! I definitely got into gay bars more easily and I definitely got fewer questions of 'why are you here?' Which I got whenever I was dressed more femme.

What does the label femme mean to you?

Being femme is often taken for weakness, which I think stems from misogyny and ideas about how people should present. But for me, femme and embracing being a femme as a queer person is really powerful. It feels like strength and sensuality and creativity and just what feels authentic for me personally.

There is something in reclaiming a way of presenting and expressing that traditionally has been seen as pandering to a male gaze. So, reclaiming that traditional femininity but at the same time rejecting the male gaze, and just living completely outside it. And there's something about that that feels very powerful.

And is there a kind of camp to femme?

I think that's really interesting because, yes, you could describe, certainly on some days, my femme-ness as camp, in a sense. A lot of my closest friends are straight women who are all feminine-presenting, but I'm definitely the highest-voltage feminine. I'm femming on a higher frequency!

While sometimes in the past in lesbian spaces I haven't felt necessarily a sense of belonging and I've detected a bit of a scepticism around my validity to be in those spaces, I have always had a lot of close friendships with gay and bi men who I've always felt really celebrated my feminine glamour. In terms of looking for style icons in the queer community, the only living ones I find are on *Drag Race*.

With the butch/femme binary, are we aping hetero dynamics or are these binaries becoming obsolete?

I have a lot of thoughts on that. Going back to when I first delved into the history of butch and femme, so in the 1940s and 50s, there was an underground bar scene for lesbians and bi women, queer women and non-binary people. Back then, for some of them, particularly for working-class queer people and lesbians, butch and femme was like creating our own codes of desire, our own structures, our own dating culture, our own way of knowing how you would attract a woman, or who would be the one who'd ask who to dance, and all of that stuff.

You could see that as, *well, you're just aping the traditional man and woman in a heteronormative relationship*. I personally don't see it as that. I feel like there's something in us creating our own ways of being.

For some of us, it feels the most authentic to be in this binary, but I don't think the binary is as simple as it looks on the surface. You can't kind of just look at a femme person or a butch person and know everything about them.

I think people are nuanced. And I also think that what we are moving towards is, yes, more playing between the binaries. Absolutely. But what I'd like is a world where everyone can just be themselves. And surely that's the point of us being queer people in the world – to be as true to ourselves as we can and live authentically.

What's so attractive about femininity?

I suppose I've always felt more comfortable around femininity than masculinity. I grew up in a family of women with two cousins who were like my sisters, and my aunts, their mums, neither of whom had particularly present men in their lives. My dad also was not the kind of textbook, beer-swigging, football-loving dad that greetings cards would have you believe is the norm. Our relationship was about art and literature, music and cooking. He took on the majority of the domestic chores in our house and made all the meals. I don't think of that as feminine, but I do think of it as not traditionally masc.

I love being around femme energy, but it feels *other* to me. I adore nothing more than being in the presence of a diva, it's why I loved working in women's magazines that were populated by a fabulous cast of larger-than-life women.

But it's not like I feel that I'm particularly masculine either. Unless my desire to link arms with a girl in heels, hold her handbag or help her slip into a faux-fur coat counts? Sports, DIY, cars, errrr . . . arm wrestling – not for me. I'm much more comfortable in feminine spaces and around femininity, even if I do feel a kind of distance from it. I'm beginning to think I might just be a bit camp.

Where I sit on the butch/femme continuum confounds me. But I might find some answers at the club night Fèmmme Fraîche. The lesbian DJ Michelle Manetti invited me and Stu to her monthly night at Dalston Superstore. It bills itself as FLINTA, which was a new term for me. It stands for *female, lesbian, intersex, non-binary, trans and agender.* (*Adds to queer dictionary*)

I arrive alone on a cold night in early March. Stu bails (you'll find out why in Chapter 15). I'm wearing a soft-butch outfit of jeans, vest top and sleeveless denim jacket. And I feel sexy in it, like I'm projecting the right message about myself. Even though I'm definitely not a butch lesbian . . .

The bar upstairs is pretty chilled out, with groups of queers drinking cocktails and yapping. I bump into some old friends and am soon three cocktails deep and heading to the dancefloor downstairs. The energy is, as the name suggests, decidedly queer and femme compared to the gay boys' nights I've been to.

I'm introduced to a friend of a friend called Flora Parkin. She's a trans woman and is wearing fishnet tights, heels and bra top. She looks fantastic. We exchange numbers as I've got so many questions for her about her own relationship with femininity, but the music is too loud to ask them here.

Here's the chat we had over email a few days later.

As a trans woman have you ever felt like you have to prove your femininity to those who gatekeep your access to gender-affirming treatments?

When getting a private gender dysphoria diagnosis, I had to jump through all the hoops I'd been told to expect of medical transition pathways; being evaluated by cis GPs, and through a gender-binary lens. My diagnosis report notes that I presented as a 'well-kempt, appropriately dressed transgender woman', with 'appropriate' carrying a lot there. Conversely, in the five years that I've been waiting for access to the NHS gender identity services, the landscape of care has changed in some positive ways. Initiatives like Trans Plus (run out of 56 Dean Street, in London) and the Sussex Gender Service (SGS) employ trans GPs, are self-conscious of the outdated approach to diagnosis and service referral, and are more open to non-binary gender and plural gender identities, providing services that match. Their approach has been to help me access the services I need to live comfortably in my body, whatever that looks like for me.

Do you feel a pressure to be 'femme' as a trans woman, and that you might need to hide the less traditionally feminine sides to yourself?

I'm a sporty femme, and I tend to dress understated and gender neutral in my day to day. I've consciously tried to resist any pressure to perform aspects of femininity that don't feel authentic to me, as if to meet expectations of proving myself as a trans woman. Things like painting my nails aren't very me. But it quickly becomes a slippery, regressive slope when categorizing examples of trad femininity seen as 'expected'; everyone performs, reclaims, expresses and rethinks components of fashion and gender in a unique gorgeous cocktail according to their life and how they want to exist in society.

In your own journey to becoming the woman you are, how have your ideas about femininity changed?

I've gone back and forth between tomboyish neutral aesthetics, to floral prints, to sporty athleisure, to hyper-femininity, often thinking I had to find my way of authentically communicating all my inner genders permanently and authentically. Now I understand that femininity can be a display, and fashion a way of moving through the world as a performance of gender. I've arrived at a place where my femininity is fluid and multiple.

Am I butch? Am I femme? Am I neither, or both? Personally, I'm happy circling these identities and never quite landing on one. But it's been fascinating to learn about how great a sense of self and of belonging some queer people can find in butch lesbian, stud or femme communities.

Chapter 7

Serving Body

Stu

I wake up in a strange room. I'm not quite sure where I am, and I feel like I've been wrapped up like an Egyptian mummy. I'm bound tight. Am I dead? Is this gay afterlife? If so, where are the spicy margs and Princess Diana? Things slowly come into focus and I look down at my body, which someone else has squeezed into a black body suit. I'm having major *Death Becomes Her,* 'Ernest, why am I in the morgue?' vibes (If you don't get the reference, well, you need more queer education than you originally thought.) I try to move, and I feel an immediate soreness in my chest. It's then that I remember where I am and why I'm here. You see, reader, I've had my own version of top surgery (the term for chest reconstruction within the trans community).

I was seven when I started putting on weight. I was comfort eating due to some changes in my family life, and these changes ended up turning into emotional and physical abuse by a step-parent. By the time I was thirteen, I was severely overweight, and that thirteen-year-old has lived inside me ever since. My stepfather would call me fat and bully me about my weight constantly. I think that thirteen-year-old will always be part of me, I'll never escape him and his sadness at being the 'fat one at school', and the 'fat one' at home. I then became the 'fat one at college' and then the 'fat one' on the dancefloor at Revenge in Brighton at age eighteen, even though by that point I'd lost five stone because of my militant approach to the 'new' Atkins diet. I never saw the five-stone loss in the mirror, and I felt it even more when I tried to squeeze into the top my skinny friend suggested I wear for our entry into the gay scene.

Body dysmorphia is a mental disorder which causes persistent, intense focus, shame and anxiety over perceived *body* defects. But I find it impossible to admit that I might have dysmorphia, because to have it would mean that my view of my body is 'distorted'. Whereas I truly believe, to my core, that I am fat, not the right shape, and completely unattractive. It's also ironic that after losing five stone and starting to feel slightly better about myself I then entered the gay scene and felt like I'd taken five steps back. Here was a world full of toned, buff bodies, sweat glistening on the pecs of guys as they merged on the dancefloor, firm skin touching firm skin as they caressed one another while the latest Madonna remix pulsated through the club.

Do I fancy you or do I want to *be* you?

When I was growing up, magazines like *Attitude* and *Gay Times* celebrated the six-pack hunk in pages filled with body types that were utterly different from my own. I wanted to find out whether seeing these supposed role models had the same sort of effect on others as it did on me, so I've asked Ian Howley, from mental health and wellbeing organization LGBT HERO, about how common body dysmorphia is within the gay scene.

'It's a subject that has both changed and stayed the same,' he tells me. 'About ten to fifteen years ago, we used to see a lot of criticism towards gay magazines for constantly putting hot, shirtless guys on the cover. Then they changed their approach and stopped doing that as much because they saw the negative impact it was having. Then social media exploded. Suddenly, you have all these people on OnlyFans capitalizing on Instagram's algorithm, and they're essentially gaybaiting. Because of the way the algorithm works, you interact with one, and it starts showing you more and more. Essentially, nothing's changed; we've just moved from magazines to social media. I think what's happening is a lot of our younger community members are seeing that and believing it is the best way to be validated – by looking good and over-sexualizing themselves. We praise people for looking good. People want that validation. I don't think body dysmorphia stops or starts at a certain age. It can happen at any time. I just turned forty and even I, with all the knowledge I have, still fall into that trap.'

It's a trap I find myself in daily when I look down at my body. And for those of us who fancy people of the same sex, it's some-times tricky to identify whether what we're feeling is gay attraction or body envy. It's a fascinating push and pull that I'm sure contrib-utes to the complicated feelings that many queer individuals have in regard to body image. On Instagram, for example, when I'm served an image of a hot guy, part of my brain falls into lust mode, whereas the other part is jealous and makes me feel inadequate in comparison. It's a bizarre sensation and one that's fairly unique to LGBTQ+ people. I ask Lotte if she feels the same way: 'Luckily, for me, the women I'm attracted to are not at all how I want to look myself. I get more body envy of men – particularly their chests and arms. I *kind of* fancy them but I also really would love to have tiny hips, a muscular flat chest and good arms myself and enjoy the freedom of taking my top off in public.'

Would you take your top off in a club?

Ahhh, taking your top off in public. What a luxury that would be. The thought of feeling free enough to whip my top off without even thinking about it, even by the pool, even when alone, is an alien one. Much of this, for me, is because my 'moobs' [aka man boobs] developed in a spectacular way when I was a fatty teen and no matter how my weight has yo-yoed they have remained a permanent fixture, always making me feel out of place and insecure. My t-shirts would feel tight against my chest, my boobs would bounce as I ran at the gym, and I could squeeze them together in a beautiful display of cleavage. At school I'd hear the taunt 'you've got bigger tits than my mum' on a near-daily basis. Like most things about myself, I learned to try to mask them with comedy. I'd reference my moobs before anyone else had a chance to and pretend I was in on the joke. 'Wanna cop a feel?' I started to retort to the bullies on the playground, and I'd watch them run, squealing 'eurgh'. That approach may have looked like it gave me a form of power, but in reality, my moobs made me feel powerless, and sad.

I once went to see my doctor as I'd read about how some men genuinely do have a condition called gynecomastia. This creates breasts because of hormone and testosterone imbalances in the body. I'd got myself quite excited about this idea: could my breasts actually be the result of this, and if so, perhaps there would be a fix? I was referred to a breast clinic in Paddington and it was only when I arrived that I realized they predominantly dealt with breast cancer. So, there I was, sitting with a group of women who had come to the clinic fearing the worst. I felt like such a fraud and wanted to hit an escape button. But before I could eject, I was quickly called through. I then had to sit in a room wearing a backless gown next to a woman wearing the same who looked petrified at the potential test she was about to have. The doctor took me through to a side room and had me lie down on a bed. He covered my chest in jelly and started an ultrasound. 'Hmmmm,' he kept going, then, 'Yep, just fat. Yes, lots of fat here, and here.' He moved to the other one. 'More fat. You've got lots of fat here.' I lay there mortified, just wondering how many more times he could utter the word FAT.

Clearly, I had no hormonal imbalances, and as I walked out of the clinic my shame and fat, saggy boobs felt heavier than ever. Ever since that incident I'd been thinking about having surgery, privately paid for, to get rid of my 'man boobs'. So, as a present to myself ahead of my fortieth birthday I decided to take the plunge. I was tired of them. I was *'Je suis fatty gay'*. I'd spent almost thirty years feeling rubbish about myself and I decided to take action, so here I am lying on what I'd thought, for just that moment when I woke up, was a morgue slab, with my moobs no longer attached to my body. The surgeon had removed 5kg of tissue from my chest and I instantly felt lighter, in more ways than one. Should I have done it? Is surgery the answer? These are questions I've gone over lots of times with my therapist. It wasn't a quick fix to my weight insecurities, and I know no matter how much I had pumped out I would forever have thirteen-year-old Stu looking back at me in the mirror.

Is it really possible to be body positive?

I applaud those who promote body positivity and seem to feel happy in their own skin. But because of my own feelings, I often have a hard time believing them. I decided to have a chat to Bethany Rutter, a bisexual author who has written many fabulous books that cover the topic of weight, and also the writer Essie Dennis, who wrote the incredible book *Queer Body Power*. I ask them first about the term 'body positivity', which, as I say, always feels at odds with how I feel about myself.

'"Body positivity" often gets projected onto people who are not thin and don't hate themselves, both of which apply to me,' Bethany tells me. 'But I don't really love it as a label. It's always felt very self-serving, like, "I feel positive about my body" and that's the end goal, whereas for me the goal is liberation for all bodies, which means that people of all sizes have equal access to healthcare, justice, employment, clothing, humane treatment by their fellow people.'

Essie has similar views: 'I go back and forth on this term because I feel like the meaning has often been changed or stripped back. I do describe myself as body positive on a social and political level. As a framework, I believe that we all fundamentally deserve respect regardless of how our body looks or functions. This applies to issues from clothing size to availability of healthcare. Body positivity to me is not just a personal thought process but applies to us all.'

I share my own experience of body dysmorphia with Essie and she says, 'Body Dysmorphic Disorder is something it took me a while to accept because, like you said, I believed my body was disgusting or abnormal. Sometimes, my feelings about my body would even stop me from leaving the house. However, it's not just about having a distorted view of your body but being far too pre-occupied with your body. BDD means you end up worrying about your body and its perceived flaws to an extreme degree, so it takes a lot of work to unpick that.'

My issues have deep-seated personal origins, but worrying about how other gay men view me and my body has definitely fed into them. I wonder whether queer women have that same feeling? With the male gaze removed, do they feel more liberated? 'It's hard to say,' Bethany reflects when I put this to her. 'I think queer women are probably more likely to be doing some kind of "unlearning" work around social norms, and that often crosses over with body image, but I think it would be inaccurate to say that queer women are free of (internalized) fatphobia or body image issues. When I was dating in my early twenties, I was often around women who were adjacent to a queer punk scene at the time and I felt a lot more comfortable with things like not removing body hair or not conforming to feminine gender stereotypes in how I presented myself. But I don't think that is true of all queer social scenes or queer women in general.'

'Although queer women do struggle on a societal level with their presentation, being somewhat divorced from heteropatriarchal beauty values means that there is generally less body dissatisfaction within sapphic communities,' adds Essie. 'However, there are a lot of different experiences within the "queer women" umbrella, so that has to be taken into account: a cis lesbian may have very different experiences with their body than a trans lesbian, for instance.' But, Essie, do you feel that being queer liberates you from traditional notions of what a female body should look like? 'Definitely! I feel like I was boxed in by arbitrary body rules for most of my life and when I came out, I was able to look at myself and decide what I wanted. Queerness saved me.'

And from a bisexual point of view? How does Bethany feel men and women respond differently to her body? 'I think in general the response is the same,' she says. 'But maybe I would say that there was a touch more curiosity from women, especially thin ones. I think I projected more expectations onto how women would view my body and assumed it would be negative because of the social conditioning women get, but I don't think my experiences really mirrored that in any meaningful way. I do feel that being queer is a form of body liberation to a certain extent. I can't really explain why, but it's something I've always felt. Maybe I've found queer spaces more celebratory and fun and liberating for my body?'

What body pressures do trans men take on?

When I think about my own body issue as a gay man, I can obviously only relate from a cis point of view. What's it like to be a trans man, in a gay world, full of the same pressures?

I talked again to Harry Nicholas, author of *A Trans Man Walks*

Into a Gay Bar, about the body pressures they face. He says: 'I am trying not to, but I find it very difficult to not compare myself to cis men. I try to embrace the queerness that I do have. It can be quite tricky with gay underwear, especially with jockstraps, and because they sit quite low down on the hip, which means that for me, as my hips are quite curved, I have to wear extra large just for it to fit right. The dysphoria for me is not from wearing XL size, but rather that in most other clothing I wear a size small. There is a contrast that feels like an alarming jump. There is an expectation of gay underwear companies that everyone has (or should have) this perfect body and if you don't, well, these clothes simply aren't for you.'

I ask if he feels held to even more impossible expectations to prove his strength, virility and masculinity as a trans man. 'Yeah, it can be exhausting. It's only recently that I've felt comfortable to go to the gym. Even though I'm nine years on testosterone now. I haven't had the confidence to know what I'm doing and be in that space and be in a changing room. There is an expectation to have that perfect male body, but also there are the limitations of not being able to go and exercise and achieve that, especially because with surgeries, you are looking at four, five years in terms of waiting lists on the NHS. You are having to exercise and bind [the practice of flattening the chest] at the same time, which is just hell.'

'Strangely, starting the gym has made me more hyper-critical of my body,' adds Harry. 'Sure, occasionally I feel some real joy and euphoria from filling t-shirts slightly better around the shoulders and chest than I did before, and I like seeing and feeling progress, but equally I'm even more conscious of my body than I ever have been – and even more conscious of how my body compares to cis men. I can restrict my diet and do all the exercise in the world, but it's confronting to realize that there are some things I simply cannot change. There isn't any amount of exercise or surgery which can make my hip bones smaller, for instance. Despite how much I do love my transness – the life experiences and the people it's brought me towards – there are moments, especially in the gym, that these realizations hit and my body becomes difficult to be in.'

The struggle trans people have with accessing the appropriate healthcare is certainly not helping things in terms of the body issues that arise pre-, post- and during transition. In a wide-ranging student study, the British Psychological Society recently reported that 'genderqueer and gender non-conforming students were most likely to be at risk of eating disorder (38.8 per cent of this group showed "clinically relevant" eating disorder symptoms), followed by trans women (37.1 per cent), gender expansive students (34 per cent), and trans men (34 per cent).'[1] They also found that 'Trans men who identified as gay, bisexual or queer were more likely to be at risk of an eating disorder than straight trans men.'

Charlie, a trans man who lives with an eating disorder, told the charity Young Minds that when he reached out for help he was turned away from the eating disorder service. 'They told me they could not help because of my issues around gender dysphoria. In place of actual support or treatment, I was told I should consider starting to eat three meals a day. At the time, I took this as a sign that I wasn't "sick enough", but I now realize that I was not the problem. Instead, the issue lies with services that are unequipped to deal with anyone who falls outside of the cisgender female archetype of what eating disorders look like. For a while, I thought I would never recover.'

I think when cis people consider the healthcare 'treatment' that trans people face, most of us think only of gender realignment surgeries, but this focus on eating and body issues demonstrates the very real struggle they face across every aspect of our health-care system.

What does it feel like to be both queer and disabled?

My struggles have been about weight and body image, but there are plenty of other ways in which our bodies can feel like they're failing us. Lotte introduces me to one of her oldest friends, Will Simpson. He's a perfect illustration of someone who's so good-looking that I don't know whether I'm more attracted to him or jealous of him. He has a beard that is big and bushy in a sexy woodcutter way, and he has gorgeous blue eyes. Very dashing. But what he presents on the surface is only part of the story.

'A few years ago,' he tells me, 'I was making the most of my life and was pretty normal healthwise – not particularly healthy, not particularly unhealthy. I used to run, but I used to drink. I used to smoke a couple of rollies here and there, but by no means was I considered problematic. But then the doctors found a mass in the upper section of my colon, which had been causing a blockage. That mass was cancerous and had spread.

'They performed a major surgery called a "Whipple procedure". It meant nothing to me at the time and so I said, "Great! That's fantastic. I'm really pleased to hear." But what happens with the Whipple is that it is a complete re-plumbing of everything. They cut a whole bunch out and basically give your digestive system a completely new route.'

Following this surgery, Will went on to have multiple month-long stays in hospital, a number of fistulas (an abnormal passageway that develops to carry waste from inside your body to outside the skin), had a stoma bag fitted (collects body waste in a bag outside your body) and now has to get nutrients from a TPN feed that's connected to him three times a week, for twelve hours at a time. Total parenteral nutrition (TPN) is a method of feeding that provides nutrients and fluids to a person through a vein, bypassing the gastrointestinal tract. It's used when someone can't or shouldn't consume food or fluids orally. So after an emergency pancreatectomy, being diagnosed with Type 1 diabetes, along with managing three stoma bags (one obstructed stoma, two fistulas) and TPN, he had to quit his job in corporate hospitality.

I ask him how things have changed for him, specifically as a gay man living with this life-altering, yet invisible disability? 'I was just starting off a relationship when it happened. I was in my prime and, let's say, I was definitely sowing my wild oats around town. I was very happy with my sex life, my relationships.'

Is Will getting back into the dating scene now? 'It's complicated,' he says. 'After major surgery, your brain goes into survival mode and switches off your libido. Thoughts of sexuality disappear. That had some benefits because I wasn't worried about having a relationship or sex. It was a non-issue for a long time. It took over a year before I could even consider anything sexual. Essentially, I was asexual for a while. You could have convinced me I could be married to a woman because my brain wasn't registering anything sexual. Thankfully, when I started trying to get things working again, my initial responses to pornography were definitely with men, which was a relief.

'Now I am exploring dating, but having a hidden disability does complicate things. You can present yourself as very able-bodied, though you have to put yourself in the shoes of the person you're wanting to date. I feel obliged to be fully open and tell them everything about what they'd be getting into in terms of my body and the stoma bags and fistulas I have. This puts me in a vulnerable position and takes away the fun or pleasure of dating. I have to be as transparent as is necessary, rather than telling them "everything" they'd be getting. Socializing in public comes with its own risks, real or perceived, when it comes to stoma management. Leaks, changes, smells, cubicle visits. Bar life, straight or gay, brings its own set of challenges.

'Ultimately, though, this procedure saved my life. Would I go through it all again? That is a question I'm not sure I know the answer to, but I do know that I'm grateful to be here and even with the radical changes in body, my soul is very much still intact. If you are in any way worried about changes to your poo and digestive regime, go and see a doctor ASAP.'

After my chat with Will I reflect on the ways in which his body has affected his own sense of queerness. I think it's an easy trap to fall into to think, 'Oh, I have it so much easier than others, why am I worried about eating crisps or wearing a tight-fitting t-shirt?' I wish I could think like that, but someone else's condition doesn't immediately fix my own, although it does, of course, provide some useful perspective, and I think we could all benefit from being more aware of the double discrimination faced by queer disabled people.

So, is the LGBTQ+ community predominantly ableist? Cis, white, able-bodied people have always been portrayed as the face of queerness and our queer spaces don't seem to fully accommodate those that have additional needs.

Let's meet . . . Simi

Simi Roach is a queer, Black, gender non-conforming lesbian, and a permanent wheelchair user who can share some interesting insights on whether the LGBTQ+ community is predominantly ableist.

Simi, how do you define your disability?

I was born with a disability, but it was progressive. It didn't really show any signs or symptoms until I was eleven. I tend not to use my diagnosis because it's really long and no one really knows what it is. So I just use 'disabled' mostly.

At that age people typically start questioning their identity and figuring out their queerness. What was that experience like for you, dealing with both your queerness and your body changing so drastically?

It was really tough. I used to call it 'reverse puberty', because everyone else's bodies were changing in typical ways, but mine was deteriorating. My body felt very separate from me, and that's something that comes into play with transness too. There are studies that show a correlation, and many disabled people I know are trans. I think it's almost easier for disabled people to discover their trans identities because they experience that separation from their bodies. I have a stranger come to my house every day to give me a shower. My body feels medicalized, and it helps me realize it's not fully who I am. Other disabled people have said similar things to me.

For so long the idea of being gay or queer has been dominated by the image of the cis, white, able-bodied people, particularly in the media. Would you agree that disabled representation is still lacking, especially in queer spaces?

One hundred per cent. Disability representation is still in its infancy. It's frustrating, I still haven't seen a Black woman in a wheelchair in any film or TV show. We're still at the point where just having a disabled person on screen is a step forward, and intersectionality is lagging behind. But it doesn't have to be that way.

How do you feel about having so many labels? Does it ever exhaust you, having to explain who you are all the time?

It's not as difficult as it may seem. I talk about this a lot with my trans disabled friends. There's a whole spectrum of expression, and some focus on passing. I exist more in the confusion of gender. I might wear facial hair but not a chest binder, or I might wear an obviously fake moustache. I'm comfortable with that confusion and weirdness. As long as I get to be free and express myself, I'm fine with it. The toughest thing is finding community. The queer community can sometimes be more ableist than they realize.

How can it be like navigating things with family?
It's a very different dynamic. My queer disabled friends some-times feel unsafe because some of them rely on their parents for everything – whether they eat that day, get washed, everything. And if your parents are very clear about being against trans and gay people, you start to worry about how coming out could affect you. So you feel trapped because you can't take care of yourself on your own – you need your parents for everything. When you're so dependent on them, it's terrifying. Even dating can be complicated. My parents had to drop me off at dates – you can imagine how for some that might be a problem.

How do you think the broader queer community can better support disabled queer individuals?
It starts with education, representation and communication. Most people, even disabled people, have internalized ableism. Society teaches us that disability is something bad, but so much of what we learn about disabled people is a lie. Many wheelchair users can walk, but when we stand up, people yell at us in the street. It's a huge gap between perception and reality. I wish people would engage with disabled media, support disability Pride, and see us as valuable contributors to society.

Do you think some people are nervous about approaching disabled people because they don't want to get it wrong?
Definitely. I feel people overthink it, but it's completely fine to approach us. Some people tell me they were scared to come

over, but honestly, it's always OK. I appreciate people's support. For me, my queer identity, my Black identity and my disabled identity overlap a lot more than people might think. I'm incredibly proud to be queer and disabled. I see so much beauty in disability, but others often see brokenness. I wish people could see the beauty that I see. We add to the beauty of the world. I just wish more people saw that.

There's often a lot of vanity in the queer community, with certain beauty standards. How do you feel about that?
It's tough, especially in dating. The beauty standards are so high, particularly in the gay and lesbian communities, and I'll never fit that standard. I see so much beauty in disability, but other people see brokenness, something wrong, something that needs to be fixed. Even with the people I know who try so hard to 'pass', like some of the trans people in my life. It's such a stress for them – worrying about how they're perceived, to the point where it's detrimental to their health. The standards are tough. But that's why I love being part of the disabled community. They teach you, more than anyone, that how we are naturally in our bodies is already perfect.

It's now been almost a year since my surgery. Do I feel happier? I don't regret it and I do feel more confident, but even this week I've resisted the urge to take off my top while sunbathing on a hot summer's day. Of course, modern-day queerness is showing that there are so many ways to fit into mainstream gay male culture, even if you aren't a Ken doll. Bears embrace bigger bodies and hairier chests, daddies are old, or at least act like they are, and chub has become a popular porn category. I don't think I could ever comfortably define myself as one of these. It would almost be like admitting defeat.

But should I try to embrace the 'thick' me? I feel I'm still in the battle and will be for quite some time, possibly for ever. As a community we have an in-built shame that makes some of us desire to prove that we're just as good, just as valid and just as strong as cis straight people. So, we work harder, we count calories, we go to the gym every day, some even take steroids to bulk up the appearance of our muscles. So many gay men were bullied as kids for not fitting in with the other boys, or maybe being a bit less interested in sport. Some of us were called 'weak' or 'sissy' at school and now we are adults we want to exorcise that shame through . . . exercise. And, of course, the AIDS crisis, as we'll explore more in Chapter 11, had a seismic impact on gay culture – wellness, fitness – it wasn't just aesthetics, it was survival. So in the aftermath of that epidemic, being fit and strong was perhaps a response to the sickness that we had seen ravage our community. The whole issue is incredibly complex but, like everything else, hopefully we can learn to understand each other's bodies a bit better, respect them, and love ourselves more.

Chapter 8

Fundamentally Frivolous? Understanding Camp and Drag

Lotte

It's amazing what a bit of contouring can do. As Jen (they/them) swipes the makeup across their cheekbones, their drag alter ego Adam begins to emerge. I'm at the south London home they share with wife Elly (aka Apple Derrieres), to watch them get ready for a show and chat about all things drag, including the performance of masculinity and femininity. Jen applies volumizing powder to their hair and sculpts Adam's trademark quiff.

Their modest London home is (in my view) a temple to camp – their cat sits on a throne, they have a hand-carved Edwardian mahogany four-poster bed in their boudoir, and a portrait of themselves created with gold glitter on the wall of the dressing room. But when I mention that it strikes me as quite fabulously camp, as interiors go, they look a little bemused. I don't think that was their intention and now I'm worried I've offended a king!

'I don't know what camp is any more,' says Adam. 'It's been so disentangled and changed and championed and mocked . . . People call me camp. They can have that if they want. Whatever.'

Adam's reaction goes to show how slippery camp is as a concept. It's hard to pin down or to describe with a single definition. Kenneth Williams, a camp icon in British comedy in the 1960s and 70s and star of the *Carry On* series, told a BBC interviewer at the time that camp meant something 'fundamentally frivolous'. Maybe. But there's more to it. Camp keeps you on your toes, it can't be captured or distilled, it's so big and so amorphous, and isn't that larger-than-lifeness in itself just so camp? I think before we talk more about drag it's worth dipping our (twinkle) toes a bit deeper into camp, because in the words of the camp crooner classic 'Love and Marriage', you can't have one without the other.

Should we carry on camping?

As soon as I finished reading Paul Baker's book *Camp!*, I knew I had to speak to him. It's such a brilliant romp through the history of camp and is full of high and low cultural moments that are woven together with a flourish. Paul is a professor of English Language at Lancaster University. We spoke over Zoom the day after Stu and I had been to a *Priscilla, Queen of the Desert*-themed party together, which was probably the campest thing I've been to, ever, given its heady cocktail of drag queens, disco music, Kylie, tins of bad wine and a room full of huns and gays on the razz wearing feather boas and sequins.

> **Hi, Paul! Let's start with that elusive definition of camp. You explore a few different ones in your book – is there one definitive explanation that feels most right to you?**
> Camp is about excess or exaggeration. Not conforming to society's standards of expected behaviour for the gender that you were assigned at birth, artificiality, and also silliness or ridiculousness. Then there's a question about intentionality. So if it's all of those things, and it's funny and it's not intended to be, then it's camp. But if it's all of those things and it's intended to be funny, then it's more campy (an American term). I think it is a useful distinction to make.

Is camp genderless?

That's a tricky question. Anyone can be camp, or anything can be camp. Objects can be camp. So it can be genderless or it can be extremely gendered, depending on who's doing it and whether (if we think of gender as an assigned set of behaviours) it is going against type in some way.

So in that case, can the presentation of masculinity from masc gay men and butch lesbians be camp too?

I think so. It's probably a less common way of being camp, but it's not even just gay men. Think of cis, straight men who have this exaggerated masculinity. I think Andrew Tate is very camp, for example. Because of the ridiculousness. And Donald Trump as well. Camp is not always a force for good.

Do you think camp is becoming increasingly separated from gay maleness?

I think gay maleness is still a big part of it, but I think there's a wider understanding of camp now. So maybe it's not separation, maybe it's more like an addition. There are more people getting it and finding it funny and creating it as well.

Gen Z has a generalized reputation for being quite earnest and political. Is there a place for camp there?

I hope so. Part of the reason why I wrote my book was for Gen Z to get an insight into the history of camp. I teach this generation, nineteen- to twenty-three-year-olds, in my role as a university lecturer, and I've noticed they love history, whether that's Polari (a form of gay slang that gay people used up until around the 1970s as a way of conducting conversations in public spaces or just to have a camp laugh with each other) or the abolition of Section 28, a lot of young people love the fact that they've got this aspect of their identity, which can be traced back quite a long way, and there are all these other people who have fought for the rights they have.

It's a bit of a difficult one, though, in that camp is the opposite of earnest in a way. Maybe my generation, Gen X, was more open to camp because the 90s were a period of irony and of making fun of things and not really feeling that we had much of a culture. So we had to just borrow it from the past and then we made fun of it.

The point of this book is to really unify our LGBTQ+ community and shine a light on all the different intersections within it and get us understanding a bit more about each other. Is camp something that can transcend some of those intersections and bring us together?

I would love it if that could happen. I've never tried it. I've never got a load of different people in a room and said, 'What can we find to laugh at and with?'

But looking at some of the movements camp has helped in the past, like fighting back against economic depressions, or just finding a way to laugh when there wasn't a lot to laugh at, lets me think that camp does have that power.

I think we queer people are under attack. Not just in the UK, but around the world. Different governments want to erase us or ban us. And then there's a little bit more infighting or a lack of cohesiveness than maybe there was, say, twenty years ago, which is a shame. It would be nice to think that camp could be the thing that lets us laugh a bit more and laugh together.

Stu's told me about being very camp as a child and how that was a kind of protection against being bullied . . . is that often the case?

Camp is definitely an armour. Fighting back comes from being witty and being able to pick on someone's flaws or talk about them in a funny way. So I think there's definitely a sense of camp being used as a form of defence. It's an amazing feeling when you meet a fellow camp kid when you're young, especially if you've felt so isolated for such a long time, and then you find that one person who's maybe a bit like you and gets the world in the way you do and is also a bit of an outsider. It's the first time you realize, I've been having to do all the work to fit in with these normal kids. And then suddenly I can be myself around this other kid. It's the best friendship you'll ever have.

CLOSER TO GOD (IN HEELS)

We couldn't have a chapter on camp and drag without hearing from Stu. He's always wanted to embrace the drag queen inside him, but something's been holding him back. Here he shares why and what happened when he leaned into, and toppled over in, his desire to wear high heels.

It feels such a cliché to think of a young gay strutting around in his mum's heels but, hands up, I very much lived up to this stereotype. I remember trying to totter around her bedroom in a pair of ugly 80s courts (sorry, Mum). I loved them. I still do. But as a young, closeted, gay boy I was hyper-conscious about being seen as too feminine, or camp.

By the time I was in my late twenties my sense of self had completely taken hold and my high-heeled dreams slipped away. As I've got older, even as I've gained more confidence in areas of my queer appearance, the heel has remained firmly off the table.

Until now.

I've been put off – at least in part – due to the lack of skill

I presume I have in this area. But can you teach an old gay new tricks? I really hope so, because as soon as we decided to explore the notion of camp I knew I wanted to dust off those heels and give it all another go, with the goal of being able to strut it in stilettos by the time I hit forty (if not sooner). But this time, instead of raiding my mum's shoe closet, I head to ASOS to browse.

At this stage in my heel journey I avoid the strappy options and plump instead for a simpler pair of black stilettos. I click order and sit patiently at home for my purchase to arrive. While I wait for my new shoes to come, I message *Everybody's Talking About Jamie* musical star Layton Williams for a spot of advice. He's just made his debut on *Strictly Come Dancing* and slayed it in a pair of killer heels. He too embraced his mother's shoes when he was a boy.

'I would always run around in my mum's heels when I was a kid,' he tells me. 'There was always a slight bit of shame attached to it, so if ever I thought someone was going to catch me I would hide them. But as soon as I got the opportunity to actually perform in heels I made them remake my shoes because the heel was too small. I'm not gonna be running around in kittens, I can tell you that much! If I'm going to give you any tips, Stu, then it's all about sinking in the hip. It's like a sense of armour when you put them on. You really do feel way more feminine. And it's about the way it makes you feel. In shows it has helped me really bring my characters to life because I really felt the femininity. Do start slow, slowly but surely, just start strutting and you'll feel more confident with it. It's really about the energy that it makes you feel, not necessarily what you look like. The more confident you get, you'll start feeling fabulous.'

And then the big day arrives. My new heels are here! I slip them on. But as I totter around in my bedroom like a baby fawn on ice, with my kids laughing at me, I know it's time to seek some professional help. As helpful as Layton's words were, I look up the dance group Rainbow Nation Dance Academy online. They are a queer dance company run by Alex Scurr. Alex sets me up for private heels tutorials with one of his choreographers, Tatiana. I drag Lotte along, who, on the day, informs me she actually doesn't own a pair of heels. I gasp and drag her to the nearest TK Maxx to pick out a cheap pair so she too can prance around a dance studio to perfect her sashay. As we head to the venue in south London I'm excited yet nervous, and I wonder if I'm being a fool to try something like this.

We meet Tatiana, a queer Russian firecracker with bright green hair, and she's ready to put us through our paces. We spend a lot of time warming up to get our heels, legs and core ready for the runway. As per usual, I'm overthinking it. My hips need to match my straight leg, but my leg can't stay straight, then I keep messing up my heel pose and my ankles apparently have a life of their own. Lotte's whipped off her white jeans and donned her shorty shorts. The legs are out, girls, and she looks hot!

The session is over in a heartbeat, and while I feel more confident than I ever did in a pair of heels, I want to spend longer sashaying around the room. My inner diva has been unlocked! While Lotte has to dash for her adult swimming lesson (reader, she's getting more Jodie Foster day by day), I find out that Tatiana is just about to teach a 'vogueing' class. I decide to throw my inhibitions out the window and ask if I can join. She wisely advises me to ditch the heels for this one. 'Maybe try a lower heel next time,' she tells me. What can I say? I felt it was a go hard or go home situation! So, I pack my new shoes back into my bag and slip on a much more sensible pair of trainers.

I step into the larger studio, which looks like something out of Madonna's 'Hung Up' video and watch as the incredibly confident men start strutting into the room, dressed in vest tops with biceps bulging. Something strange then happens – well, strange for me, at least. One comes up and says hello and gives me a warm hug, asking if I've ever done anything like this before. Then another, called Rodrigo, tells me that if I get through the warmup all will be fine. The class is a joy from start to finish. I feel so confident and, weirdly enough, sexy, despite my body and confidence issues. I think a large part of this was down to the energy of the room and the encouragement I received from the queer guys around me. I'm so used to being in gay spaces that make me feel uncomfortable and anxious, but they made me feel confident, camp and glorious. At the end of the class, where we have been sashaying around to Beyoncé's 'Cuff It', I chat to Elliot, who was one of the kind guys that welcomed me at the start. 'The wonderful thing about vogue is the confidence it gives you,' he tells me. 'Even if it feels delusional, you have to believe you are the most gorgeous thing in the room. That's the attitude you need.'

Is camp the same as 'feminine'?

Camp has often been understood as synonymous with femininity. But I don't think it's as simple as that because it comes with an artifice, a specific hyperness, like the kind Roxy Bourdillon spoke about in Chapter 6. 'Femming on a higher frequency,' as she put it. It's this that elevates regular femininity to high-camp status.

In the 1980s and 90s, boys of my generation were told there was something wrong or shameful about showing any femininity or campness. Today, I notice boys in my daughter's playground with painted nails, wearing Elsa dresses, like it's no big deal, which it obviously isn't. But what about when they get older and are maybe finding their place in the queer community? Will they want to explore their femininity? Will they embrace camp?

And anyway, gay male masculinity is so over the top. A room full of muscle men with their tops off all snogging each other? It's masculinity on steroids – literally! This whole Masc4Masc short-hand, and the Grindr lingo 'No femmes', is designed to project an image of being manly and masculine, but isn't it just, I don't know, a bit silly?

I first met Jen, who performs as the drag king Adam All, and their wife Elly, whose stage name is Apple Derrieres, when they did a drag show at the launch of my children's picture book *My Magic Family* – Elly is one of the few cis women queens on the scene. Adam All (the character, not Jen, the artist behind him) is one of those men who just desperately wants to be perceived as manly but is actually quite sweet and sensitive and nuanced. The humour of his character in performances comes from the tension.

'I've always been interested in why is that masculine? Why is that feminine? Why is this that I'm doing, or the way that I look, why is that wrong for the body that I have? What is every-one's bloody problem?' Adam says as he slips on his blazer and adjusts his bowtie. 'Trying to work it all out has got to the point that, for me, it can't be anything but art now. Masculinity is very often completely misunderstood as being a neutral ground and people think of it as, *oh, that's just people being people*, but as drag kings naturally prove – masculinity is just as performative as femininity.'

Jen says that if they didn't have Adam as an outlet for their masculinity, they'd be struggling. 'My gender identity is fascinating to me, but that's why I got into drag. Because I wanted to explore and express it, dissect it. And then try to explain my findings.'

Elly has been helping Adam get ready for the show. She's his manager as well as a drag performer in her own right. I think cis female drag queens present us with another really interesting argument for separating gender identity from biological sex. Why shouldn't a cis woman be able to perform as a drag queen if it's a send up of gender anyway? Why does a drag queen have to be a man? Many drag queen performers have transitioned in their day-to-day life and identify as trans women, which is inherently different from the version of hyper-femininity they perform on stage. But Elly hasn't always felt accepted by the drag queen scene as a cis woman and she uses this as material for her own show. 'With my own performance, I'm often trying to knock the kinks out of a lot of really negative stuff that some other drag queens do. With some drag queens there can be a kind of bashing of females. It can be a bit misogynistic. Apple, my character, is very, very assertive. I call her an alpha femme. It's all about big breasts and curves and big hair . . .'

What's been the impact of *RuPaul's Drag Race*?

Apple and Adam are disappointed that *RuPaul's Drag Race* has not, at the time of writing, featured many cis women queens or drag kings for that matter. But there's no denying the show has radically transformed the landscape of drag around the world and elevated the artform from queer clubs to mainstream TV sensation. And it's had a profound impact on the LGBTQ+ community as a whole, increasing visibility for drag culture, fostering greater acceptance of gender and sexual diversity, and empowering count-less queers through its celebration of self-expression. There are now twenty-seven versions of the show produced in seventeen countries and it has won thirty-one Emmys.

Queens have built massive followings and launched successful careers on the back of appearing on the show. But since becoming an entertainment behemoth, *RuPaul's Drag Race* has had various criticisms levelled at it. From not being trans-inclusive to using misogynistic language or jokes (both of these things have, however, been addressed in more recent seasons and changes have been made).

It felt like a good time to speak to Fenton Bailey, an executive producer of the *Drag Race* franchise, about how the show has evolved over its sixteen seasons and how this reflects changes in the drag world more widely.

Fenton calls me from his LA home.

'Above all I see *Drag Race* as a kind of Trojan horse, because it comes on our screens as a "knives out" reality competition show. But it's hard to resist the love and joy that bursts off the screen. And sure, it's frivolous, but it's also fundamentally life-affirming in that everyone involved with the show has heard someone saying it changed or saved their life. That's important in a world where LGBTQ+ lives are in danger – even in America evangelicals and conservatives want to ban drag. So the fact that our community has a show that's been on the air for fifteen years in multiple countries – that's queer power. It gives the finger to the prejudicial belief that we do not belong. So the show is a Trojan horse because in the guise of something fundamentally frivolous is something that changes and saves lives.'

I put some of the criticisms of the show to Fenton, particularly his thoughts on the potentially offensive language previously used – such as 'fishy' to describe a feminine-looking queen. Fenton studied English Literature at Oxford. He tells me, 'Language is always in flux and always changing. So it makes sense that as words shift and change their meaning, they don't get used. And then, on the other hand, new words do get used. And the approach of the show – the whole idea of *Drag Race*, really – is that it's about dressing up, trying things on, making fun of things, so it does that with language too.' He adds that drag has always sampled all different kinds of things from all different kinds of places. 'The language might come from ballroom culture or it might come from advertising slogans, or it might come from jingles, or lines in movies.'

> The gay ballroom scene is an underground subculture that originated in New York City during the 80s, primarily within Black and Latinx LGBTQ+ communities. It features elaborate drag performances, dance battles and runway competitions held in 'balls', where participants, often from various 'houses' led by a 'house mother' or 'father', compete for trophies and recognition in categories that celebrate fashion, dance and identity, all within a supportive space that challenges societal norms and celebrates self-expression.

I ask if the show has become more inclusive since its origins, when trans women were not allowed to compete. 'When the show started in 2009, it was a different world,' he reminds me. 'There was never any intention to exclude and the show has been increasingly trans representative. The reason we have the mantra Charisma, Uniqueness, Nerve and Talent is that it isn't a show that works by ticking boxes or filling quotas. It's all based on the creativity of the individuals who apply.'

I recently came across a letter that had been written into *The Guardian* in April 2024 in response to a piece about the wonder of *Drag Race*. In it the woman, who we shall call 'shocked of Tunbridge Wells', wrote, 'Drag can be compared to blackface and yellowface: those holding the reins of power utilise performance to mock those without power through a demeaning parody. This reassures the dominant group of their superior status while effectively silencing the group being parodied.' To me, this comparison lacks any real understanding of drag and the lived experience of queerness – power? We wish! I think it also misses the point entirely. If drag is parody, as this letter writer believes, what it really sends up is patriarchy and the male gaze.

I ask Fenton what he would say to the challenge that drag is inherently misogynistic. He explains, 'I've always seen drag as a sampling from all of popular culture, rather than something that is about gender. The act of cross dressing into drag is a ritual inversion of norms that says "beyond this point there are no sacred cows". I look at Caesars Palace in Vegas and think, that's a building in drag. Vegas itself is an entire city in drag. It's at once celebrating the architectural lewks of herstory while also sending them up. As RuPaul famously says, "You're born naked and the rest is drag." Meaning, and this is just my interpretation, that everything we put on is a statement, a choice about who we think we are or how we want to be perceived. Drag is a great way to take the massive amounts of incoming data and content, and to filter it, and, very much in a collage-like way, take bits and pieces from it, and create something that can be a mirror or shine a light back on it.'

What are some of the challenges of being a drag artist?

Back at Adam and Apple's not-so-humble abode, they are almost ready to head off to a drag bingo event in Soho. I ask how Adam is perceived by drag queens on the scene. 'They think I'm cute. Which is good, because when they think I'm cute I get more gigs. I think I was, to begin with, tolerated. And then, sort of, mothered. And now I'm just one of them. But I'm also not one of them at all. Because I don't do wigs and nails, and heels, so they think I'm getting off easy. I do like to run around in my flats, just to wind them up.'

Adam doesn't feel that drag kings get the respect they deserve. Why has RuPaul never included them in *Drag Race*, he wonders? I ask him to elaborate on the most annoying misconception people have of kings like him. 'That all drag kings are trans. And it's about you wanting to be a man. And it's not about performance.

I'll get told, *your makeup is too harsh*, or *it's too campy*, or *it's too cartoony* – you don't pass as a man. But I'm not bloody trying to pass as a man, you moron! You're supposed to see the strings, that's the point. If you think I'm just a dude, it completely fails.'

There are tons of challenges for drag performers; simply getting from a cab into a venue without being abused is one of them. Tom Rasmussen, a singer, performer, activist and writer, used to be a successful drag queen. I asked them why they gave up their fabulous alter ego and, well, it turned into a rather interesting conversation about performance, authenticity, femininity and queer hero complex.

'I think creatively, I had explored every avenue of drag and I'd come to a dead stop with it, it had stopped being enriching. I had accidentally made it very easy – a sort of pay-as-you-go formula, where it's like, I'll sing these songs and go on stage and get paid this amount of money. That meant working in spaces and with brands that, increasingly, as different offers came in, I felt uncomfortable about. I felt like it betrayed the politics that I'd spent so long learning and discussing and fighting for. I felt like a hypocrite really. So I cut off that opportunity at the source basically.

'We often assume because someone's a drag queen they are pure of heart and politically right on, but there's monstrous drag queens and there's monstrous drag kings and there's amazing, political drag queens and amazingly political drag queens. We've amalgamated the image of a drag queen with a political leader. And that isn't fair.'

I ask Tom how their sense of themselves changed once they no longer had a female alter ego as an outlet. 'When I quit drag, I remember my singing teacher said to me, "It's all you. Every note you sing is you. Every word you speak is you." If I'm honest, drag was an easy and hard route to explore the femininity I felt inside. I think maybe my female personae exists slightly more internally now. Since quitting drag, I've started oestrogen and I've been thinking a lot more about my changing transness but I think it's all just one long, quite complicated spaghetti roundabout of a journey.'

Tom adds, 'Drag is sort of a package, isn't it, of all the queer things about you. I think maybe I'd also got a lot of healing from it. Drag is so interesting because I'm on stage being celebrated for all the things that I was once really berated and criticized for, and I felt such a lot of shame about. And now I'm in a different place, and that is because of drag. You can't deny it has an incredible power to heal because it's such an act of bravery and commitment.'

Can you imagine queerness without camp? Without drag? Gah, it would be so worthy and boring. These things are the backbone to our culture, bringing lightness and wit and playfulness and, perhaps most importantly, a way to laugh at ourselves even in the hardest times. Yes, camp might now be found on TikTok and in memes. And yes, drag might be constantly evolving and challenging *itself* as much as it lampoons the society around it, but these mediums are here to stay. Please join me in thanking our queer higher power for the kings, the queens and the camp warriors who remind us what a silly old performance it is to be a human.

Chapter 9

No One Is Alone:
Our Queer Minds

Stu

It's large, it's pink and it's mighty impressive. Oooh Madame, get your head out of the gutter! I am, of course, talking about a much more important, and more powerful organ than whatever ran through your filthy minds! Our brains. Wonderful, yet incredibly flawed.

From the horrors of electroshock therapy, which was commonly used in the 1960s and 70s as a 'treatment' for homosexuality, as if it was something that could be 'cured', to the modern-day belief that gender dysphoria is a form of mental illness, queer brains have been misunderstood and maligned throughout history. The assumption that our minds are any different to cis heterosexual (aka cishet) people's is obviously problematic. But part of me hopes that if you did cut our gay skulls open, Cher's 'Believe' would come flooding out like a child's music box.

Though one thing that does seem different about us, is how we queer people care (or don't care) for our brains, and the effects that being queer has on the inner squishy bits of our head. Gay literally means 'happy', right? We skip around, dancing to our pop anthems, we love who we want to love and look fabulous while doing so. What's the issue? We are surely a community made up of happy-go-lucky frivolous people and we can leave mental health issues for the straights to deal with, right? Right???!

Evidence consistently shows that if you are queer, you are more prone to suffer from poor mental health. The last report, conducted by Stonewall in 2018,[1] makes it clear that over half of all LGBT people experienced a form of depression over a one-year period – that's double the UK average. A similar report found that a whopping 79 per cent of queer women[2] feel sad or miserable, which in turn makes me feel sad and miserable, and when it comes to the transgender community, a sobering fact – 46 per cent of trans people have tried to take their own lives. So why is this? The answers might be obvious for some, but I don't want my assumptions to get in the way of truly understanding why so many of us, quite frankly, feel like we don't want to be here any more. And does the average hetero, who only sees us waving our Pride flags covered in glitter, realize what is lurking beneath the rainbow?

I, for one, know my rainbow is not always brightly coloured, and often I'll find a bucket of anxiety and depression waiting for me at the end of it, rather than the promised pot of gold. Like many queer people, I have really struggled with mental health issues over the years. In fact, 'struggle' would be the better word as it is still a daily battle for me. I have major anxiety which manifests itself through stress, irritability and a huge heap of self-esteem issues, all created from the various psychological abuse I've experienced at some pivotal moments over my life. It's only thanks to recent therapy sessions that I've even been able to address the word 'abuse' and recognize that it is time I called a spade a spade. Being queer with this level of mental health issues has made everything all that much harder. I've never felt good enough for the community and never felt like I fit in. A large part of this, as covered in Chapter 7, is down to how I feel about my body image and weight. Lotte gets angry with me sometimes, and rightly so. 'If someone else was talking about you the way you talk about yourself, I'd punch them in the face. I won't stand for anyone being so unkind, so don't be like it to yourself.' She's right, but for some reason I like to mentally beat myself up daily. I talked about discovering the drug sertraline with my doctor's support in our previous book, *The Queer Parent*, and how game-changing that was for me. Since then I've moved onto a drug called citalopram, as I felt I needed something that directly targeted my anxiety. Again, it was another game-changer, and I take one every night to help settle the overwhelming emotions I was experiencing when I woke each morning.

I won't go into the full specifics around the abuse I suffered, abuse that I feel sparked a lot of my issues. That's not because I'm not open about it, but because I'm still not too sure how 'queer' the abuse was. By that, I mean the experiences didn't seem to be *directly* linked to my queerness. I am still slightly unsure, and perhaps still need more therapy sessions to unpick it. The different mental health issues we have as LGBTQ+ individuals are not always the direct result of our sexuality, identity or gender. But, like me, being LGBTQ+ can define how we react to the issues we have. Our queerness, and our relevant space within our queer communities (or lack of!), can only exaggerate these problems even if they are not the root cause.

WHY ARE WE NOT OK?

The stats on LGBTQ+ mental health show that queer people are disproportionally suffering. Here are some examples of the most common issues experienced by queer people:

- Depression: Persistent feelings of sadness, hopelessness and a lack of interest or pleasure in most activities. This can be more prevalent in the queer community due to the social rejection we have historically experienced.
- Anxiety disorders: Intense and persistent worries and fears about everyday situations. We can also suffer from higher levels of anxiety due to fear of discrimination or harassment.

- Post-traumatic stress disorder (PTSD): A mental health condition triggered by experiencing or witnessing a traumatic event. Some of us may develop PTSD as a result of hate crimes, bullying or abusive environments.
- Substance abuse: The harmful use of alcohol and drugs can become a coping mechanism for other mental health issues, and can intensify them.
- Body dysmorphia and eating disorders: An obsessive focus on a perceived flaw in appearance. While not exclusive to LGBTQ+ people, body dysmorphia and related eating disorders can be more prevalent. (See Chapter 7.)
- Internalized homophobia/transphobia: Internalizing society's negative attitudes and beliefs about LGBTQ+ identities, leading to self-hatred, shame and low self-esteem.
- Minority stress: Chronic stress faced by members of stigmatized minority groups, resulting from social exclusion, prejudice and discrimination.
- Isolation and loneliness: Feeling disconnected from others, often due to rejection from family, peers or society.

Let's meet . . . Ian Howley

Clearly these issues highlight the importance of having dedicated support for queer people. I spoke to Ian Howley, CEO of LGBT HERO (the Health, Equality and Rights Organization), a charity dedicated to queer wellbeing. I wanted his perspective from being on the frontline of mental health care within the LGBTQ+ community.

Ian, why do you think there's such a prevalence of mental health issues within the queer community?
It stems back to childhood. LGBTQ+ people live in a world not designed for us. We're inundated with negativity towards our

community. When you realize that you're part of that community, it can lead to mental wellbeing issues like anxiety and depression, among other complex issues. We are not given the tools to deal with this as young people and we get through our teenage years, into our twenties, and then we explode. We don't deal with childhood trauma, which then affects our ability to form relationships, manage alcohol or drugs, and build lasting friendships outside of sex. While some are fine, most of us deal with unresolved issues from childhood and therefore we need to build support from a young age to help people with issues related to their sexuality or gender identity, so they can manage life better as adults. We are stuck in a cycle because we have not tackled the root cause.

Why are some of these general mental health issues so specific to the queer community?

A lot is based around anxiety and depression, leading to feelings of isolation and loneliness, which worsen these issues. Isolated and lonely people often neglect their health and wellbeing, and this includes how they view sex and relationships. For instance, people with body dysmorphia might have more sex, but it's often not the sex they want. They might turn to places like dark rooms and saunas, using alcohol and drugs to mask their issues, leading to riskier behaviours. It's all interconnected.

Why do the stats point to mental health being worse for bisexual people in particular?

Bisexual people often do not feel connected to the community. They might feel excluded from both mainstream society and the queer community, especially if they're in an opposite-gender relationship. Their identity is often not validated or accepted, leading to higher mental health issues. We need to have more conversations about bi-erasure and we need to better support bisexual people. People often don't understand or support their bisexual siblings and it means we need to have more open conversations about bisexuality and share people's stories to break down this stigma. Real stories help people connect and understand each other better.

I experience social anxiety and as a gay man I know I'm not alone in that. Why is it so common?
I experience it myself, and it's very common in our community. A lot of it stems from not learning how to build solid relationships and communities. Our social spaces are often based around alcohol and nighttime venues, which can exacerbate social anxiety. If you're nervous, you might drink more to connect with your community, which is often found in pubs and clubs, and this can lead to alcohol and substance misuse because people struggle to control their emotions. People sometimes end up in situations like chemsex by accident. [There's more about chemsex on page 238.] They move to a big city, don't know many people, and get invited to a party where drugs are involved. They might not have the capability to handle drugs and end up addicted. We see a lot of overdosing on GHB in our community, and chemsex is more prevalent now than ever.

When I was researching our chapter on HIV, I was talking to a nurse at 56 Dean Street who mentioned a chemsex rise in older men, even in their seventies and eighties. It surprised me.
Yes, it's linked to loneliness and HIV prevention. Men over sixty are often the hardest to convince to use condoms because they feel disconnected from the community and have self-esteem issues. We lost a generation of older men during the AIDS crisis, so we're only now learning about the needs of older people in our community. Many older men might feel

isolated and they turn to chemsex as a way to connect.

In places like West Hollywood, there are more opportunities for sober activities, but here in the UK, it's different. Most queer spaces are pubs and clubs. We're trying to work with councils to create more ally spaces that are queer-friendly but not alcohol-based. It takes time, but we need more community spaces outside of pubs and clubs.

Do you think a historical lack of positive LGBTQ+ role models has had an effect?

In the gap between accepting myself at sixteen and becoming comfortable with my identity by eighteen, what helped me were the role models and the community I found. Meeting people in long-term relationships contradicted what I had been told – that I would be lonely and never have a relationship. This broke down a lot of the stigma I had internalized as a teenager. Organizations like Diversity Role Models, who take queer people into schools to talk about the positive aspects of their lives, are so amazing and important, but this needs to be done on a larger scale.

There are so many political issues and ideologies that we face as a community, it can feel quite overwhelming at times. That must have an impact?

Right now, you go on social media and it just feels like every day is a punching bag for our community, particularly trans people. We are seeing our lives debated and a lot of people feel like they can be negative towards us and get away with it. Social media is a big part of that but it's seeping into society, and I don't know how we can fix it. I don't know if it's just going to be a societal shift over time, in the same way that acceptance happened for the rest of our community previously. Maybe it will happen as certain groups of people get older and pass on, and younger people have a better attitude towards trans, non-binary and gender-diverse people? I'm worried that it might even get worse over the next ten years. I don't think we will lose rights, but life is not going to get better for the trans, non-binary and gender-diverse community over the next five years.

And what do you think all of this does to people within the community, to their mental health?

Your existence is being debated on shows without your opinion being considered. When you see these shows, it's all groups of cisgender people talking about trans people. Why are trans people not being included in the conversation? They're not. They're being dehumanized. That's what we're seeing. I can't imagine being someone who is trans, non-binary or gender-diverse and seeing this on a daily basis, feeling like they don't matter. That's going to play into self-esteem issues and self-worth. There's going to be a lot of work needed with the trans community over the next ten years to support them. They already deal with a lot of mental health issues, and having this on top of it is going to be difficult.

Do you think we'll ever reach a point where mental health issues are not related to our sexuality or gender?

I don't think it'll happen in our lifetime. Decriminalization of homosexuality was only about fifty-two or fifty-three years ago, and look, we are still dealing with homophobia and transphobia. It takes generations for shifts to happen. What I hope for is that as society progresses, we move more towards where we need to be, but nothing ever changes in one generation.

Can anyone hear us?

Sadly, the suicide rate amongst LGBTQ+ people is incredibly high, with 68 per cent of LGBTQ+ young people experiencing suicidal thoughts, compared with 29 per cent of young people who were not LGBTQ+, according to the findings of youth charity Just Like Us in a 2021 survey.[3] In my own journey with mental health, I feel incredibly privileged to have not only a wonderful, understanding and resilient husband who helped me finally get the support I needed, but also a group of friends who help me out of my dark days. But what if you don't have that? Where do you go to for help?

To find out, Lotte and I visit the team at Switchboard, the national LGBTQIA+ support line, to learn about the incredible work they do to support those in the queer community who are struggling and need someone to speak to. Founded in the early 1970s, it was set up in response to the increasing numbers of people calling the Gay Liberation Front following the decriminalization of homosexuality in 1967. As we head upstairs to meet volunteer and training manager Henry, we take in the timeline that's illustrated on the walls, showing moments of queer crisis from throughout the organization's existence. Switchboard has been there for our community through HIV/AIDS, Section 28, the aftermath of the Admiral Duncan bombing in Soho and the development of technology and the explosion of social media.

We meet Henry in the upstairs call centre, which is a space for those volunteers that like to come in to take the calls together. 'Pre-pandemic, it was more physical phones in a room,' he explains. 'Whereas now, obviously, volunteers are able to dial in wherever they are in the UK and so it makes it more accessible to different people who are interested in volunteering with us. We get anywhere between 15,000 and 20,000 calls a year, but the demand is actually a lot higher, so we are trying to recruit more volunteers so we can have more conversations.' But how many volunteers do they have, we ask?

'We have 300 at the moment, and our hope is to get that to 500 by the end of 2025.' Admittedly, while we know there are other LGBTQ+ volunteer organizations out there, we do find this number lower than expected compared to the number of queer people. In perspective, over 30,000 people marched in the 2024 London Pride. Does Henry hope more people will join the ranks of dedicated volunteers that are helping people in vital need?

'Yes, we would love to have more people join Switchboard! I think our volunteers feel a great sense of pride in being able to offer people a safe and open space to talk about whatever is on their mind. With everything happening in the news you can feel so help-less, and you don't really know how to tangibly care for the community or care for each other. I think just volunteering at Switchboard gives people a tangible way to feel like they're doing something positive for the community in times of crisis and struggle.'

So, over an always-therapeutic cup of tea, we begin to chat about the work that the volunteers do at Switchboard. 'It really is so broad in terms of the types of mental health issues that come up,' Henry explains. 'It could be anything, and that is because our remit is so big, it's almost like looking at us like we are generalists. It could be anything from conversations where people are in crisis – and by that we mean planning to die by suicide or even in the process of doing so – to someone having an anxiety attack or bouts of prolonged depression. Because mental health services are at max capacity within the NHS, and as going private is some-times outside of people's financial capacities, Switchboard becomes a place that people feel like they can be listened to. One of the quotes we have on the wall is from a service user that said, "Honestly, Switchboard was a lifeline for me", which I do think is true for a lot of folks who can't access the mental health services that they need.'

Henry is also keen to impress on us that Switchboard is a support service, not a helpline. 'Our volunteers never give advice. They may signpost resources, and I often think people start their journey with us, but then they won't often finish it as they may go onto somewhere like Gallop (the LGBTQ+ anti-abuse charity) or Mermaids (who support trans, non-binary and gender-questioning children). We are non-directive, we are non-judgemental. It's very much about being more of a backseat passenger and asking questions.'

Non-directive, non-judgemental. Are these things we should be taking on board to support the rest of our community who are struggling? Do we too often try to solve our friends' problems when we are not the experts? Should we be taking a leaf out of Switchboard's book and just listen and ask the right questions?

'It's so hard to catch yourself and just suspend that judgement and assumption,' reassures Henry. So, often are we trying our hardest to fix things? 'Most people who come to volunteer do it because they want to help. They want to give something back to the community, and often at the beginning they'll have a conversation with someone and question if they actually did anything. There could be no resolution or marker signs that someone has progressed in any way. But just holding that space with another person, just being available to listen, that is doing something. By being there, and being active, and listening, is a real gift to someone.'

I ask Henry what the future looks like for Switchboard and how they're planning to recruit more volunteers. He tells us that in the coming years technology such as webchat, email and other such forms of communication will be more and more important to the organization, which hopefully makes it more accessible for people to volunteer. 'Not only is it accessibility, a lot of people, especially young people, can't find a safe space in their surroundings to talk on the phone. And when it comes to volunteering, different people have different skills. Some people have beautiful writing skills but may not feel confident with their verbal literacy. By giving the option to volunteers to volunteer on our chat or email channels, and not only the phone, it will be able to draw a lot more people across the board and bring more people in, hopefully. The more volunteers we have, the more people across the UK we can support. If people reading this book are looking for a way to support the LGBTQIA+ community, volunteering for Switchboard might be the place for them. If people are interested, they can check out our website to learn more and apply.'

MindOut, an LGBTQ+ mental health service, gives us some invaluable advice on how to help a friend who is experiencing suicidal thoughts.

- Take the time to *really* listen to them.
- Don't judge or force advice or opinions, but give them your undivided attention.
- Respect them and don't try to take charge.
- Treat everything in complete confidence.
- Care, make yourself available, put the person at ease and be calm. Reassure, accept and believe.
- That person shouldn't be alone in their thoughts. Rejection can make the problem seem ten times worse.
- Lectures don't help. Nor does a suggestion to 'cheer up' or an easy assurance that 'everything will be OK.' Try not to analyze, categorize or criticize.
- Don't interrogate them. Don't change the subject, don't pity or patronize.
- Talking about feelings can sometimes be difficult. People who get the confidence to speak to you about suicide won't want to be rushed or put on the defensive.

Are queerness and neurodiversity linked?

We've looked at how the various pressures of being different, of being other, can affect the mental health of LGBTQ+ people. But what is it like when your brain works differently to the norm (whatever that is) anyway? And are queerness and neurodiversity linked somehow?

It's a controversial question, I know, because our community has an incredibly long history of being labelled and stigmitized as 'mentally ill', so I feel the pressure to tread carefully here. In fact, when I bring up the subject of the queer neurodiverse hangouts with Ian, he is keen to address straight away that 'we have to be careful not to link queer and transgender identities with neurodiversity, as if one causes the other.' If you are reading this book I'm sure you don't need educating that being queer is not a mental illness, so I'm not going to give it to you. But while it's clearly not the cause, the fact is queer people do live with neurodiversity. There are approximately one in seven people who have some form of neuro-difference (according to Mind) within the UK (queer and cishet) according to the NHS.

So, what is it like to be neurodivergent and LGBTQ+? Do past and previous stigmas around mental disabilities still affect them when talking about their diagnosis? Is it another helpful double whammy of shame? I found it fascinating to learn that, according to The Brain Charity,[4] evidence suggests that those who are neurodivergent, particularly those diagnosed with autism, *are* significantly more likely to identify as LGBTQIA+ than those who are neurotypical. While it seems that no one really knows why that might be, the predominant theory is that the overlap is down to the fact that 'neurodivergent people tend to be less aware of or inclined to follow societal norms.'

I pick up the phone to John Anderson (he/they) who works as a fundraiser at The Brain Charity to hear more on their thoughts on queerness and neurodivergence . . .

Would you mind telling me a bit about your own journey to recognizing your neurodivergence?

I'm currently on the autism diagnosis pathway through the NHS. At our charity, we promote the benefits of neurodiversity, and many of our staff members are neurodivergent – some assumed I had already been diagnosed. It wasn't something I considered growing up, but working at the charity made me recognize certain traits in myself that align with autism, like finding large groups intimidating and hyper-focusing on tasks. These realizations led me to seek an assessment. It's a fairly long process on the NHS, it can take up to two years for an assessment.

Can I ask about terminology? Is it still correct to say 'on the spectrum', or is 'neurodivergent' more appropriate?

I hear 'on the spectrum' less frequently now. Neurodivergent is more of an umbrella term, like 'queer' for people who aren't straight or cisgender. Some autistic people prefer to identify as autistic rather than neurodivergent, but the term neurodivergent is becoming more widely recognized.

It's interesting to see the parallels between queerness and neurodivergence. Both are about personal identity, but neurodivergence often involves a formal diagnosis.

Yes, but we emphasize that support shouldn't rely solely on a diagnosis. Just as you'd support someone questioning their sexuality, you should support someone exploring their neurodivergence.

You mentioned you find being in large groups intimidating. How do you feel in queer spaces?

Many queer spaces can be overwhelming, privileging extroverts and neurotypical people. Events like Pride, while enjoyable, can be challenging due to the sensory overload. I know many neurodivergent people avoid Pride for this reason.

Are there any neurodivergent-friendly Pride events?

Not in Liverpool where I am based, but we're in dialogue with Liverpool Pride to make the event more accessible. There's no separate event yet, but it's something worth considering.

How can the queer community be better allies to neuro-divergent people?

Given that LGBTQ+ individuals are disproportionately more likely to be neurodivergent, making spaces more accessible benefits the community itself. This includes quieter events and non-alcohol-based gatherings.

Do you think there's a stigma around mental health and queerness because of the past (and current!) associations of being gay equalling a mental illness?

Yes, there's a lingering stigma due to the historical pathologi-zation of being gay. However, there's been a significant shift towards understanding both autism and queerness as natural variations of human experience, not something to be cured. I hope we can change the idea of people exploring their neuro-divergence by continuing to promote understanding and acceptance. I think our knowledge of the brain is still quite limited. There's so much we don't know about it, how it works, and so on. My personal view is that the links between some-one's sexuality and neurodivergence are influenced by various factors, including biology and the environment in which they are raised. It's a complex issue.

Yes, it's definitely complex. And coming out as neuro-divergent, do you find there are parallels there too?

Coming out is a process that happens multiple times. You come out to your parents, friends, new friends, and colleagues. It's similar for autistic people, especially those whose autism may not be immediately visible. We often assume that the person we're talking to is neurotypical, which isn't always the case. You have to keep coming out to different people and explain your needs. Doing this constantly to new people can sadly cause huge levels of shame.

Do you think neurodivergent people might be more vulnerable to homophobic abuse or other challenges within the queer community?

For sure. Neurodivergent people may be more vulnerable to being taken advantage of, socially or sexually. We help many neuro-divergent people with issues like debt, falling in with the wrong crowds, and holding down jobs. These vulnerabilities definitely carry through into the queer community as well.

Have you noticed differences between different generations in how people react to being queer and neuro-divergent?

I've seen older people try to link the rise in autism to people being more open about being trans, suggesting that these individuals are confused, which I find offensive. While some anti-trans activists have made the groundless claim that autistic youth are being 'tricked' into identifying as transgender or queer, the reality is that being neurodivergent remains a huge barrier to many people receiving the gender-affirming health care they need. Trans people often have their gender identity repeatedly questioned due to their autism. This is a long-lasting prejudice towards neurodivergent individuals that assumes they are not competent enough to understand their own sexuality or gender identity, and directly leads to under-diagnosis of neurological conditions among the LGBTQIA+ community.

I'm really glad I got the chance to chat with John and hear his views on neurodivergence and the links to queerness, because as a (presumed) neurotypical person my exploration has led me to realize the similarities that exist among us, queer or not. Hopefully more of us can be stronger allies to those that are especially both queer and neurodivergent and consider them more carefully. Again, it feels our trans siblings have another uphill battle here, and will continue to face more and more prejudice, particularly in relation to any neurodiversity being used against them to prevent them accessing the care they need.

When I've had struggles in the past, I used to listen to the Stephen Sondheim song 'No One Is Alone' from the musical *Into the Woods*. Did I mention I was gay? The lyric 'No one is alone, someone is on your side' always moved me deeply, and still does. The stats say it all. We are not alone. There are many of us feeling sad, anxious and more beyond.

If you need any support you can reach the LGBT Switchboard by phone at 0800 0119 100, by email hello@switchboard.lgbt or via online chat at www.switchboard.lgbt. Things won't be resolved overnight, but by chipping away at what is causing you to feel like you don't belong, or that you are not good enough, you may soon start to notice a difference. Some advice that perhaps I should listen to myself.

Chapter 10

The Portrait in the Attic:
Ageing Disgracefully

Lotte

As the lift doors open onto the twelfth floor of a swish new-build overlooking the River Thames in London's Vauxhall, I catch a faint whiff of hospitals – disinfectant muddled with a kind of sweet, musty, human smell. A man in a blue nurse's uniform walks past and then the doors close again and we whizz up another few floors to the communal areas of Tonic, the UK's first retirement community for LGBTQIA+ people. Here there are few signs that this is anything other than a luxury apartment block, but look a little closer and the prevalence of Pride flags and the December activities calendar on the wall in the corridor (Friday 8th – Pansexual Pride Day, Sat 23rd – Gay Men's Chorus trip, etc.) suggest we're somewhere special.

Don't we deserve a place to live freely and age well?

Tonic is a not-for-profit organization focused on creating vibrant and inclusive urban LGBTQIA+ retirement communities where people can share common experiences, find support and enjoy their later life. I'm here in my efforts to discover what happens to queer people when we get older. When I ask Raga, a fifty-four-year-old Indian woman who moved in after her (older) wife had a stroke a few years ago, how she felt living in a community of elders when she is still relatively young, she laughs and shakes her head. 'I have met some very dead twenty-five-year-olds, let me tell you that. Seriously, living with people who are in their eighties is energizing. These people are full of life. No one is boring. They're funny. They have stories to share. They're interested in you. They listen. All the things that, when we're younger, we don't really bother with. The energy at Tonic is so special.'

The initiative was set up in 2014 to address the issues of loneliness and isolation within the older LGBTQIA+ community and the need for specific housing and support provision, as there was none in the UK before 2021. In the process of writing this chapter, one of the UK's only charities supporting LGBTQ+ elderly people, Opening Doors, was forced to close due to a lack of funding. We are so glad to have had the chance to visit Tonic because, to us, LGBTQ+ culture is pretty youth-obsessed. We want to find out what happens to the older queers.

Tonic at Bankhouse comprises nineteen flats on the top four floors of a fourteen-storey housing block. You can buy an apartment for £126,875 with 25 per cent ownership (market value £507,500) and if you wish you can add on different levels of care provision, from none to daily visits from a carer. London was the site of this first project as the capital has the largest older LGBTQ+ population in the UK, estimated to be 145,000 people. Manchester is currently developing its own residential community for LGBTQ+ elders with a different housing association, which will hopefully open within the next five years.

Stu and I are hoping by the time we are in our eighties a luxury hotel brand will have opened a retirement village where a hologram version of *Real Housewives* plays on repeat in the snug, and sexy young queers serve us champagne and listen wide-eyed to our stories of the good old days. There'll be a grand piano in the corner and we'll take it in turns to sing our favourite canonical pop hits, while Adele (because, of course, it's open to gay icons too) tinkles the ivories.

The common room area at Tonic may not be quite as glamorous and star-studded as my fantasy but it is a bit like a hotel lobby or spa waiting room, with low mood lighting, comfy furniture and instead of Adele playing the piano, there's an illuminated tank of exotic fish.

When we visit, the week before Christmas, we are escorted into the bar area (of course there's a bar!) where a group of people sit waiting to chat to us.

At first, I am quite taken aback by how sprightly they seem. I would have said the majority were in their early to mid-sixties. My first thought is – why are these capable, smart, active adults choosing to live in an old people's home?!

Cue the judgement klaxon. It is really about time I challenged my idea of what an 'older person' *should* look like. Why do I have this almost cartoon version of old age in my head? Grey-haired women wrapped in shawls, men with white moustaches and walking sticks. My mum's in her late seventies and she's one of the coolest, most stylish and sassy people I know. I guess I see her as the exception rather than the norm. And anyway, this isn't an 'old people's home' like the ones I visited my grandparents in. It's a place where you can truly live and be yourself, with a bit of friendship and support on your doorstep.

Although you don't *have* to be queer to move in here – it bills itself as 'LGBTQ+-affirming', so as long as you're not a homophobe and sign a contract to agree to LGBTQ+-affirming values, you are welcome – the majority of residents do identify as gay. Willie is the oldest. A jolly character in his late eighties, wearing a red jumper and exhibiting the quickest of wits despite being a little slower on his feet than he used to be, he tells me about the shoot and interview he's just done for *Vogue* magazine about Tonic with the photographer Tim Walker. 'It's wonderful here,' he told the magazine. 'You don't have to worry about what folks are going to think about you.'

Raga is the youngest resident. She is in her fifties and far from retirement. She runs a speakers' bureau and is a chair of the London LGBTQ+ Community Centre. She works flat out, but after her wife Nicola suffered a stroke, it made sense to move somewhere they could access care should they ever need to. You have to be over fifty-five to qualify for an apartment here, but an exception was made for Raga because her wife did meet the criteria. The decision to buy was about future-proofing. The pair just wish they weren't the only lesbians in the retirement village (the other female residents are straight, but gay allies).

As I'm handed a cup of tea, I do the maths and figure out it'll be another fourteen years before I can officially move in myself. I shudder at the thought because, yes, I'm sorry, I'm not thrilled about ageing. I'm not ready to 'embrace' it. Honestly, since turning forty, I've realized I'm struggling with my attitude to getting older. It blows my mind that the first series of *The L Word* aired twenty years ago! I remember that scene when Bette and Tina 'make a baby' like it was yesterday. Two decades is evidently no time at all – but then that scares me because the equivalent time, in the other direction, takes me to sixty-four years old. I'm confident I'll continue to feel like *me* at that age, but how will I look? Will I still be able to wear a baseball cap and tracksuit without evoking Gangster Granny vibes?

There is perhaps no better allegory for the vanity of being youth-obsessed than Oscar Wilde's *The Picture of Dorian Gray*. A beautiful, narcissistic young man behaves with impunity, believing he will stay forever young. He is given a portrait of himself and laments, 'I shall grow old, and horrible, and dreadful. But this picture will remain always young. It will never be older than this particular day of June . . . If it were only the other way!' In a mystical turn of events, he hides the portrait away in the attic and this image suffers the effects of ageing, and the flaws of his character, so that he doesn't have to. It becomes grotesque. When he finally attempts to destroy the portrait, he's reminded that in reality no amount of beauty or youth will ever protect you from mortality. Substitute Dorian for any looks-obsessed queer with a face-tuning app and Botox doctor and the story carries a dark resonance today.

The fact is, like Dorian, I still expect the person I see in the mirror to look like the person I was in my late twenties and thirties. I spent a long time with that youthful face, this forty-something face is newer, less familiar, and honestly I need to get used to it. I'm not saying I dislike it, but I'm still figuring out how I want to show up as a queer person over the next few decades – baseball cap or not. I wish I had more role models.

As much as I would love to be besties with lesbian actress Holland Taylor (who is stunning and in her eighties) – I'm not actually friends with any queer people over the age of fifty-five. I don't have any templates for living as a non-binary queer person in my sixties, seventies or eighties.

Is it that people like me disappear at fifty, Botox and all? Are we simply transported to an alternate universe where we live among other lost, abandoned things – odd socks, loose change – down the side of the sofa? Orrrrr is it more the fact that people currently in their eighties would have been young adults in the 1960s, which wasn't the most LGBTQ+-friendly of decades, let's face it. There must have been so many gay people in this generation who lived ostensibly 'straight' lives, were married, had children and perhaps even now haven't come out to friends or family.

And let's not forget that there have been almost 20,000 deaths from AIDS in the United Kingdom since the epidemic began, with the peak being reached in 1995 when more than 1,700 people lost their lives. This has had a significant effect on the elder gay male community's numbers, because many simply didn't survive.

It's not unusual for queer people to enjoy multi-generational friendships or relationships, but the lack of mainstream representation makes it seem like LGBTQ+ people over fifty don't exist. The fact is, we are only just starting to see queer people presented unproblematically in culture and society, and it's no surprise that it takes the youngest, most beautiful and most successful queers to make the first dent in the zeitgeist.

Over the next few decades there will be more and more examples of queer people not just living, but thriving into old age – I'm hoping I'll be one of them.

Friends with (pensions and) benefits?

While I've befriended a handful of queer and trans people who are twenty years younger than me, I've yet to make a bestie who is twenty years older. But I love the idea of the kind of mixed-age social groups and sexual encounters that have been so well documented by gay authors like Armistead Maupin and Alan Hollinghurst. It's certainly far less loaded to see age-gap relationships in the queer world than it is in straight society. I wonder why this is? I think a big reason is that our queerness transcends the specificities of our age and there is so much we can learn from each other. It's why and how we have historically built our own chosen families – we have found our parental role models, our *daddies* and our '*mothers*' (cue Moira Rose calling us Bebé), in friends and created a new kind of nuclear.

It's an interesting conundrum, then, that despite this fabulous queer, non-linear, intergenerational community, youth is still so prized. In Evelyn Waugh's *Brideshead Revisited,* the character of Anthony Blanche, 'aesthete par excellence', aka hot gay, is described as being 'ageless as a lizard'. That's the dream! If my gay male friends are anything to go by, the Peter Pan effect is real. Lizards, the lot of them! Now in their forties, single (or in open relationships), child-free, home-owning, professionally successful, they have the time for facials, to work out for an hour a day, have money to take holidays and look sun-kissed and healthy. The fifty-year-olds pass as forty. The forty-year-olds pass as thirty. They party most weekends and many have a lot of sex. Maybe that's the truth behind the glow.

By comparison, I feel haggard. But then people who aren't men seem to have a harder time getting older, both physically and societally. As we've seen throughout this chapter, queer men are silver foxes, sexy daddies. Queer women are . . . what? Non-existent. 'Hello mummy' doesn't have the same ring to it.

I was a major fan girl of Stella Duffy when I was in my early twenties. She wrote sexy lesbian detective thrillers and we often found ourselves at the same lesbian networking event or party. Since then, Stella has had cancer twice, been through early menopause as a result, and, like Chance, who we met in Chapter 1, she has retrained as a therapist (and yoga teacher) with a specialism in the lived experience of post-menopausal women.

She's sixty when we speak, but as beautiful as ever, with long greyish hair and a face that looks weathered in the best possible way by sea swimming, being outdoors and leading, or trying as best as her body allows to lead, a good, a happy and a grounded life. I'm excited to speak with her after all these years and quickly remember why I loved the snatched conversations we used to have at cocktail parties. She's so sharp and funny and challenging and swears like a trooper. During this conversation she really introduced me to some new perspectives on the subjects we tackle.

Stella, hello! Forgive me for jumping straight in but why is the menopause presented as something that really affects only straight women with children?

I've got two theories here. One is that biomedical research has been done on this demographic of women, which is true. But two, and this was borne out by my own research: if you're a privileged white, straight middle-class woman, not many things have been that shit for you, other than sexism.

Seriously, this is awful and I feel bad saying it, except it's also true. Queer women, women of colour, non-binary people, trans people, disabled people, the whole fucking gamut of the rest of us, have had to put up with being marginalized, being outside, being left behind, being not considered throughout our lives.

It's the white feminism thing, right? So what happens when women of a certain class and status suddenly realize that it's even worse – even if they've been alert to sexism and misogyny – it's worse than they thought because when you throw in ageism, you really are on the scrap heap.

Hence we get celebrities on the telly saying it's the worst thing that ever happened to them. Quite possibly because it *is* the worst thing that ever happened to them. They're not queer women. They're not Black women. They're not disabled. In a culture that is pronatal [values child rearing above all else], anti-disabled, anti-Black, anti-Asian . . . all the other shit things associated with these identities hadn't happened to them.

In my research, women of colour and working-class women commented that the people who are in their circles who had complained the most about ageing tended to be, not always, but tended to be middle-class white women. And that's not to say the working-class women and the queer women and the Black women weren't having difficult physiological symptoms.

They were. But they just had more fucking perspective because life had insisted they have more resilience.

Why don't we talk about what happens after menopause?

To date, menopause has largely been seen as a problem, a deficiency disease. By the same logic, you might as well call nine-year-olds who don't have periods yet *deficient* in oestrogen. This is what the body does. You're not deficient.

The other problem here is that for the global majority, menopause is fantastic because it's the first time they don't have to worry about getting pregnant. It's an extremely wealthy white thing to say that menopause is awful and it's the end of our lives, because for the vast majority of people around the world, as long as we're having periods, we are having unwanted pregnancies.

And that's not to say we're not allowed to say it's hard. It's a transition. It's uncontrollable. But, then, you know, I've had cancer twice – that too is an uncontrollable transition.

Where does queerness intersect with menopause and ageing?

My generation grew into our gayness thinking we weren't going to have children to look after us in our old age. For a long, long time, until very recently, as gay people, we knew that it wasn't going to happen for us. And therefore we had to make provisions for ourselves in our old age. So what we did was we began to understand that there were other ways of creating family.

I think queering everything, queering childlessness, is so useful because it reminds people without children that actually, here's an entire group of people who've managed to survive and thrive despite society being so against us and find ways of living full and brilliant lives without children for millennia until very recently.

Similarly, when we look at queering the ageing body, so your body is no longer procreative, but that was never its only value. So what else can we learn from queer communities who, until very recently, were never having children? How can we learn from our gay elders of eighty-five and ninety about how they created families? How they dreamed their futures?

How does ageing and menopause affect lesbians specifically?

Something lesbians need to reckon with is our own internalized ageism, because as lesbianism became sexy (thank you, the middle-class white women of *The L Word!*) there was an assumption that we had to stay young otherwise you were just an old dyke.

As lesbians we were always treated as a bit weird and *other* and different and strange and witchy, so when we get old, we fit that stereotype even more.

It saddens me that there's a bit of a problem now, as there is an assumption that older lesbian women will not be trans-inclusive, that we will not be broader-sexuality-and-gender-informed, and that we are stuck in some time warp, which is a shit lie, as far as I'm concerned, and one promulgated by the straight women who say they're *speaking up for lesbians*, more than lesbian women are ourselves.

How can older queer people find a place to belong?

Back at Tonic, one of the men at the table who seems barely of retirement age is John. It turns out he is sixty-four. He looks like a kindly professor, or someone you might see propping up the bar at a local gay pub. He's got smiling eyes and a white beard and such a relaxed, jovial demeanour that I'm tempted to climb onto his lap and tell him what I want for Christmas. I'm really trying to be sensitive and open-minded but the question of *why* this man is living in an old people's home is going round and round in my head. We give John space to talk and eventually he finds his way to the reason.

He says, 'I was in a dark tunnel, I would say for three years, lonely and all that. Because I had a forty-year relationship, and my partner passed away in August 2020, so I was stuck at home. Doing the talking to walls thing. Now, sad though it was, when I think of him, I smile because I had a great life. *We* had a great life.'

The way John talks about discovering Tonic makes it sound like, in many ways, it saved his life. With it he has found a sense of friendship and togetherness and pulled himself out of grief and back into the light.

We talk about how, for some older gay people, when their partner dies they essentially end up going back into the closet. John wanted to stay connected to the gay community. He tells me, 'I had a forty-year relationship, going through all the AIDS epidemic and everything, seeing all your friends die. All that stuff. So when I came out in 1981, AIDS came out as well. My partner and me – we did the journey together. It was a very sad journey, a lot of good people died. I'm one of the lucky ones, I suppose, because I met someone and we were safe. I'm very happy to be here. I don't ever want to go back to a dark place.'

We learn that some of the residents frequent the iconic south London gay pub and club-night venue the Royal Vauxhall Tavern and have even popped their head into some of the more hardcore Vauxhall nightclubs like XXL and Fire. With a cheeky smile Clive tells me that last time he went to a nightclub with his friend David and his partner the couple brought their two grown-up daughters and their two boyfriends clubbing with them. 'One of the girls said to David, *"Daddy, Dad, can I have a drink?"* And David screamed, *"Don't call me Daddy in here!"'*

The question of why these ostensibly cool and capable queers are living at Tonic is gradually being answered. While at first I found the closeness to medical facilities and vaguely institutional feel a little confronting, the whole idea of a post-retirement community filled with LGBTQ+ people and allies is becoming increasingly appealing as a later-life choice.

It's different for everyone, of course, but the sense of community is at the heart of each resident's reason for being at Tonic. Queer people have always been lifted up by each other, and just because you're not going to nightclubs full of people like you any more, there's no reason to miss out on that same sense of belonging. In fact, it has been proven that people who lack social connections have 50 per cent higher odds of dying than others who are more connected, according to a review of 148 studies. Being isolated was also shown to have a greater effect on high blood pressure than having diabetes in old age, according to a recent study. A queer retirement home seems a no-brainer.

It makes me think of Ted Brown and Noel Glynn, a couple who weren't so lucky. Ted is a veteran LGBTQ+ campaigner – in the 1970s as part of the Gay Liberation Front he famously helped organize London's first Pride march and staged a mass queer 'kiss in' on Trafalgar Square. When his civil partner Noel moved into a London care home a few years ago, his horrific experience at the hands of homophobic staff highlighted the issue of elder abuse and how vulnerable LGBTQ+ people can be in these spaces.

Noel was beaten, taunted and mistreated by care home staff. He has also talked of how they refused to recognize their relationship – referring to Brown as Glynn's 'friend' or, bizarrely, his 'father'. Since Noel's death in 2021, which was unconnected to the attack, Ted has said, 'I was incandescent with anger and I haven't been able to express that to anybody.'

Do I really want to be forever young?

I keep coming back to the portrait in the attic in *The Picture of Dorian Gray* – which unsurprisingly was written by a gay man, Oscar Wilde. Do we want to stay young for ever to be fuckable, because this is where our value lies? Or is ageing just another transition that actually a queer life has set us up well to enjoy – if we can relinquish our ego? Or are we scared of being forced back into the closet because society's services aren't set up to treat us as LGBTQ+ people? Being old becomes the 'identity' that trumps all others, that bulldozes the intersections of our selfhood. But is the real problem that there aren't enough gay role models over sixty yet to give us a sense of who and how we can be?

I ask Raga, 'What's the greatest thing you've learned from living in an LGBTQIA+-affirming retirement home?' She takes a beat and then answers, 'That this moment, this right now, this is it. There is nothing beyond that, before, or after.'

'At Tonic, they live for this moment, in this moment they are fully present. They are fully aware of what's happening and they are fully there. Nothing else matters. They don't think about the future when they may not be here, or traumatic things that may have happened in the past. There is no yesterday, there is no tomorrow. There is today and in the today there is only the now and it will never come back. And that's a beautiful lesson to learn from the elderly around you.'

Chapter 11

Undetectable, But Does the Stigma of HIV Live On?

Stu

I snake my way through London's Soho and turn right down Dean Street. I've walked down this road a thousand times, yet I've never really noticed the clinic nestled between a couple of obscure clothing shops. This centre, 56 Dean Street, is a renowned sexual health clinic, and for the first time in my life I take a step through the glass doors and put on a show of confidence as I tell the friendly receptionist that I'm here for an appointment.

It's a generic office reception, with a pinewood desk and some nice lilies in a vase. A few queer-seeming characters drift in and out as I sit and wait. Then a handsome nurse steps out and introduces himself as Jason. He leads me upstairs to the clinic rooms. I'm here for my first ever HIV test. I'm a bundle of nerves.

What about the *other* pandemic?

In 1985 more people were diagnosed with AIDS than in all the previous years of the pandemic combined.[1] It was an 89 per cent increase and this was also the year I sashayed into the world. I was born in a year in which 8,406 people died of AIDS in the US alone. One of these was the closeted Oscar-nominated actor Rock Hudson. I was two years old when adverts depicting gravestones and warnings of imminent death started playing across UK TV screens. When I was six, the man who wrote the lyrics to the songs that shaped my youth, Howard Ashman, died of AIDS. I didn't know who he was when I heard 'Part of Your World' at my first cinema trip to see *The Little Mermaid*, nor, at the time, did I know he had died, or how, but I'll always remember the tribute to him at the end of one of my all-time favourite films, *Beauty and the Beast*, just a few months later:

'To our friend Howard, who gave a mermaid her voice, and a beast his soul.'

Howard Ashman died before *Beauty and the Beast* was finished. I then was eight when the movie *Philadelphia* was released, with Tom Hanks winning an Oscar for his portrayal of Andy Beckett, a gay man living with HIV and AIDS. As I was very young when I watched it, it stayed with me, becoming one of my first real memories of HIV and AIDS. Global deaths from AIDS peaked in 1997 when I was twelve, with 3.3 million people dying of the disease. At eighteen, I started university and watched, loved and cried at the brilliance of Mike Nichols' AIDS-themed TV series *Angels in America*, which was, poetically for me, set in 1985, the year of my birth.

So I spent my early, and formative, years growing up alongside the AIDS epidemic. While I was trying to get a sense of my self and my identity as a gay teenager, I knew that there was this dark, sad and painful disease that could strike at any time. These few films, TV shows and public figures formed my only education around HIV and AIDS. There was no mention of it at school, there were no role models to listen to, no social media or internet to explore. It was a petrifying view of gayness. But although fear of this illness, this 'gay plague', was always present growing up, it has never actually become part of my life. I was, perhaps, a decade or so too young. And as a basic, vanilla, monogamous gay who practically got married at the age of twenty-one, fear of the illness has never been part of my day-to-day sexual life in terms of protection, or even thought process. So, with an education of HIV built solely from media depictions, I am ignorant as to what HIV and AIDS really means to our current queer generation. I still live with the 1980s legacy of HIV as a death sentence, a trauma deep inside me.

I have never had an HIV test. Ever. Aside from the obvious health implications, it also weirdly feels like another gay rite of passage that I've missed. Before I met my husband, at twenty-one, I had a few years of promiscuous sex with strangers and I did think about testing a lot. But I was too scared. This was back in the early 2000s, and while there were medical steps being made in order to live a life with HIV, the stigma and trauma from the 1980s and 90s were still strong. All I could imagine was the moment when a doctor would take my hand and utter the diagnosis that I still believed was a death sentence. So I took the stupid decision to not get tested. I believed that I was being safe, although there were occasions where I was definitely at risk. I realize, looking back, how ridiculous that all now sounds. Because if I was in fact positive, I could have got the medication I needed and not passed the virus on to anyone else. It wasn't only stupid but selfish.

When Lotte and I discuss writing about HIV and AIDS for this book, she's the one who suggests that now is the right time for me to finally get tested. My first feeling when she brings it up is that familiar one of fear. Could I have been incubating the HIV virus for eighteen years with no symptoms? Is that even possible? Surely I had to be negative, right? But what if I wasn't? While my education on this subject was minimal, I know enough to understand that medical intervention has progressed so much that if I do have it, I really should be getting treatment. I made my mind up, took the leap, and booked an appointment for a test at the Dean Street clinic.

So here I am now, in Soho, starting to discuss my situation with nurse Jason and prep for the test. Jason tells me he has worked at 56 Dean Street for eight years and before that was an A&E nurse in Manchester, but his goal was always to work in sexual health following his own experiences when he was younger. I take the opportunity to quiz him about the process I'm about to go through.

One of my fears is how long HIV can lay dormant without symptoms. Could I have had it since the age of twenty-one and never known?

Some people are elite controllers, meaning they suppress their own viral load and are HIV-positive but undetectable. It's rare, but it happens, and also, it's rare for someone your age to have never tested.

What does the test involve?

There are now two tests: a fourth-generation HIV test, which is a serology blood test that looks for the virus and antibodies and gives us your status from six weeks ago. And there's also a rapid test, which is a finger-prick test that tells us about your status from three months ago.

What's the difference in giving these tests to people? Which will I have today?

If someone had risk exposure seven weeks ago, the rapid test wouldn't be accurate. We'd use the serology test instead. The serology test is more accurate and used when starting patients on PrEP. We will do the finger-prick test for you today.

What are the test result times for both tests?

The rapid test is instant. The serology blood test goes to the lab and is processed within six hours. If the result is reactive, the lab retests it for confirmation.

So it's a lot quicker now? One of the hangovers from my basic TV and film education on HIV is the long waiting period and having to come back in. I have that image so clearly in my mind.

Yeah, it used to be like that. You'd do an HIV test and if you didn't hear anything in two to three weeks, it was negative. If you did get a call, then it was bad news. It was horrible. You'd see missed calls from unknown numbers and panic. Even coming here for the first time as a patient, I was petrified, convinced I had HIV.

Now, for things like gonorrhoea or chlamydia, we usually just text and say, you know, you've got gonorrhoea, you need treatment. Follow this link to book an appointment. With HIV, though, we've got health advisors and a recall team who contact the patient directly via phone. They'd probably say, 'Your HIV test has been reactive, we need you to come in for more tests.' At that point, we book them a doctor's appointment, they see a health advisor, and we do a whole set of blood tests. One of my biggest fears when I started here was delivering that news to someone. But what surprised me was that we tell them their test is reactive, do another confirmation test, and then, if needed, have them talk to a health advisor right away. I did think it would be more . . . dramatic. But they go home the same day, which seemed so odd to me for such a life-changing diagnosis. I say life-changing because you are going to be on medication every day for the rest of your life. Though there are now injectable antiretrovirals that patients can take every two months instead of daily pills, which we have been doing for the past eight or nine months. It's amazing and gives patients a new sense of freedom. But the stigma is still there. We're lucky in London, we live in a bubble where most people know someone who is HIV-positive.

It feels like stigma is still such a big part of HIV. Can everyone get to a stage where they're undetectable?

Yes, as long as they take their medication as prescribed. We say 'U equals U', meaning undetectable equals untransmissible.

I feel that must be a big decision when deciding whether or not to mention you are positive, yet undetectable, to someone you might want to sleep with. I wonder how the younger generation approaches it, given they don't have the same stigma or history to contend with?

Well, flip it, if you were to have sex with someone undetectable who didn't tell you, how would you feel?

Right now, I think I'd be upset. I'd want to know. But maybe that's because I don't know enough about being undetectable?

It's actually safer to know someone is HIV-positive and unde-tectable, because they can't pass it on.

Interesting. Does that mean that in the years that you've been doing this, your approach to delivering the news to people has changed?

No, I just have to remind myself that it's not about me. It's my job to deliver the news and support the patient as much as I can in that moment. Most of the time, patients just get quieter and withdraw while they try to process it. We also have support workers. They help patients understand how they can live with it and reach an undetectable status. We answer any questions they have in the room and reassure them. We usually tell them it's like a chronic illness, similar to diabetes.

But do people still die of AIDS, if medication has progressed so much?

AIDS is the end result of untreated HIV. When you have a weakened immune system you're more likely to contract co-infections. It's less common now because of effective treatment, and we rarely see it. People still die of AIDS, but usually because they haven't been tested or treated. Or sometimes they stop taking their medication because of misinformation from non-medical sources, which is sad.

So, Stu, are you ready for your test?

I tell Jason that I am. I feel a little shaky, but honestly Jason is so lovely I'm soon quite at ease, although the idea of being the rare person who has suppressed my viral load over the years keeps bouncing around in my head. Jason tells me we will do the fingerprint test and that today he will just test for HIV. Just!! He starts to prep what looks like a COVID test. It sits staring at me on the desk. He needs to ask me some routine questions about my sexual health and all I can think of is the Samantha Jones scene in *Sex and the City*. 'Do you have oral sex?' 'Yes.' 'Give? Receive?' 'Yes, Yes.' 'Do you swallow?' 'Only when surprised!' I'm sure mine will be a lot less interesting!

What's your full name?
Stuart Oakley.

How many sexual partners have you had in the last three months?
One.

Was that a regular partner or a casual partner?
A regular partner.

When was the last time you had sex without a condom?
Over six weeks ago. We've been married a long time . . . regularity isn't a thing (I laugh).

And your last HIV test?
Never tested.

You're not currently taking PrEP?
No.

Any symptoms or concerns today?
Just the general nervousness from never having had a test, but otherwise, no. It's just been something I've thought about since I was twelve.

You'll be absolutely fine. So, let's start asking about your sexual history. The last time you had unprotected anal intercourse?
God, not sure I remember. I'd say about a month ago.

And were you the top, bottom, or both?
Both *(now there is a revelation for you, reader!)*.

Have you ever had syphilis before?
Not to my knowledge.

Now, a question we ask all our patients: Any fisting, injecting drugs, or chems?
No, no . . . and no. I'm very basic. Very vanilla.

Okay, so that means you are low risk for hepatitis C. And the sex you're having, you're consenting to all of it?
Yes.

And no one's harming you or hurting you?
No. Not intentionally anyway!

And then it's time for the test. Jason does a rapid finger-prick test. It is exactly that, a prick, and I don't even feel it. He lets my ruby red blood drip onto the test and adds it to a solution sitting in the white plastic container. He gives it a mix and then takes his surgically gloved hand to wipe the blood from my finger, pressing firmly with the cotton wool. A few seconds pass and he asks me about my kids, but then all of sudden he says, 'It's negative by the way. Congratulations on your first HIV test!' And it's that simple. I've been tested. Years of stress and worrying about it suddenly flood out of me. I realize how much I've been holding in regarding this subject that has affected our community for so many years. I find it incredible how quickly I get the news as well.

PrEP?
During my chat with Jason he mentions PrEP. I initially nod like I know what he is talking about, but then I have to stop him and ask exactly what is PrEP? I mean, I've heard of it and I'm vaguely familiar that it acts as some sort of anti-HIV drug, but I admit I'd like some more information. He hands me the Dean Street clinic's FAQs, which help to answer some of my questions . . .

What is PrEP?
PrEP (Pre-Exposure Prophylaxis) PrEP is a modern medicine designed to help prevent HIV. It stands for Pre-Exposure Prophylaxis, and it works by stopping HIV from getting into your body and making copies of itself (replicating). PrEP can be used by anyone from a community or group that is most at risk of HIV, or people who have sex with people from those networks. PrEP is typically prescribed to people at high risk of

HIV, such as those with HIV-positive partners, gay and bisexual men, and individuals who engage in sex without consistent condom use.

After my appointment at the Dean Street clinic I meet up with my friend Dan Harry (and star of BBC's first gay reality dating show *I Kissed a Boy*), who has presented a ground-breaking documentary for the BBC on PrEP. Dan is continuing his own exploration of HIV following him volunteering, as an HIV-negative person, in ongoing vaccine trials.

'My interest in LGBTQ+ sexual health started in school,' Dan tells me. 'In sex education, gay sexual health was never talked about. Gay wasn't a word used by teachers or anyone. It made me scared and led to a lot of fear of the unknown. From that age, I started to become curious about sexual health as a gay man and did my own research. Moving to London, I met friends who understood sexual health better. That's when I learned about PrEP, and I've been taking it since I moved to London three years ago. It's really changed the face of sexual health for gay men, giving them confidence that HIV is not a worry if they take PrEP.'

In the UK, there has been some controversy over making PrEP available on the NHS. Initially, funding was delayed, with some critics questioning whether NHS resources should be used for preventive medication. However, after several legal battles and public advocacy, PrEP was made available across the UK. Despite this, there have been issues with consistent access and awareness. And that's not the only controversy. 'There's also the false argument that because people are taking PrEP, they are actually engaging in riskier sexual behaviour, and then this potentially increases the risk of other STIs,' Dan tells me. In fact, one of the studies on PrEP, the iPrEx trial, observed that participants who were taking PrEP did not significantly increase their risky sexual behaviours (e.g., condomless sex) over time. Instead, many continued to engage in protective behaviours while on PrEP. The PrEPX Study, conducted in Australia, also found that PrEP did not result in increased STI rates among participants, largely due to the increased frequency of testing and medical follow-up.[2] 'There's still a lot of work to do regarding education of PrEP,' adds Dan. 'The awareness is definitely growing, especially in the gay community, but we need to reach other at-risk groups as well. More education and more accessible testing and treatment options are key.'

As it turned out, I was not HIV-positive. But I wanted to know more about what it is like when the story is different; what it's like to actually be diagnosed with HIV today. Yes, it's life-changing, but it's not life-threatening in the way it used to be. It sounds like everything is a lot more upbeat than I'd expected, but I'm sure there is still a lot of complexity to the situation. After all, the younger generation may not share the same trauma as older folk, but stigma around HIV and AIDS clearly still exists.

Let's meet . . . Alan

The fabulous people at the National AIDS Trust put me in touch with Alan O'Neil, who was given a positive HIV diagnosis at the age of twenty-seven. He's a gay man with 'undetectable' status. I meet him in Essex, where he lives, and he tells me what happened when he learned he had HIV.

When I first learned about my diagnosis, I had been struggling with my mental health and used casual sex as a way of coping, rather than getting support for how I was feeling. I was just having lots and lots of sex as it made me feel good, but then I ended up getting HIV from it. It was 2019 so I was diagnosed just months before PrEP became widely available. I was quite angry and disappointed about this at the time. It's not that I think that if PrEP was around I wouldn't have caught HIV, as there are other ways I could have protected myself, but a consultant once remarked how close I was to avoiding HIV if PrEP had been available sooner. 'Such a shame,' she quipped. 'A mere few months.' The shade!

I had been regularly testing for HIV and had a feeling I had contracted it even before the diagnosis confirmed it. I just felt it. Someone I had been seeing for sex regularly told me that they had HIV, and I suspected I had contracted it from them. I always tried to be safe but there were moments, like being blasted on a Saturday night, where I knew we hadn't used protection. The test confirmed my suspicion. It was a finger-prick test that took sixty seconds, but I was already crying before the test results came back positive. I couldn't accept it. It was one of the worst things.

Throughout 2019, I spent about four and a half months on psychiatric wards because I kept trying to end my life. I took it so badly because I was just not educated on the subject. When I came out as gay, my best friend's mum said to me, 'You'll just get AIDS and die.' That always stuck in my head. Growing up in south-east London, in a travelling Irish Catholic community, was challenging. I didn't have any gay friends, which made it hard for me to come out. My stepdad beat me because, in our community, it was OK to do that if someone came out.

I finally started exploring my sexuality in my mid-twenties. I became reckless. It was overwhelming to discover the gay social scene after being hidden away for so long. I chose not to educate myself about HIV because I was scared. There was no proper education in school. And then when I got diagnosed, I was given a book on ART (antiretroviral therapy). The first page talked about tens of thousands of cells multiplying in my body. It was terrifying. I looked at my skin, imagining all these cells inside, and I remember scratching at my skin. I felt like I'd fallen into the gay stereotype, as my friend's mum had suggested. People in my area expected gay people to get AIDS and die. Surprisingly, my best friend's mum did loads of research and became an HIV expert, proving me wrong about her beliefs.

There is still a stigma about HIV based on horror stories from the 80s and 90s. There's stigma and trauma. The older generation lost so many people and received scary leaflets through their doors. My gay uncle was angry at me when I told him. He lost friends in the 80s and 90s, and he could not believe I'd got HIV. He thought it was reckless, but I understand that his feelings are more about the trauma of losing friends rather than anger. The younger generation's reaction to my HIV status is mixed. Sometimes, I wish I didn't tell anyone. I'm out there doing a lot of activism work, especially around HIV fertility laws (which up to 2024 prevented HIV-positive homosexuals donating sperm but allowed HIV-positive heterosexuals to donate), and educating people, but being public about it has been challenging, especially now that I'm back on the dating scene. There's this whole spectrum of reactions. Some people still don't want to know, and as soon as I mention HIV they shut the door on our relationship. And that's hard, but I get it because I used to be that person. I'd block someone if they told me they had HIV because I was scared and ignorant. Now, I feel a bit lost in limbo, I'm stuck between older people who went through the worst of the crisis and younger folks who don't even think about it because they have PrEP. For them, HIV is almost non-existent. Then there's my generation, caught in this world of outdated, discriminative laws and social stigmas. We're not accepted by the older generation because we didn't endure their struggles, and the younger generation sees us as branded, unworthy. It's a lonely place.

And I am undetectable – it means you can't transmit the virus. Once your viral load is below fifty, they can't even detect it under a microscope. My immune system is actually healthier than the average person, thanks to my medication. So, do I have to tell people? No, not legally. But it's tricky. My consultant advised me to be selective because once you tell, you can't un-tell. Responses vary. I've had someone walk out mid-dinner after I disclosed my status. But I've also dated someone who was knowledgeable about PrEP and supportive. For casual hookups, I sometimes don't mention it because if I'm unde-tectable, there's no risk of transmission. My consultant com-pared it to my anxiety, as I live with anxiety but there is no way they are going to catch my anxiety, so do I need to disclose it to them? It does mean that dating with HIV means navigating mixed reactions, educating others, and sometimes facing rejection. But it also means finding those who understand and support you, and that makes all the difference.

When I think about my journey, especially after being diag-nosed with HIV, people need to understand it's going to be really tough. There's no sugar-coating it. It's going to be shit, really shit. But not because of the condition itself, but because of how you will let it affect you. It takes time for your mind to heal. It took me two years before I could talk about it openly. My healing process began when I started speaking up.

I drive out of Essex after my chat with Alan, a little less positive than when I first met him. Or maybe I am just leaving more educated? More aware of what it means to have HIV today? I drive round the M25 thinking about the road that I've been on over the last few months. I spent my teenage years and early twenties being petrified of this 'disease' because of everything that was fed into my brain over the years. I then went into a denial mode and my privilege meant I never had to think about it. Jumping into an exploration of HIV, and even my own test, I was surprised and heartened by the sense of hope and progress that seemed to have been made.

Is the stigma still strong?

But it's clear that there is still so much stigma around HIV, especially for gay men and trans people, and things are far from equal or up to date when it comes to the law. 'The impact of the virus itself has never been lower,' Dan Harry tells me. 'If you test regularly and catch it early, you can take medication, become undetectable, and live a normal life. However, stigma remains strong. People still receive nasty messages on dating apps, and there's a misconception about someone's sexual activity based on their status. It can happen to anyone, regardless of how often they have sex. The AIDS crisis was reported as a 'gay man's disease', and there's still a hangover from that. The reality is, it's not a gay virus. The rate of HIV cases is actually growing more among the heterosexual community in the UK now. In fact, the UK Health Security Agency reported in 2022[3] that in England the number of new HIV diagnoses among heterosexuals was actually higher than among gay and bisexual men.

When we wrote *The Queer Parent*, I was shocked when I found out that an HIV-positive cishet man can donate his sperm for fertility purposes but a homosexual cis man cannot.[4] It's simple discrimination that's only been overturned in 2024.[5] Alan tells me that 'we need basic access to services that many take for granted. There are still home insurances I can't get, travel insurance that's ridiculously expensive, and life insurance? Don't even go there. And it is all because of outdated laws and a lack of education. Laws that still see HIV as a "gay disease", which is absurd given the current statistics. We need equal rights in policy, especially regarding insurance, so people can buy homes and live their lives without unnecessary barriers. In short, we need to update these old, discriminatory laws and educate people. Only then can we move towards true equality for those living with HIV.'

As I reflect back on what I've learned about HIV today, something Alan said when I met him really stays with me. 'We don't live with HIV, HIV lives with us.' Let's not be blind to the continued stigma, but let's not let HIV cloak our community within darkness any more.

Chapter 12

Just Like a Prayer: Queering Religion

Stu

I find myself in Milan on a work trip. It may sound glamorous but honestly it is freezing cold and the rain is heavier than it is back home in London. On my afternoon off I escape the rain by ducking into the grand Duomo cathedral in the centre of the city. This isn't an unusual occurrence for me, as I'm always visiting churches or cathedrals on my travels. Yes, I love the architecture, and they are often top tourist attractions, but I find the peace within so calming, and an antidote to the feelings of anxiety that are often pulsing through me.

I sit on a pew in this grand place of worship and take a minute to marvel at just how *gay* churches are. I mean, there is so much drama, the opulence is off the scale, there are naked torsos on display, Jesus is giving major thirst-trap vibes with his ripped abs and peek-a-boo loin cloth, and let's give some snaps for the lighting, which is always just so good. It makes me wonder why more queer people are not religious, and then I remember that most religions are not known for being overly accepting of a bit of queer love. Yes, the age-old 'man should not lie with man' argument.

I don't have a religion. I didn't grow up in an overly religious house, although I was christened and my mum did the typical middle-England, middle-class thing of starting to go to church when she decided she wanted to get my sisters into the local church school, but that was the extent of it for me. Knowing I was gay from a young age, I've just never embraced the idea, but, as I've gotten older, I've started feeling a longing for the faith that comes with religion. For me, faith means a sense of self and inner peace as well as feeling connected with others, a community. For example, and I'm aware it's a light touch, I love listening to Radio 2's *Pause for Thought*. It's a daily message on the breakfast show from a religious figure spanning all faiths, and it's always calming, thought-provoking and enlightening. This is the part of religion I relate to and unexpectedly find myself being drawn to. It makes me question how many of us have potentially sacrificed our own journey of spirituality or faith because we never believed it would be possible to be both queer and religious?

In their paper, 'Shaping Attitudes about Homosexuality: The role of religion and cultural context',[1] Amy Adamczyk, a Professor of Sociology, states that 'Across the world, personal religious beliefs and affiliation are typically seen as powerful predictors of attitudes about homosexuality. Most religions tend to categorize behaviors associated with homosexuality as "unnatural", "ungodly", and "impure" (Yip, 2005). Because of this framing, active religious involvement, regular exposure to religious literature and frequent interaction with religious friends are likely to encourage anti-homosexual attitudes.'

With this in mind I want to know how one can be queer and religious when it seems religions, and religious people, have a history of being anti-LGBTQ+? For Christianity, Catholicism and Orthodox Judaism, the Bible states, 'If a man lies with a male as with a woman, both of them have committed an abomination; they shall surely be put to death; their blood is upon them.' Leviticus 20:13 (Old Testament). For Muslims, the Islamic readings the Hadith says, 'The Prophet (ﷺ) cursed effeminate men (those men who are in the similitude [assume the manners of] women) and those women who assume the manners of men, and he said, "Turn them out of your houses"'; and according to the Church of Latter Day Saints' Law of Chasity, Mormons believe that 'sexual relations are to be reserved for marriage between a man and a woman. Any sexual activity outside of this context, including homosexual acts, is considered a violation of the Law of Chastity'. It's worth adding that some of these translations are contested, and in the case of Hadith, their authenticity can be questionable too, as my new Islamic friend Deenah (who you will meet very shortly) tells me.

What space is there for LGBTQ+ people in religion?

For all these teachings it does seem that LGBTQ+ groups within various major faiths are becoming more and more commonplace, creating safe and welcoming environments for those who are queer and religious, so perhaps it's not too late to find a faith that would welcome me? Groups and individuals are doing amazing work in this area across all religions – see the resources section on page 254 for some of these. Many branches of Christianity have begun the process of creating LGBTQ+ spaces, and Progressive Judaism now fully embraces LGBTQ+ individuals, emphasizing the evolving nature of Jewish law and tradition, and prioritizing the contemporary values of inclusivity and equality. In fact, I am lucky to know many Jewish friends who have fed my inquisitive mind with facts and details of their religion over the years. I have loved discovering their traditions and often chewed their ear off to hear about their rituals, especially those that revolve around the family, such as the Friday night dinner held to celebrate the coming of Shabbat – the sabbath. The family will gather to share food and drink that have symbolic meanings, read blessings and use the occasion as a time to be together. There are various rituals that form part of the Shabbat dinner, all of which create a sense of belonging and togetherness with one's family. The nearest my family has to a tradition is to order a pizza while watching *Gladiators*.

I find the idea of Progressive Judaism really intriguing. For them, this sense of progression means applying the teaching of the Torah to modern times and applying context to the faith in the current world. And this isn't a new progression, either. It actually started in the 1800s. So to understand the queerness within Progressive Judaism and find out how one can be queer and Jewish, I met with Rabbi Elli Tikvah Sarah. She was the first lesbian to lead a mainstream congregation (in the world!) and was Rabbi of the Brighton and Hove Progressive Synagogue for over twenty years.

Rabbi Elli, I'd love to know about your journey of becoming a rabbi. I believe you came out before you began embracing your Jewish heritage?

I came out as a lesbian radical feminist in 1978, in the context of the Women's Liberation movement. I didn't actually want to have anything to do with mainstream Judaism, because I saw it as totally patriarchal and excluding me. But I also didn't want to be defined by anti-Semitism. I wanted to make sense of anti-Semitism as a Jew on my own terms, and that's what precipitated me taking a journey into my own Jewish heritage. Saying it belongs to me and I'm going to make it work for me, and make it work for other people like me. I decided to become a rabbi to make Jewish teaching and Jewish life more inclusive, and that means, in a sense, buying into something which I then transform. And that's what I've been doing, and what I encourage people to do. I have devoted my professional life to making Jewish life and teaching more inclusive.

In what ways was Judaism not inclusive?

Jewish teachings have traditionally been patriarchal, about men maintaining control of women. At a very simple level, why does it say that one man should not lie with another man as with a woman and that it's an abomination? Why does it say that? One of the reasons it says that is because there's nothing worse you can do to a man than treat him like a woman. When we began to look at these things with LGBTQ+ eyes, and you read that as a gay man, you think, 'Oh, God! I'm not included. This is ghastly and horrible, and I am going to run a million miles in the other direction.' And this is what so many people do. Then what has happened over the past thirty-five to forty years is people have said, 'Wait a minute, I'm Jewish, or I'm Christian, or I'm Muslim, or this is part of my culture, and I'm just not going to allow them to say this to me. I'm going to get into there, and I'm going to make it make sense to me on my terms.' And that's been a whole journey.

And now?

The Progressive Jewish community has now advanced very far on the journey of inclusiveness. The Progressive rabbinate is now composed of over 20 per cent LGBTQ+ rabbis. Progressive Judaism is genuinely embracing, but there's a long way to go in the Jewish community as a whole. LGBTQ+ people can grow up in families where they feel afraid that if they come out, they'd be rejected. So you need people around you, as it takes a lot of courage and determination. It can be much harder for minority communities to come out. Cypriots, Muslims, Jews, you're already a minority, so the thought of rejecting your family is not an easy option.

I get the sense that there is a kindred spirit between Jewish people and the LGBTQ+ community. Would you say that's true?

What Jews and LGBTQ+ people have in common, even if the Jews are not LGBTQ+ themselves, is coming out. As a Jew, the minute I let someone know I'm Jewish, I'm likely to deal with anti-Semitism. So, Jews stay in the closet, just like LGBTQ+ people stay in the closet. We are a minority too. There are only 270–290,000 Jews in a country of 68 million, so there is a real kinship between LGBTQ+ people and Jews.

What would you say to a young person who knows that they're LGBTQ+ but struggling with that and their Jewish faith?

I'd say, come and speak to me. Anybody who wants to come and speak to me, I speak to them and help them to find a home in the Jewish community. I tell them: You can belong here.

Next time I'm in Brighton I plan to visit Rabbi Elli's synagogue. Is Judaism the faith I've been missing in my life? But before I go full Charlotte from *Sex and the City* and decide to convert, I want to know what other religions, especially those that Rabbi Elli points out are not potentially as progressive as Judaism, do offer to queer people.

Adam and Eve not Adam and Steve?

I touch base with the Reverend Jide Macaulay who founded the group 'House of Rainbow'. Originally the House of Rainbow started as a weekly gathering for LGBTQ+ Christians in Lagos, which soon became known as Nigeria's first gay church. Jide, a gay British-Nigerian Christian minister, has faced intimidation and death threats and now lives in Manchester developing the house as a global organization that supports people through online services.

He tells me first that the people in his community call him 'Mama Jide', which he loves, especially because of the toxic masculinity that he has experienced previously within the church. 'I've had to work through the abuse I received from my father,' he tells me as we chat. 'I was born and raised in a very conservative Christian home in Nigeria. My father is also a religious leader who has just never understood my sexuality. Even today we don't see eye to eye, and I've been disowned. So the fact I've been able to find my own way, especially around my sexuality, is an incredible joy and a continuous journey. I say continuous because there are obviously still people within the faith that would say we are an abomination and you should give your life back to God. I think it's important to know that LGBTQ+ individuals are often misrepresented in religious contexts. The belief that LGBTQ+ people are condemned as an "abomination" in scripture stems from a long-standing misinterpretation of biblical texts. However, a deeper understanding of scripture reveals a different story, one rooted in love, acceptance and humanity.

'First, it's important to recognize that the Bible, written thousands of years ago, reflects the social and cultural contexts of its time. Furthermore, Jesus never specifically condemned LGBTQ+ people or spoke against same-sex relationships. His teachings emphasize love, compassion and inclusivity, particularly for those who are marginalized. In the New Testament, we see a focus on how to treat others with kindness and understanding. For LGBTQ+ Christians, this is the core message of their faith, a message of unconditional love and acceptance. The misconception that LGBTQ+ people are condemned by scripture often comes from selective readings of certain passages, coupled with cultural biases that have developed over centuries. Religious homophobia emerged because of these misunderstandings, combined with societal norms that viewed homosexuality as unnatural or immoral. This homophobia has been perpetuated by religious institutions that, instead of evolving their understanding of human sexuality, have held on to outdated interpretations. I want people to know that they can live their lives joyfully with God.'

Reverend Jide adds, 'We have been told so many things that are wrong. We've been told that God made male and female, and that is it. We've been told that God did not make Adam and Steve, but Adam and Eve. That is wrong. We've been told that God destroyed two cities because of homosexuality. That is wrong. You know, we've been told that as homosexuals we are not going to inherit the kingdom of God, and now we're learning so much more. There are people who are LGBTQ+ who have left religion, and now they're coming back to Christianity. It's about changing minds and opening up spaces. It makes so much difference by just creating safe spaces and having somewhere people can be a partaker of their community and faith. However, I really doubt that in ten years' time, globally, Christianity will be more embracing. Although I have hope that maybe in five to ten years the Church of England will fully accept LGBTQ+ people and we will be able to marry within the denomination.'

As of right now the Church of England does not permit same-sex marriages to be performed in its churches. However, it does allow for prayers of blessing for same-sex couples following a civil marriage or civil partnership. The Church continues to discuss and debate its stance on this issue. 'I expect people to remain homo-phobic,' continues Reverend Jide. 'If it does change it is going to take quite a bit of time, maybe a completely different generation. But it will be a disservice if we don't share our voices today, if we don't speak out.'

I tell Reverend Jide that I often have my own preconceived notions when I know someone is religious. It's like something tenses in me as I just immediately assume that, because of their religion, whichever faith it might be, they must be homophobic. Is that something he has experienced from the non-religious queer community? 'I've had non-religious LGBTQ+ people attack me. We live in a world that is so polarized, with so much information that shapes how we see religious communities behave. We are associated with corruption, or with the religious leaders who have made our lives hell. I've been told that I am a disgrace. I've also been told that because many Black queer people see it that I am embracing the colonizers who forced their religion on our community. I just have to think about my own human rights. I think that it's time to rescue the Christian faith from those that are abusing it. I'm not saying make it presentable, but present the truth.'

Can you pray the gay away?

I feel such a strong sense of positivity from both Rabbi Elli and Reverend Jide. It radiated from them, and I carried it with me for the rest of the day. I can fully understand how religion gives people hope and happiness, which is why it's so hard to reconcile this with the extreme and fundamentalist notions that exist within these religions, particularly the idea that you can 'pray the gay away' with conversion therapy.

Conversion therapy is the process where people believe they can enact a change to someone's sexuality via various techniques, which include talking therapies, aversion therapy (pairing same-sex stimuli with negative stimuli), prayer and physical methods including hormone treatment. While not exclusively a religious exercise, according to the UK government's LGBTQ+ survey in 2018[2] those from religious faiths were more likely to be offered some form of conversation therapy, with 10 per cent of responders to the survey being Christian and 20 per cent from Muslim backgrounds. More than half of those who had received the therapy said it had been conducted by a faith group, while a fifth received it from health-care professionals.

For many, the idea of conversion therapy transports us to an image of 1950s asylums with people strapped down to a gurney, not the cozy, modern living room of a friendly-looking therapist in 2024. Though, at the time of writing, the latter is very much happening, and legal, within the UK. There is a fight for a bill to ban the insidious practice of conversion therapy with an MoU joint document (a Memorandum of Understanding) having been signed in 2017 by over twenty-five health, counselling and psychotherapy organizations including NHS England and the British Psychological Society. They called to end the practice of conversion therapy in the UK, making it clear that this practice, in relation to gender identity and sexual orientation (including asexuality), is unethical, potentially harmful and not supported by evidence. A call to ban conversion therapy was included in the King's Speech to the UK parliament in July 2024.[3] We've been here before, though, with the late Queen mentioning it twice previously, and still nothing has been actioned by the government. At least the latest conversation is now referencing an additional ban on transgender conversion therapy within the proposed bill, as previously our trans siblings were being left out to the wolves.

But even if, by the time you are reading this, the law has changed and the 'practice' is banned, will that stop the many different forms that conversion therapy can take being used? One interviewee told me about the experience they had at their family church when they were younger. For ongoing legal reasons they do not wish to be named or have their full story shared, but they used the word 'gaslighting' when remembering what happened. They describe what felt like 'a subtle form of conversion therapy', with trusted elders in the community telling them that 'if they loved Jesus enough' they wouldn't act on their queer tendencies, and all this took place in informal, familiar settings.

So while conversion therapy itself, as a formal therapy, might be banned, will that really stop some folk taking advantage of vulnerable queer people? Will it really stop some people, potentially led by religious beliefs, making others believe they are fundamentally broken and need to be cured?

Indeed, the Christian Institute states that '[we have] been at the forefront of opposition to a ban on conversion therapy and have warned that such a broad ban would threaten gospel freedom and would inadvertently criminalize the ordinary work of churches.'[4] Additionally, 250 British imams and Muslim leaders signed a letter stating, 'We believe any future legislative plans must uphold the right of individuals who don't identify as lesbian, gay or bisexual and have unwanted same-sex attractions, to explore their potential for opposite-sex attractions.'[5] The fact that these religious institutions want to find loopholes to continue gaslighting those questioning or discovering their sexuality says it all.

What's it like to be queer within a religious community that doesn't accept you?

Some people are able to remove themselves from a situation, and a religion, with little backlash from their family or community. We all know that is often not the case, especially for religions perceived as less progressive. I really wanted to gain some insight from someone within one of the perhaps most misunderstood and misrepresented religions, Islam. Muslims, rightly or wrongly, are known for potentially being one of the least-accepting religions, but I found the Hidayah, a charity and a non-profit organization that runs projects, events and activities for the needs of LGBTQ+ Muslims. Their mission is to provide support and welfare for queer

Muslims and promote social justice and education about the community to counter discrimination, prejudice and injustice.

Hidayah literally means 'guidance' in Arabic. So I think, perhaps naively, 'This is great. You can also be totally queer and Muslim and I can't wait to hear all about that!' One of their team, Deenah, agrees to speak to me and we organize an online chat, with cameras off. Early in the interview Deenah, who is in her twenties, tells me she lives at home with her family. When I ask her about how she identifies, she goes quiet, then tells me to check my chat box. The word 'lesbian' has appeared. Deenah isn't open with her parents about her sexuality and, as she is conducting the call at home today, she needs to be careful about what might be overheard. My immediate reaction is to think 'how terrible!', but Deenah explains how this impulse to be out to family and the 'world' feels like a very Western idea.

'It's a very Western expectation,' she tells me. 'It doesn't necessarily fit into my worldview.' Deenah points me to an incredibly interesting article she wrote for *Metro*.[6] In it she talks about the privilege often associated with coming out. 'These narratives assume you have an emotional and financial support system,' she writes. 'Ignoring how so many people of colour depend upon and lean on their families or cultural communities. There are privileges that we need to deconstruct.' She goes on to explain how it is the implication that someone's identity is only valid when everyone knows about it which is an interesting viewpoint, and one I'd never really contemplated before. She tells me, 'I know a lot of people who see things differently from me, and I think that is the beauty having an intersectional identity. People, even people who are of the exact same demographic as me, may have a different view on things than me, and I think that's fine and totally valid.'

I'll admit it is fascinating for me to hear this perspective on things, as I clearly subscribe to the narrative that in order to be 'happy' you have to be out and that equates to being proud, and

I've never even considered that's my cis-white non-religious privilege speaking. There is nothing in Deenah's work or life to indicate that she isn't proud of who she is, or is in fact lonely. In fact, it is quite the opposite, with the thriving group of friends and chosen family she has at Hidayah. 'When you have people in your circle who are very much aware of your circumstances, and are even in similar circumstances to me, then there is a solidarity. There is a shared love. I have met people who are going to be friends for life, people who I consider my siblings.' And there it is again. That sense of community that people from any religion seem to feel, it feels powerful. Dare I say, even more powerful than the general queer community? So, being queer and religious perhaps even gives you some form of community superpower?

I tell Deenah I'm not aware of how open and progressive parts of Islam might be. For example, is there hope in the future that more LGBTQ+ people can be accepted into the religion? 'There is definitely progress,' she says. 'There are some Islam scholars out there, including Dr Amina Wadud, Imam Daayiee Abdullah and Imam Muhsin Hendricks, who are much more affirming of people's identities, they are adding weight to the conversation for sure, but it's still very much on the edge of things. Something you need to also understand for context, especially in terms of UK Muslims, is that many British Muslims are people of colour, with most being second- or third-generation immigrants. Many of our families came here as migrants looking for a better life, safety and security. but they were often met with violence and racism. So, we assimilated, we tried to adjust to make ourselves respectable, for want of a better word. This has left a sense of shame in a big part of who we are. It's always a question of what will people think? Will this harm our family's representation? That definitely feeds into the anxiety of rocking the boat too much. In terms of shaking things up and being more progressive, I'm not sure how likely that is to happen in the immediate future, but I hope that it can happen one day.'

It's interesting to me how Deenah brings the word shame into our conversation. A word also so seeped into the very fabric of our queer identity, and how as an LGBTQ+ Muslim you face a double helping of it. It also makes me sad to think how we've made so much progress in the queer community, but how the very notion of being queer and Muslim is still seen as 'rocking the boat'.

Prior to exploring religion for this chapter, and having never grown up in a religious family, I had found it hard to understand why some people would continue to practise a religion that didn't accept them. But speaking to Deenah, I completely understand the nuance involved, especially as a marginalized community. I can never truly put myself in her shoes, but I do want to know, especially as someone trying to find my own faith, what is it that she loves most about being Muslim? 'It comes down to a sense of oneness. There is a concept in Islam called Tawhid, which is essentially a oneness in God. We are a monotheistic religion, so we only believe in one God. And for me the oneness is also about the community. While I do obviously have certain objections to the way Muslim communities are run and led by, generally, cis men, it's the actual community itself. I've seen when those communities have come together in times of need and who have banded together to help provide a sense of comfort when you don't expect it. Having our rituals and our traditions that unify us.' I think this goes back to the 'Western' views that Deenah explained before. I, for one, had to question how she will manage in the future with being 'closeted' for her entire life to her family. But that's just my projection, and some people may not find a problem with masking part of their life in order to allow the other part of them to survive and thrive. It is not something, with my own upbringing, I can fully get to grips with, but after speaking to her, I get it. Family and belonging are vitally important.

The interviewee who told me about the 'unofficial' conversion therapy they felt that they had received also spoke about missing the sense of community they used to find at church after they left it. Singing songs together, having tea and coffee with peers and the older generation.

I wonder if queerness is another type of religion. We find our sanctuaries and our communities, and maybe these places are gay bars and clubs, not churches or mosques, but they function as safe spaces all the same. There are some very interesting parallels between religious and queer communities. But as someone who doesn't enjoy queer nightlife, and for others seeking a sober place to unite, is this our moment to start our own queer religion, which, as I discussed with Reverend Jide, could take elements from many different faiths? I mean, this could be my own L. Ron Hubbard moment. My chance to create the Church of the Latter Day Queers, perhaps? If Jedi can be recognized on the census as a religion, why not queer? With mental health issues, loneliness and family rejection being so rife within the queer community, is it such a bad idea to have somewhere we could congregate weekly to listen to messages of hope and love? A place where we can be sober together to have a sense of belonging and compassion for one another. Somewhere we can sing songs and bring joy to each other's lives. A chance to make friends and socialize with intergenerational gay people and embrace our differences and similarities. And, most importantly, a place that doesn't discriminate, that celebrates the love that it preaches? Can I get an amen?

Chapter 13

What's Your Pleasure?

Lotte

I'm writing this chapter while my five-year-old daughter is off school with a temperature and a sore throat. She's lying on the sofa listening to a bonkers Enid Blyton audio book about a magic tree and every now and then climbs onto my lap and reads out a word from my computer screen. Thank goodness so far it's only been the word 'dull' and the word 'queen' that she's chosen to sound out.

I can't help but feel there's something a bit wrong and inappropriate about me sitting here writing about sex while my child lolls around in a Calpol-induced daze. But this is the reality of the queer experience. We are the light, and the shadows. We are monogamous queer parents and promiscuous singletons. We have boring married sex in bed and wild, boundary-breaking sex with strangers. We have wild boundary-breaking married sex *and* boring sex with strangers. We are all of these things and none of these things, and we have a vastly expansive spectrum of sexual preferences, practices and predilections. It's impossible to distil queer sex into anything even close to a singular experience (especially when Kate Winslet is narrating a story about someone called Moon Face and his slippery slip in the background, although come to think of it that does sound like something you might find in a gay sex club). So what I hope to do over the next few pages is give equal credence to a diversity of queer sexual experiences and explore some answers to the question of whether queer people really are more sexual than straight people, and if so, why?

The very act of coming out means we are having to publicly announce our sexual preferences in a way that straight people just don't have to. But is it that queer people are having *more* sex than our hetero friends, or are we just more open about it and better at talking about it? I'm not sure, because on one hand I know a whole culture that revolves around sex has been created by queer people *for* queer people and this has been the case for hundreds of years – thousands, if we count those Ancient Greek shenanigans. Cottaging, dark rooms, orgies and saunas have long been part of gay (male) life. Transactional or casual sex has always been a greater part of gay male culture than it has lesbian, though that's not to say queer women are less sexual, maybe it's just that women, because of, y'know, the patriarchy, etc., aren't as confident in prioritizing their sexual desires, nor might they feel as safe about meeting up with strangers. Throw into the mix 'dating' apps that mean you can organize a hookup within the hour pretty much anywhere in the world, which is possible for gay women but definitely more normalized for gay men, and it could easily seem like queer people are sex obsessed.

Have we had to desexualize queerness for mainstream approval?

As a queer parent I am faced with a ridiculous backlash to my very existence, which comes from right-wing politicians and keyboard warriors but has had an insidious impact on so many aspects of our society. I've sometimes felt the need to completely desexualize queerness in order to prove to these bigots, who think

LGBTQ+ people are indoctrinating children and dismantling the sanctity of family life, that sex and sexuality exist in a totally different space to wholesome family time and day-to-day parenting (aka the majority of my life).

To justify the appropriateness of drag queen story time, for example, which is literally just a fabulous drag performer captivating kids with an animated reading of a picture book, we have to categorically assert that there is nothing sexual about drag queens.

We've lost all nuance. Drag queens can be kinky and funny and sexy and outrageous, just like anyone can, but they read the room! And when it's a room full of toddlers, they're going to moderate their behaviour just like any adult person would.

I'm beginning to wonder if we have worked so hard to desexualize homosexuality that we've created this really vanilla version of queerness that's palatable to the hetero masses? It's all rainbow cupcakes and smiling white men in suits at their child's christening. Or it's lesbian mums clutching oat lattes and pushing Bugaboos. Or it's hit shows like *Heartstopper*, which have been criticized for showing a 'watered-down' version of teenage queer life. It's airbrushed and unthreatening.

How dull and unsexy!

Meanwhile, there's this dark, underground, leather-clad, queer sexiness that feels illicit – and never the two shall meet (at least in public, or sometimes at Pride).

I have a hunch that gay shame and the legacy of Section 28 has made some of us willing participants in the sexless gay fantasy that I describe. And maybe, interestingly, it's the same thing that has pushed others into its shadow – the underground culture of hookups and transactional sexual encounters.

It is when they talk about sex that I feel the most distance from my child-free gay friends. They enjoy a freedom and near-constant access to sexual wish fulfilment, while I feel I have to take the *sex* out of my sexuality in order to be seen as a decent and upstanding queer parent in a world of straight parents.

I find it frustrating that the biological children of heterosexual parents are (mostly) the physical result of sexual intercourse; these kids are the walking, talking products of *what goes on behind closed doors*! Talk about shoving your sexuality in our faces. And yet these parents don't ever need to worry that if they hold each other's hands or steal a kiss in a playground someone might accuse them of being inappropriate or too open about their sexuality around children.

Is this need for the outward image of queerness to be decidedly PG keeping queer sex in the shadows, in dark rooms and saunas, in Grindr hookups you might not even tell your friends about? And is this why issues of consent, chemsex and STIs are so prevalent in our community? If we had permission to be more open about sex outside our own queer microcosm, with wider society, would it all just be a bit more normalized and safer in every sense?

Gay and straight sex should be considered equal, but it was only in the year 2000 that the age of consent for homosexuals was lowered from eighteen to sixteen – the same as it had been for heterosexuals since 1885 (when it was *raised* from thirteen!). Weird, then, that it took another twenty-three years for the UK to air its first gay male dating show on prime-time TV.

I consider myself open-minded. My friendship group of mainly gay men talks freely about sexual conquests, desire and the ins and outs of their various experiences, from douching to dating, and I barely raise an eyebrow (although, as I said earlier, it does make me aware of how different our lives are these days). But in the course of researching this chapter, opening the door to the dark room, both metaphorically and literally, I have been challenged, educated, surprised and a little bit turned on by a fabulous orgy of experiences.

I know lots of people, gay and straight, have questions about gay sex that they're maybe afraid to ask. So I'm going to ask these questions for you and call on a fabulous coterie of sexy queers to help.

How do lesbians have sex?

It's a shame that googling this question most probably won't give you a very accurate answer. More likely it'll be the porn version you're confronted with which is aimed at, you guessed it, straight men, and before you know it your algorithm will have pushed you off your well-meaning cliff into a *Not All Men*-shaped black hole.

The fact is, lesbian sex is not one thing and it isn't necessarily penetrative, although it can be – strap-ons, tongues, fingers, hands, fists, vibrators, scissoring (where two people with vaginas/vulvas rub them against each other. Dear God, I hope my parents aren't reading this). All of the above. None of the above. The wonderful thing about lesbian sex, well, this is true of all kinds of sex really, is it can be so many things – as long as it feels good.

My lesbian sexual education came as a teenager via a gay and lesbian sex education video my first partner had somehow got hold of. We watched it secretly when their parents were out one day and I remember distinctly one of the lesbians advocating for placing cling film over your partner's vagina in order to perform safe oral sex. I've never looked at a tightly wrapped sandwich the same way since. My ex and I laughed, and figured we'd work out what to do ourselves with a little help from classic movies such as *Bound* and *If These Walls Could Talk*, and later *The L Word,* of course. But look, I'm no expert.

What are some specific lesbian sexual identities (not to be confused with the general lesbian 'types' Stu explored previously) I might not have heard of?

Stone butch: This term is used to describe butch lesbians who don't like to 'receive' sexually but are more than happy to give. The dyke equivalent of a 'top', perhaps. It became a bit more well known with the publication of Leslie Feinberg's novel *Stone Butch Blues* in 1993, which is about a working-class stone butch living in the US in the 1950s and is now widely considered a queer classic.

Touch me not: Known as TMN for short, this is a cultural term that some Black lesbians and queer people use. Often, touch me nots are masculine-of-centre lesbians or studs. It's usual for TMNs to keep their clothes on during sex and derive pleasure entirely from making love to someone else.

Pillow princess: A common term in the lesbian and queer women world, pillow princesses are less likely to reciprocate some or all sex acts (the insinuation being that their head remains on the pillow because their partner is doing all the 'work'!). If we were to compare this to the gay male world, its closest equivalent would be a bottom. Pillow princesses are usually femme, and while some are self-confessed pillow princesses and might play up to the sassy/'lazy' reputation, others see the term as pejorative.

Dom femme: She's the alpha in the bedroom. Most likely to call the shots and not hold back in articulating when, where and how she likes to be touched. There may or may not be an element of kink or BDSM play with a dom femme.

In my limited personal experience of casual sex with women, no one has ever told me they identify, sexually, in a specific way. Getting to know each other's preferences has been part of the fun and there have not been these fixed labels for us to negotiate. I get that when online dating these labels can be a useful shorthand if you are a TMN or stone butch, for instance, and you know you need something very specific from a sexual partner. But otherwise, it seems a little limiting to me to have to name your sexual preferences so definitively. Which is probably why the majority of queer women don't.

What really happens in a gay sauna?

I've often walked past what I thought was a gay gym on Ramillies Street in central London. There's a picture of Cain, who we'll talk more to later, in a tiny towel outside. He must be just about to change into his PE kit, I had always naively figured.

I decided to get in touch with the founders of this place to discuss the relationship gay men have with fitness for Chapter 2, but I quickly discovered that SweatBox is in fact a sauna/sex club – with a small gym in it that occasionally hosts naked fitness classes.

I love having my expectations challenged so blatantly. I had assumed the men behind this place would be beefy, BMI-obsessed fitties. But no, Mark and Jason Ford are like a better-looking Gilbert and George – avant-garde, sex-positive nihilists. Jason, who is a handsome American in his early fifties, identifies as a vampire/merman (just go with it!). And his husband Mark is a wiry, fast-talking, ex-1990s TV exec – he conceived the iconic *Eurotrash* and *The Girlie Show*. He is sixty but looks forty (I mean, they both spend a lot of time in saunas!).

My interview with them, in the sub-basement of SweatBox in their secret office – which is campy, B-movie horror meets the occult meets *Buffy the Vampire Slayer* in its décor – was one of the strangest places I've been in my life. Their black French Bulldog sat between them on the sofa and growled at me throughout. I was one of the few 'lady people', as Mark called me, to ever be let down here. No wonder their dog was on guard.

The pair delight in not being what anyone expects from the founders of a gay gym that's actually a sex club. Our conversation took in more twists and turns than a Berlin dark room.

Sex clubs for straights do exist, but dark rooms and sex-based saunas seem far more a part of the queer (or at least gay male) experience – for some people at least. I asked Mark and Jason why there are no lesbian equivalents. They say they did try to launch a lesbian sauna night on a Tuesday but so few people showed up, it didn't work. Obviously, no one told them about *Wednesday* being life's official lesbian day. In the course of my research I've not come across any female or non-binary-friendly queer saunas, but I have discovered a BPOC Trans Sauna event which is non-sexual. I have also been made aware of some more gender-diverse, queer dark rooms in certain nightclubs, although I have been told these spaces remain cis-male-dominated.

So what actually is a dark room?

A space, often underground, often within a nightclub, which is dark (obviously!) and contains beds, sofas and shadowy corners where you can have anonymous sex with people you can't really see. I have had a fun night in a dark room myself, in Duesseldorf of all places. I passed as a boy and kissed a few random stubbly faces, felt up some leather-clad bulges before worrying I wasn't enough of a boy to be there and had to find my way out – not easy in a pitch-black labyrinth dense with writhing bodies.

As I'm far from a dark room doyenne and the darkest room Stu's been in is his office when the lightbulb blew, I ask Mark and Jason to tell me more.

For someone who's never been to one, what do you think the appeal of a dark room is?

When you step into the dark room the rules of consent change, and you are consenting to be touched intimately by hands. The whole point of a dark room is you don't know who is touching you, so you don't get to go, *not you, ugly, only you.* That's what you consented to. You haven't consented to anal sex. You haven't consented to anything penetrative. That can still be non-verbally negotiated within the dark room. Penetration is a different thing, but touch, somebody grabbing you in any particular place, you have consented to.

I think the appeal of a dark room is . . . imagine being caressed by many hands at once. And men don't get touched often. And sex is often a performance. And anxiety comes with performance. Male sexuality is all about worrying, *can I get hard? Can I deliver? Can I satisfy? Can I do this? Can I do that?* In a dark room, you don't worry about anything. You just surrender to these hands, and it feels amazing. You're on a wave of tactileness.

What happens in a sauna?

Again, this is another consensual space for anonymous sexual encounters. You leave your clothes in the locker and head into the steam room. You can see people but the steam adds a layer of anonymity. You need to follow unspoken cues to gauge whether a fellow sauna goer wants to have sex with you, then you negotiate what that sex might be. But anything goes, from hand jobs to oral to full, consensual, penetration.

What are these unspoken cues in a sauna? How do I show someone that I want to fuck them?

We refer to that as the code of silence. Saunas have been around and a part of gay culture since the Ancient Romans. Unlike a bar, where you'd have to buy someone a drink or summon up the courage to actually speak to someone, this is orchestrated completely in silence. So it's making eye contact, moving closer to the person, accidentally your feet might touch, your legs, or you might go for the old yawn and stretch and put your arm around them. The steam in saunas offers just the right amount of visibility – you can get a sense of someone but it's all in softer focus than it might be in daylight.

And how do you signal no – I'm not into you?

Usually if someone's not interested in you they will move your hand. We are currently in the process of writing out the rules of consent for SweatBox. This is the first time we've needed them because I think there has been a generational shift. In general, gay guys have always just known these rules. You engage your gaydar, you know – that thing in which you make eye contact with somebody and know instantly they're gay.

This skill came from a time when we were all in the closet because it was illegal, and so the gaydar, the eye look, or the little mannerisms – all of that was about working out whether the other one was too, and so therefore sex could occur.

One of the side effects of actually having more and more acceptance, and more and more integration and freedoms, is that you don't necessarily grow up having to think about your life and who you are and where you fit in and how it works, which is terrific but these younger people don't necessarily intuitively know as much.

What happens in a sauna is it goes from look, to touch, to usually a conversation.

The polite way of rejecting someone's touch is, if I'm sat in the steam room and somebody is doing this [rubbing] on my thigh, if I'm not interested, because I'm older and I'm more confident, I would just touch their hand, possibly take it and move it, but give it a little friendly squeeze at the same time, which is my version, without having to break the code of silence, of saying no thank you. And nobody sees that rejection going on. If you're gonna break the code of silence it would be because someone wasn't getting the hint, then look them in the eye and say, 'Sorry, mate, that's not going to happen.'

Saunas are generally a silent secretive thing we don't talk about. Whereas when we were designing and constructing and conceiving the concept of SweatBox, we very much wanted to be more sex-positive. We didn't want to be on the edge of, on the fringe of our community, we were going to be in the centre and we were going to be loud. There's a sort of paradox in our culture that we talk about sex all the time and we pretend to be sex-positive and everybody associates us [LGBTQ+ people] with sex. But we're not really. We're actually quite ashamed of it.

Some Sexplanations: What you've always wanted to know but been afraid to ask

What's a bottom?

The 'taker' in anal penetration or any sexual encounter. It's more of a common word in gay male sex, but lesbians, particularly those into BDSM (**bondage, discipline or domination**, sadism or submission, masochism), will also use it. A 'power bottom', however, is a more active/dominant participant in it. Some people have reductively likened the role of the 'bottom' in gay male relations to that of a woman in a hetero relationship. Within these hierarchies someone who identifies as a bottom might also be the more feminine energy in a partnership. There are some outdated stereotypes and expectations associated with the identity being 'passive' that continue to be perpetuated among the gay male community, which is now thankfully being called out as bottom-shaming.

What's a top?

The 'giver' in anal penetration or any sexual act. Gay men and lesbians might both identify as a 'top' as well as all other genders and sexual identities, but the term is most used in gay male communities, particularly on dating apps. A top might fancy another top but sexually the dynamic probably wouldn't work if neither was willing to deviate from their preference. In gay male culture there's a bit of an in-joke about the lack of tops on dating sites and out and about on the scene.

What's vers?

Short for versatile. They'll mix it up being a top or a bottom depending on what works with a particular partner or particular situation.

What's a side?

Sides are men (mainly) who enjoy a variety of sexual acts except anal penetration. It's a relatively new term. According to an article in *The Guardian* it was coined in 2013 by the sex therapist and author Dr Joe Kort. Sides are more about emotional connection and physical sensation than simply fucking. For many who find the process of anal sex compli-cated, it also provides a way to enjoy pleasure without penetration. Stu most identifies as a side. 'A hand job is sometimes so much easier, and just as fun.' In 2023 Grindr added 'side' to its options for preferred sex position (previously just listed as 'top', 'bottom' or 'vers'). But some sides feel like they face discrimination from the wider gay male community for not participating in anal sex, as though this makes them less gay.

What has Grindr done for gay sex?

'We [gay men] kind of created the concept of online dating,' Grindr's CEO, George Arison, told *The Guardian* in March 2024. This isn't hubris, it's true. Before Grindr revolutionized the landscape, gay men sought connections through myriad inventive means: from classified ads (lesbians were big fans of the classified ad, too) and phone chat lines to the pioneering dating websites of the late 90s and early 2000s like Gaydar and Manhunt (queer women also embraced online dating but the apps didn't expand as fast and furiously as the gay male ones did). I remember using Gaydar with my best gay friend Will when we were teenagers and printing out a grainy photo of a potential suitor on Will's family PC. Oh, how times have changed! By 2009, Gaydar boasted an impressive five million subscribers, a testament to the queer community's yearning for connection at the start of the digital age.

Although Match.com debuted in 1995, it wasn't until the arrival of platforms like Gaydar and Manhunt that the concept of online dating began to truly resonate within the gay community. Meanwhile, straight people were still grappling with the idea, finding it somewhat unsettling.

Enter Grindr in 2009, a game-changing app launched by Joel Simkhai just nine months after Apple incorporated GPS functionality into the iPhone. Grindr emerged not just as a dating app, but as a revolutionary location-based tool, predating Tinder by three years. Its genius lay in its simplicity and immediacy – users could chat with other gay and bisexual men nearby, knowing exactly how far away they were, down to the foot. Fifteen years later,

Grindr's core appeal remains steadfast: facilitating spontaneous meetups, often of an intimate nature, with a precision and ease that continues to define the app's legacy. Some blame Grindr for the mass closure of gay bars. Others love how easy and efficient it makes finding someone to have sex with. All the freedom of a dark room, but with the added bonus of being able to see each other's face (or penis) before committing.

Are Grindr hookups soulless?

Who better to ask this question of than one of my own gaggle of gay male friends?

Peter (not his real name) tells me, 'Grindr hookups can be soulless and unfulfilling. But so can boring dinner parties and monotonous work projects. We accept the occasional shitty social engagement and menial work because we know how great it can sometimes be. I have truly made some of my very best friends from Grindr hookups. You get out what you put in. If you enter into Grindr looking for soulless fun, then guess what . . . that's what you'll find . . . Another soulless fun seeker. Sex is fun, not shameful. The often-maligned "hookup culture" has actually had some profound benefits for me. I've been able to explore my sexuality and learn what I like (and what I don't). I've had exposure to other people's predilections (which, incidentally, can make great dinner party stories . . . solving another problem mentioned above) and has definitely made me less judgemental. I've learnt to enjoy my body and, more importantly, that there is no shame in that.'

My friend Mo [not his real name] adds: 'I think Grindr is like most tech – it's how you use it. I have spent hours – probably months – wasting time on it. But I've also met nice people and had life-enriching encounters: platonic and not so. Some people hide behind tech in order to be toxic, some people bring their full selves, are vulnerable and want to make good connections. For me, it's fine as part of the mix of ways to meet other people – but like most things should be used thoughtfully and rationed a bit.'

Why would anyone *want* to be a sex worker?

I like the way my friends, along with Mark and Jason, have all talked to me about being sex-positive and removing the shame that has for so long been associated with 'what goes on behind closed doors'. When it comes to sex, the attitude is often don't ask, don't tell, but as we know, this apparently well-meaning phrase is designed to keep queerness in the closet.

It was with this in mind that I decided I needed to confront some of my own prudishness around sex work and porn.

So, I arrange to chat to Cain, a cherubic thirty-year-old performer and porn star. Cain is a fixture on the London queer party scene. He has run nights at Heaven, he hosts and dances at Feel It and other clubs dressed in incredible latex outfits or dolled up as a sexy fetishy clown. He supplements his performance work by running a hugely successful OnlyFans porn channel. He was awarded Sex Worker of the Year in 2023 at the Sexual Freedom Awards, and is a very kind and gentle-mannered person who your mum would love. I ask him to share a bit of his story with me, which we continue in Chapter 15, when we look at partying in more depth.

'As a survivor who's been in situations of assault and rape, I didn't even begin to process that until I started going sober. I did studio porn when I was eighteen. It was all consensual, it was of legal age, but the storylines and the scenes that I filmed, looking back now, are not narratives that I want to feed into, kind of schoolboy/headteacher vibes. I remember they would shave my body to make me look as young as possible.

'So one of the things about going sober and especially having OnlyFans and producing my own content is reclaiming that narrative and controlling completely the production that I put out. I would never film a scenario like that. I'm always really cautious to include general elements of consent in there – even simple things that you just don't find in studio porn, like lube application or awkward position changes. And I think that mentality that I have towards how I produce things with adult content also trickles into my day-to-day sexual life.

'Going sober and reconnecting with myself sexually has been beautiful because I always have bad days, of course, but I now have a better relationship with my body. I'm kinder towards myself. Things that people maybe tried to take or did take away from me in the past, through power, I've now reclaimed.'

After meeting Cain, I feel like my mind has started to open up to how sex work can be empowering. I'm put in touch with Eddy, a trans rent boy who is up for talking more to me about this subject.

I'll admit I've got a bit of a crush on Eddy. He's hot, but he's also confident and charming, and when Stu and I meet him for coffee outside Bar Italia, in Soho, on a sunny winter's afternoon, I find myself getting a bit giddy. I like how uncomplicated sex work is for him. He compartmentalizes it as his job, and he's not ashamed of it. In fact, his whole family know what he does. Eddy has a boyfriend, and is, like Cain, really sweet and wholesome – he has to dash off to his Spanish lesson after our chat. And I find that all of my stereotypes about sex work are quashed by him. He's not damaged. He doesn't hate his life. He hasn't been pushed into it through shame or trauma. And being a trans man has given him a point of difference as a sex worker and (he'll admit the male privilege of this) hasn't caused him any issues in the way it might for a trans woman sex worker.

We start by asking him to introduce himself. 'I define my sexuality as maybe just queer, sometimes gay, sometimes pansexual, depending on who I'm speaking to. I'm a sex worker, so I do escorting as well as porn. I try to be really open and use the term sex worker without shame.'

Eddy knew he was trans when he was eight. But at that age he didn't know the word 'trans'. Transitioning for him was a very gradual process. He told his parents he was a boy, started going by Eddy and cut his hair. This was over the course of about a year or two. The pronouns came after that. It wasn't overnight at all. Eddy started taking hormone blockers in his mid-teens, started taking T when he was sixteen, then had top surgery when he was eighteen.

He got into porn and sex work while working on reception at a gym in Manchester. He figured the money would be better and the hours more flexible. 'The first time I did an escorting job it was really scary. I didn't know anyone else who had done it. I just found information online about safety practices. The guy came to my house. I told my flatmate that it was happening as a safety net. It went quite well and by the time he left I was buzzing. I was doing it for a couple of months, and then lockdown started.'

Eddy's clients are pretty much exclusively gay men, or closeted men. 'I'm always very clear in all my advertisements that I'm a trans man. That I'm a man with a pussy.' He tells us he never tries to hide that part of himself, which he feels is the most safe way to be as a trans person. 'Not being honest about it contributes to a feeling of shame. I don't necessarily think there's an obligation to tell someone if it's not necessary. In the sense that, like, you kiss someone in a club you don't have to tell them you're trans. There's no entrapment there. Really, they should be coming out to me about being a bigot if they have an issue. I shouldn't have to come out to them about being trans. But if it's getting to the point of being naked and showing them my body, there's no way I would ever enter into a situation where someone didn't know before we got to that point.'

Eddy's porn name is EddyFTM, which stands for 'Female To

Male' and is the widely used porn category. However, outside of that this is now quite an outdated term because most trans people will describe transitioning as becoming the gender they've always been rather than going from one gender 'to' another. I ask him if there's a disconnect between the people that enjoy FTM porn and the way that trans men are treated by the gay community generally. He takes a sip of coffee and says, 'I guess when it comes to porn, it's very fetishy, so I think sometimes people can confuse supporting trans rights with finding trans people hot, and thinking that wanting to fuck trans people, or fucking trans people is doing enough for them.'

We ask Eddy if he's ever worked for a porn studio, and if like Cain he prefers controlling his own narratives. 'I've worked with one studio, and it wasn't the best experience. The actual filming was fine, but the way they marketed the video was pretty inaccurate. A little bit derogatory. I knew the guy who was organizing it, and I said just make sure they don't use words like 'tranny'. But then they marketed it saying 'tranny! Three holes, to use and abuse'. *I was like, I don't even do anal, so, what are you talking about? I'm not submissive in the slightest, so* . . . This doesn't happen when I make my own videos.'

Eddy takes lots of precautions to make sure he's safe as a sex worker, he takes the contraceptive pill and other drugs to avoid STIs.

He describes his job as an escort as being a bit like a therapist. 'I'm an oversharer as well, so I'm always like, *tell me more, let's keep going, this is great*. It's really nice. You can bounce off each other and share experiences and get some sort of intimacy.'

As for how many clients he has in a week, it varies. 'I might have no clients one week, the next week I might have a client every day. Most of my time is taken up with the OnlyFans side of stuff: filming, doing the editing, all of the social media side of things, and then all the admin.'

Sex work is legal in that it is decriminalized, but there are a lot of restrictions and rules around advertising. 'I was stealthed once, which is sexual assault, because someone takes off a condom halfway through sex. I didn't go to the police because I don't trust the police. I don't want to be on their radar.'

In the future Eddy would like to lead a very simple life. 'I don't want anything too exciting. I don't want any surprises. I want something cozy. I see myself moving out of London eventually, but maybe not for like five or ten years. I really don't have big ambitions. I don't necessarily want to travel the world. I'm happy with how things are, I just want things to continue. I want to have a cute place with my boyfriend and just have a nice little life and keep up the work that I'm doing and have my wholesome little life separate.'

Can monogamous queer couples still have great sex?

In my efforts to understand if it's true that queer people are more sexual, I've gone deep, so to speak, with the idea that we are. I've chosen to step outside my sexual comfort zone and meet people like Eddy, like Cain, like the SweatBox founders for whom sex is work, is life, is freedom, is power, is, well, fun.

But where does that leave the rest of us? Monogamous, married, parents. Still queer, still up for it. Can we have the kind of great sex our single friends still seem to be enjoying on a daily basis? I wonder if there's anything specific to our queerness that makes it even harder to reconcile our parent selves with our sexual selves? I ask our friend Dr Karen Gurney. She's a fantastic clinical psychologist and psychosexologist whose latest book is called *How to Not Let Having Kids Ruin Your Sex Life*. She says, 'I don't think there's anything in particular for queer parents that's drastically different than for any other parent, apart from the combined impact of minority stress on that group. So we know that minority stress [the difficulty that comes from being any minority in a world set up for the majority] has an impact on our sex lives. And obviously there are additional parts of being a queer parent, like, being excluded from the WhatsApp groups because they're all for mums, or being asked who's the real parent, etc., etc., that add an extra element of minority stress for queer parents.'

But it's not all bad news. She says, 'I think, in contrast, queer parents have more resources available to them than non-queer parents around adapting to different sex lives, because we know there's much more diversity in queer sex, less sexual scripts around who does what and a different range of sexual practices. So I think probably queer parents have got more resources available to them to survive some of the challenges of parenthood.'

She tells me it's useful to try to develop a culture in relationships around being able to check in regularly about people's wants and needs rather than wait for it to become a problem, because then it tends to be met with quite a lot of defensiveness, and it feels like you're raising something because it's really catastrophic.

It's easy to get stuck in ruts, Karen says, and get used to the fact that our partner expects us to be one way when it comes to sexuality or gender expression. And that stepping outside of that can create a situation where our partner goes, *Oh, what are you doing? This isn't you. This isn't what you usually do?* And that stops us from doing it. 'Over time we can find ourselves on a trajectory where we are comfortable to say, *I don't always want to be like that sexually. I don't always want to play that role. I don't always want to represent my gender in that way.'*

So it's about just starting to have a conversation where you might ask, if you weren't with me, if you were with someone new, what kinds of things might you want sexually? Or what might you do around gender that you feel less able to do with me because you know me so well?'

As I come to the end of this chapter, I feel like I'm opening the door of a sex club to stumble home after a wild night. The light is blinding. Reality slaps. My daughter shouts 'Mama!' Kate Winslet's dulcet tones fade back into my consciousness and she's still going on about that slippery slip, except now someone called Saucepan Man is doing something with a silk cushion. Nothing, and I mean *nothing* surprises me any more.

So what's the answer? Do queer people have more sex? I think it's more that we value sex. We centre it, and as something that may have previously caused us shame, we are very good at finding the joy in it now. Whether that means saunas and sex clubs or snatched snogs when the kids aren't looking, there's no hierarchy. Anonymous sex isn't bad, monogamous sex good. Sex workers can be empowered and happy, while others, of course, may still be exploited. Grindr can be sweet and fulfilling sometimes, harsh and soulless at others. Maybe we are more sexual than straights, and that's OK. We shouldn't have to deny this side of ourselves to be accepted.

Chapter 14

Three's a Crowd?:
The Possibilities of Polyamory

Stu

On a dark Monday night in the middle of winter I find myself dragging my oversized coat around into a packed bar. Squeezing past people smiling and engaging with one another, I spot they all have stickers identifying just what, and who, they might be into. This is no usual gathering, nor are these people random strangers chatting to other random strangers. They are all here for a purpose. And I feel like a bit of a fraud as my purpose differs from theirs.

I connected a few weeks ago with the team at Feeld, an app that's been shaking up the dating scene by creating a platform where people are encouraged to express their desires. It describes itself as 'a dating app for the curious; those open to experiencing people and relationships in new ways'. They list polyamory, consensual non-monogamy, homo- and heteroflexibility, pansexuality, asexuality, aromanticism, voyeurism and kink as some of the desires that make up their community. Feeld hosts an 'IRL experience' each month for their members at an uber-cool hotel to 'spark connectivity and a vivid connection'. I've asked the organizers if I can tag along and see if I can find answers to some of my questions on polyamory. Does it fit under the queer community umbrella? Should it? Is it inherently queer to be polyamorous? There is no P in LGBTQIA+, so is it all in the plus? Is it an identity?

Is it an orientation? Is it simply a preference? How does it fit? I want to know what polyamory is, try to understand it and question how it plays a part in our LGBTQ+ community.

How does polyamory fit into LGBTQ+?

My basic understanding is that polyamory is having an open relationship. But is that correct? Caroline Rose Giuliani, a US-based filmmaker and activist, is someone who wants to break down stigmas and shame around 'ethical non-monogamy' and defines polyamory as 'the practice of having multiple romantic and often, though not always, sexual relationships at one time, with all parties aware and consenting.'[1] I feel the part about all parties being aware and consenting is really key here. I do wonder if everyone can truly be on the same page all the time when it comes to multiple relationships. But more on my ignorant questions later.

Aside from the fact that I think anything that fundamentally shakes up the 'traditional' notion of relationships is by definition 'queer', it certainly feels like more gay men are non-monogamous, and explore open relationships, than straight ones, or than queer women. The data, as with most things LGBTQ+, is lacking. The most recent survey I can find is from all the way back in 2016, when the then health charity GMFA (originally Gay Men Fighting AIDS) surveyed 1,006 men with the results showing that 41 per cent of gay men have previously experienced, or are currently in, an open relationship. I personally have often felt the weight of expectation from others that my husband and I must be in some form of open relationship, especially from those within the community. We are not, which, at times, has made me, again, question my own queerness. Or, rather, my gayness. Honestly, I do feel like such a boring gay. I don't do drugs, circuit parties or fuck other men. Lesbians get a sub-category called 'cottage core lesbian' to describe those who embrace a cozy, quiet and idolized existence in the countryside. Where is the gay equivalent? 'Cottaging gay' has a very different connotation. Could I be a quiet life queer? A suburban sodomite? A green belt gay?

Polyamory has never even been a thought for me. For me, the jealousy and curiosity would be far too great. I can picture myself on a stakeout outside the restaurant where my husband would be courting another, slipped down in my seat, in the dark, wearing big shades, most likely with Lotte by my side, watching every move, every touch, every gesture. My levels of cyber stalking would also go through the roof – refreshing their Instagram page every five seconds and keeping a watchful eye on every story they post and comment they make. Of course, we could try anonymous poly-amory, setting rules so that we don't know who each other is dating, but the not knowing would most likely eat me up inside. Likewise, a throuple situation would probably end in tears – mine – when I convince myself that the other two like each other more than either one likes me. Quite simply, I think it would be a recipe for disaster.

But it's time to put my own feelings aside and throw myself into this world. I'm a little nervous, but Feeld, like this book, encour-ages one to embrace taking yourself out of your comfort zone. Still, I've brought my gay bestie Ollie with me for moral support. He tells me on the way about a friend of a friend who used Feeld and found it incredibly liberating. Apparently, she said it cut through a lot of the bullshit found on other dating apps – and she ended up with a most satisfying fuck on her stairs as they never even made it to the bedroom . . . The story does reinforce some of my preconceived ideas, and I'm expecting nothing short of a sex fest as we make our way to the bar. Are we about to walk into a room of people wearing bondage gear? Does Feeld provide a dark room in the corner? Is there a bowl for keys next to someone who looks like your Aunt Shirley in a leopard-print top, red lippy on and buxom bosoms heaving?

But the only bowl we're faced with is one full of stickers, which help other attendees identify what you are looking for from the event. We have the options of poly, LGBTQIA+ and kink. There is a further colour-coded sticker allowing people to choose from blue (friends), yellow (friends and lovers) and red (lovers). We each opt for a simple blue sticker – after all, we are not here to trick or mislead anyone. The room is packed and it's a total vibe. It feels diverse, fresh and fun, and there is a fizz of promise in the air. Most importantly, it immediately feels welcoming. It's a room you want to be in. Every time I've set foot in a gay bar I feel judged, uneasy and on show. I felt not one of these things here. We get a drink and find Lyu, our host for the night. She tells us that there is no singular 'type' of person that comes to these events and that it's essentially a community of different communities. She explains that while she is predominately attracted to men, she feels over the years coming to these events she may now see herself more identifying as 'queer', a statement reinforced by her LBGTQIA+ sticker.

Queer or not queer?

This is one of my burning questions for the night, and Ollie and I spot two guys near the door that don't seem to fit the fluid aesthetic that the rest of the room is giving. Ollie suggested 'bankers'. We swoop in, fully disclosing why I am there. Ollie was right, these two handsome strangers are indeed bankers who immediately tell me they feel like they should have changed outfits before coming. These two have no LGBTQIA+ sticker and they scream 'straight'. However, they tell us they want to bend the norms in terms of relationships. They don't want a monogamous relationship and the trappings that come with that. I suggest that perhaps the 'bending' of the norm they describe could be viewed as fitting under the queer umbrella? It's at this point that I worry I've kick-started their own existential crisis when it comes to their identity, and I notice a small flash of panic in their eyes. They immediately tell me they are, of course, very pro-LGBTQIA+, and I feel they are a sentence away from informing me that they know some gay people and to them it's 'cool'. I leave them to enjoy their night, but as I do the taller one looks at me and says, 'Well, however we define it I do know that to be "normal" is boring.' Amen, Mr Banker.

We next chat to Mark and Ebele. It's not immediately clear if they are a couple or two friends, but they tell us that they have been in a relationship for two years, and they have always enjoyed spending time with other couples. They are gorgeous and have a radiant energy. I ask for their number, not because I want John and I to be their next couple, although if I had to pick anyone in this room it might have been them, but I want to hear more about their story. They input their numbers on my phone and disappear into the room.

Later, as the night starts to draw to a close and I'm a few barrel-aged negronis in, Ollie and I reconnect with Lyu. We stand next to a throuple who are enjoying a three-way snogging session. I wonder to myself if all three arrived separately and they found each other via sticker, or perhaps it's a couple looking for a third? Sadly, for me and not them, they are too deep into it for me to tap them on the shoulder and enquire.

With Lyu we discuss that while polyamory is one of the things people do explore within Feeld, it doesn't mean that everyone there is exclusively poly. She actually tells us that she doesn't like the term 'polyamorous' and says many people now just prefer to use 'ethical non-monogamy' when explaining their relationship preferences. I find this fascinating, especially as polyamory itself is a relatively new term (its first use was reported back in 1990, with it entering the Oxford English Dictionary as recently as 2006). For it to be already outdated shows the speed with which our quest for self-definition can move.

Single and ready to mingle?

I feel like I've had my eyes opened, in a good way. Lyu reveals that part of the purpose of the IRL events is to find a connection, but that could also be a connection with yourself. You'll perhaps never discover who you really are until you begin having those conversations and explore. Even setting aside the poly exploration, I've realized that I perhaps had some unconscious biases about what it must be like to be single. I'd never quite describe it as a pity, but I it was moving in that direction. As someone who has been in a monogamous relationship for almost twenty years, *Oh I can't imagine how hard it is to date* or *Must be so daunting to go out and meet people* are thoughts that have run through my head. What coming to this event has made me realize is that being single can be fun and that this new approach to relationships really does feel like Queer 2.0.

Lyu also points out that many people are single by choice, and for good reason. While I think I will, for now (never say never!), remain in a monogamous relationship with my husband, I found myself thinking about my kids, and what their dating patterns might look like. I think about how proud, and even encouraging, I would be for them to explore different ways and communities. It feels like the future.

What are the rules of polyamory?

After the event I connect with Mark and Ebele, the radiant couple I met there. They both identify as bisexual and I ask Ebele if she feels they identify as polyamorous too. 'We don't actually use the term polyamorous. Like, what actually falls within the category of polyamory? I feel polyamory means having more than one partner consensually, but I don't think we are open to having other people join our relationship. Two is enough already! We just had a desire to explore a bit more outside of what we have known to date. It felt a good opportunity to do that together.' I tell Mark and Ebele that I think that, like queerness in general, being polyamorous has its own many varied rules and definitions. For them, it's purely about experiencing sexual relationships with others, but for others it can also be about having romantic connections. Mark refers to it as a bit of a secret society – 'the illuminati' – which reminds me to state that, for the record, at their request, I am using pseudonyms for them as they want to remain anonymous. I ask them if there is a certain amount of shame tied into non-monogamous relationships. 'I wouldn't say shame,' says Mark. 'It's more about being guarded. You'd only do it in certain spaces. And it also depends on the kind of environment you're raised in as well. There is a lot of discretion that needs to be used, because not everyone is given the same kind of grace.'

And what are their boundaries? Have they got set rules in place? 'For us,' Ebele tells me, 'it's like, if you want one, you want both. If it's not that, then we're not really interested. We like to do things together as a unit. We don't mind guys and girls, because we're both bi. We don't mind other couples as well, or groups.' And knowing they are not interested in inviting someone into their relationship romantically, what boundaries do they put in place to stop this happening? 'In terms of not seeing someone more than once, that's something that's not been mentioned,' ponders Ebele. 'At the moment we haven't done that.' The romantic in me wonders if one day someone might wriggle themselves into Mark and Ebele's hearts, but they are so gorgeous as the pair they already are, I can see why they are only up for guest stars.

Can polyamory work long-term?

Not long after my night out at the poly mixer, Lotte decides to treat me to tickets to the play *Afterglow* at the Southwark

Playhouse. The play focuses on a gay couple in a poly relationship. Spoiler alert: it doesn't end well. As we sit there looking out at the sea of gay men crammed together to watch a so-so play about three ripped men who get fully naked on stage and simulate sex (honestly, I couldn't put my finger on what the appeal was for the audience?!), we note that there really don't seem to be many depictions of polyamorous relationships in mainstream culture, and those that are don't seem to be portrayed that positively. Mark and Ebele only wanted guest stars, but is it possible to have a positive polyamorous relationship, long-term?

Let's meet . . . Abby
Abby is one-third of a long-term throuple.

Abby, how would you describe your relationship?
I have been with one of my partners for thirteen years and we have all been together as a three for four years. We're a throuple, which I sometimes describe as 'like a couple except with three people instead of two'. In our dynamic we are all dating each other, which is different to other throuple set-ups, where one person might date the other two but they are not dating each other, for example.

What do you think is the secret to a long-term poly relationship?
One word: communication! You have to be open to having honest conversations, even when it's uncomfortable – poly people aren't immune to difficult emotions like jealousy, you just have to be able to scrutinize your feelings and communicate them to your partners. Communication should be a big part of any relationship – breakdowns in communication are what lead to a lot of monogamous relationships falling apart, too, so in that way polyamory isn't that different.

How do you manage the dynamics on a day-to-day basis within the relationship?

We live together so really our relationship doesn't feel that different from that of a monogamous couple. We share household tasks and cooking pretty evenly. My partners work at offices whereas I work from home, so during the day I have the house pretty much to myself (apart from the cats, who dislike me and each other!). In the evenings and at weekends we also do 'normal' stuff that couples might do. An average weeknight might be watching Netflix or having friends over for dinner, at weekends we like to go on walking trips, or to exhibitions in London. Being three people does come with a little more life admin – we have a shared Google calendar for things like family events, birthday parties of friends, and so on, just so we don't have awkward situations where one of us agrees to something and then the other two forget. And agreeing on a movie to watch is sometimes more difficult than it might be for a couple. We're quite independent (I think this should be the case for all relationships) and will sometimes do things like hang out with friends without the other two. In this scenario, if I'm out having dinner with a friend one evening, my partners might go on a date together, and vice versa.

On the whole we enjoy the same things, but sometimes we might do things in pairs that the third person wouldn't enjoy. A great thing about being in a throuple is that you get different things from different partners in this way – but we also make sure to give each other our own space too, as well as spending quality time all together as a three.

Do you find that people have preconceived notions of what it means to be poly? Do you face any prejudice?

Now that we've been together for a few years and live together, people seem more convinced by our relationship, like we've passed some kind of test. But in the beginning we'd get a lot of comments like 'that'll never work'. It's worth noting that people's comments were deeply rooted in sexism – people would imply that Paul and Andrea would run off together, that Paul would realize he 'prefers' her to me, but nobody ever suggested us two women might leave the man. On the whole we were very lucky (we live in a liberal part of east London; I feel like our experience might have been very different some-where else) but people did ask a lot of the same questions, which got a bit tiresome. People always say, 'But don't you get jealous?' and everyone always seems to want to know about our sleeping arrangements, for some reason. (We sleep in the same bed, but it's huge.)

Have you experienced challenges from your respective families in terms of understanding your relationship?
We've been wildly fortunate in this regard. My parents, and even my grandparents and extended family, were very accepting – they could see I was happy and that was all they cared about. Andrea's parents took a little longer to come around, initially they were worried for her safety and thought there could be a dodgy power dynamic at play in her dating a long-term couple (they live in another country, which perhaps contributed to this anxiety as they're far away from their daughter). But after meeting us they saw that our relationship is much more equi-table than they thought and they quickly came around. Paul's mum and sister reacted in a similar way to my family – they could see he was happy and so were curious but accepting of the relationship. His dad took a little longer, but this didn't come from a place of bigotry or small-mindedness. Our dynamic is just very outside of his life experience, so he felt a little uncomfortable at first and didn't seem to know how to react or behave, so he buried his head in the sand and just pretended

it wasn't happening, which was frustrating for a while. But as soon as Paul started to talk about it with him more, and he started to ask questions and understand better, he was accepting too.

What's the best thing about being in a poly relationship?
Having more support and in different ways. I think it's kind of wild to expect a single partner to give you everything. Even in monogamous relationships, people should have people outside of their partner (family members, friends, etc.) who can offer them things their partner can't, but it's very common to expect a partner to be your rock, your everything. In our dynamic, we all bring different things – some of these are kind of frivolous: Andrea is great at interior design (our house looks fabulous because of her), Paul is great at gardening, I'm great at planning holidays and (if I do say so myself) cooking. But we also have differing approaches to life that often come together, Power Rangers-style, to make us a really great team in a crisis. I think I'm good at helping everyone see the bigger picture and calm down, whereas Andrea is good at organizing logistics and Paul is a real do-er, he'll get stuck in and get things done. We all bring different things to the table day to day, as well as when we have challenges to face.

Would you define your relationship as queer?
Yes, though I'm well aware this is a controversial topic. A lot of people who talk about polyamory call it 'queer-adjacent' because a dynamic won't necessarily be queer in its gender dynamics (for example, you might have a throuple where the woman is dating two men, but they are both straight and are not dating each other). However, I feel that queerness is about a lot more than just the literal facts of who you have sex with. I'd call our relationship queer for two reasons, one of them is

very simple: within our dynamic, Andrea and I are dating each other, and we are both dating Paul; we're both queer women who are attracted to people of all genders. It gets more complicated, I guess, when you consider Paul, a straight man with two girlfriends; ostensibly this is very not queer. However, our relationship shakes up the status quo of what relationships look like – our relationship overall is queer because it's different, and, vitally, it's unique to us. Polyamory is sometimes called a 'choose your own adventure' – in poly relationships, you make it up as you go along by doing what feels right for you. I think there's something fundamentally queer about that.

What do you see is next for your relationship?

We're starting to think about buying property (at the moment we rent) so this will add a slightly different financial aspect to the relationship, but we haven't quite worked out what this will look like yet – we won't be buying for a few years and how we work this out will naturally depend on all of our financial situations at that time. Obviously, marriage between three people isn't legal (in the UK anyway) and a traditional kind of marriage isn't something that appeals to us, but we have jokily talked about having some kind of queer commitment ceremony – basically an excuse for a very lavish party. None of us want children, this was the case before we became a throuple and isn't likely to change, so kids of our own aren't in our future, but we have close relationships with our friends' children (we are godparents for two of our friends) and we all have nieces and nephews, who we are excited to see grow up.

And are you now a monogamous throuple?

We're mostly monogamous as a three – we discussed how we would feel about opening up in a sexual way and decided that in exceptional circumstances (i.e., someone objectively hot hits on you at a party) we're comfortable with pursuing casual sexual encounters outside of our relationship, but we don't actively date other people or actively seek out sex with other people. It's more like it's not completely vetoed if a super-tempting scenario presented itself, kind of a hypothetical. We also attend spicy parties sometimes and are open to encounters with people we might meet there, which would likely be something we'd be doing together and would be a one-off kind of thing. But emotionally we're monogamous, we wouldn't want to bring a fourth person into our relationship. Some people have much bigger polyamorous groups than we do and that works for them, but we discussed this and all agreed that having two partners already feels like a lot sometimes – we don't feel we'd have emotional capacity for an in-depth romantic relationship with an additional person.

What can the monogamous learn from the non-monogamous?

We met Dr Karen Gurney, known on Instagram as @thesex doctor, in the last chapter. I got in touch with her again to ask for her top poly relationship tips that anyone can take on board.

Communication

Keeping channels of communication open at all times is key. Even figuring out when and what you would like to communicate about, and what are the topics or events that you might choose to not communicate about and keep to yourselves. It can be useful to have a sense of regular check-in about communication itself, say, for example, every few months you set a time aside to review how well you feel communication is going and whether any tweaks are needed. After all, your needs here are likely to change over time, and it's good to create a culture of adaptation to allow this.

Effort

One of the problems with monogamy is an idea that just because you've said you'll love each other for ever, you will, or just because you want to be together for ever, you will. And sometimes what comes with that is a lack of intentional effort into creating a relationship culture that you would continually choose if given an option.

Choice

In open relationships and poly relationships, there is an idea that you're continually choosing a relationship or perhaps navigating a new one based on where you want to put your efforts. And bringing that idea into monogamy, it's useful to think about whether the relationship culture you've created is one you would continually choose if you met that person again now.

Sexual Communication

We have quite a lot of research in sex science that the more we're able to communicate about our inner sexual world to a partner, the better our sexual satisfaction. For example, couples who watch porn separately, but then talk about the porn they watched together, generally have higher levels of sexual intimacy. And so in monogamy even acknowledging that you fancy someone else can be seen as such a huge threat. We can't have a blanket statement, but perhaps this happens a bit more freely in poly relationships. If you're in a monogamous relationship, discussing things like, 'I had a sex dream about someone at work and this is what happened. It was really hot.' That's bringing sexual content into the relationship as well, which is saying something about interest and desires and can act as sexual stimuli for you both. It is about navigating insecurity, and also attachment.

Relationships

There is an idea that sometimes, but not always, monogamy can look like we do everything together. We don't have any other relationships that are extremely important to us. We have to meet each other's every need. And obviously one of the features of poly relationships is that with different people, you can do different things, and meet different needs, but it can be very threatening in monogamy to do that, but it's also very good for relationships.

Is Poly a sexuality?

One thing I've still not really been able to get a good steer on throughout my 'poly journey' is if polyamory is an identity, an orientation, or a preference. I went back to Dr Karen Gurney for her thoughts:

'I wouldn't define it as a sexuality, but I would say it could be both a preference and an orientation, in that some people are more naturally inclined to feel comfortable with more open relationship structures. Some people may have a preference for that because it suits them for that time or for one particular reason. I haven't seen any data that represents it as a sexuality. But, you know, it wouldn't shock me too much if that emerged over time.'

I ask Karen about the word 'preference', as I feel it sometimes has negative connotations within our community due to the fact that it indicates we have a choice in our sexuality. 'I don't see why we shouldn't use the word preference,' she says. 'I often find that the term orientation is quite a helpful way for people to feel less shame as well with polyamory. The idea that some people might have always struggled with monogamy, and blamed themselves a lot for that, can sometimes feel less shamed by the idea that this might just be part of who they are. And in some ways, preference then makes it sound like they're choosing it. I think both of those words could suit different people in different scenarios.'

I think back to those two straight bankers at the Feeld event, and I wonder how they would view it? Would it be a preference for them? And while it sounds like I'm trying to recruit straight people into the queer fold, if you are straight and poly, are you queer? Dr Karen thinks so.

'Yeah, definitely. I think, you know, queerness is really about subverting norms, isn't it? And monogamy very much fits into cis-heteronormativity as a kind of societal norm to be subverted, and I think there's something essentially queer about that.'

And has this experience led me to question if polyamory is a preference I could explore? Let's just say I've had my eyes opened and my prejudices quashed, but I think I'm a one-man gay at heart – a family of five is already enough for me to handle!

Chapter 15

YOLO:
Why the Party Never Dies

Lotte

In the end it's all just bodies; moving, gurning, twisting, kissing, spilling drinks. As dry ice rises and the beat drops, it's harder to make out where one person begins and another ends. I'm in it. Dancing in the basement of a bar. The music is electro, the atmosphere electric. Everyone is free to be themselves and there's an absence of the usual peacocking and pec-flexing I'm used to in gay clubs. This is a FLINTA night (as you'll recall from Chapter 4 this stands for female, lesbian, intersex, non-binary, trans and agender) and I know from having hung out in the bar upstairs first that there are trans women, butches, lesbians, non-binary folk, fat people, skinny people, older womxn, twenty-year-olds fresh to the city . . . while most are white, many aren't. Dancing together under the velvet glamour of darkness – we're one. Stu was supposed to be here with me, and I wish he was, wearing his new pair of heels, buoyed by the love and expansiveness of this crowd who would see him and celebrate him and show him a good time.

Here's what happened
STU

I am not a party gay. I never have been. Even back in my late teens the only club nights I used to enjoy were pure bubble-gum-pop dance parties. Me and my best gay mate Tommy used to find ourselves in Bar 150 on a Monday, a sweaty and smoky club above the infamous Charles Street Bar on Brighton seafront, where we would dance to unremixed Britney songs. I loved the dancing, but I quickly started to judge if the night was a success by the amount of men I did, or more importantly didn't, get the attention of. As I talked about in Chapter 7, I have severe issues with my body and although, at this stage in life, I had lost a significant amount of weight, my self-esteem was still lingering on the sticky floor. If I didn't end up snogging the face off some poor soul, I would end up going home in a deep depression, fuelled by a fried chicken burger binge. Poor Tommy – he put up with a lot. As did my best friend Laura, who I often went crying to at 2am when Tommy had managed to cop off with someone and I found myself alone, sobbing into my bottomless bucket.

So, my clubbing life burned out pretty quickly. The enjoyment of dancing was completely overshadowed by feelings of rejection. Tommy started exploring the more dance-music-heavy clubs, and soon I found myself standing in the middle of topless, ripped gay men despising the *doof doof* of the hardcore DJ beat, as well as myself. Meeting my husband at the ripe old age of twenty-one was the final nail in my dancefloor coffin. Fast-forward to my near forties and you could say I'm a born-again nightclub virgin. Like anyone about to lose their virginity, I'm nervous about this planned night out with Lotte even though it's a FLINTA night and ever since Chapter 3 I've embraced my inner lesbian! I do agree I'm missing out on a huge part of gay culture by not partying. The number of times I feel like such a simpleton in a group of gay men for having never setting foot in Fire, stepping over the threshold of the iconic Royal Vauxhall Tavern, or even venturing down Canal Street. It feels like being a devout Christian, yet never going to church.

While I initially agree to go with Lotte to the club night, the anxiety, ultimately, becomes too much for me and I decide to bail. It was inevitable really. There was a reason I hated clubbing when I was nineteen and that reason is still very much within me. The moment I let Lotte know I feel a sense of peace wash over me. I decide that, you know what? It's OK to be a gay worshipper without going to church.

I've never been one for clubbing or late nights myself. Ask any of my university friends and they will tell you I was known for leaving parties early, or not going at all. But I think it was more that I was *discerning* than actively against gay clubbing. I've always known what I enjoy (glamorous venues, fun people, pop or house music, maybe a smattering of C-list celebs) and what I don't (electro/trance music, messy drunks, crowds, too many straights). I've had some life-changing, soul-expanding, legendary queer nights out, I just haven't ever made partying habitual. And now I'm a parent it's not a realistic part of my social life as it is for my happily child-free queer friends, who have money to spend and no real responsibilities beyond showing up to work on Monday morning. Clubbing has never been part of my personality in the way it is for some people, and now I'm a parent there's even less of an incentive to hit the dancefloor. However, in the spirit of discovery, I feel like I really want to understand what the queer scene is like today, and how it's different from when I went out more often in my twenties. I just wish I had Stu, my wingman, by my side.

I'm interested in why the spirit of hedonism is so integral to queer life. Why does the journey from *coming* out to *going* out feel as vital a life stage as womb to cradle? Are we not even truly born as LGBTQ+ people if we don't go to a queer club within hours of first embracing our sexuality or gender identity?

I'll be slipping on my glad rags and hitting the town as I try to score some answers to this on the dancefloors, in the dark rooms and queuing for the loos of the queer scene.

Do we need to get out more?

I'm disappointed when Stu pulls out of our planned date because his anxiety around his body seems to be holding him back from exploring the queer scene, and that feels like a gaping hole in his life experience. It could end up being where he *finds* his body confidence and meets people who lift him up and celebrate him. It could also be where the music, the mood, maybe the amyl nitrate transport him for long enough to forget his body, his anxieties, his real life for one night of hedonism.

I also feel clubbing is an important stepping stone in anyone's queer journey because it connects us to our LGBTQ+ forbears. It writes us into the same history. From the symposiums of Ancient Greece to the 'Molly houses' of eighteenth- and nineteenth-century London, to the first drag balls in Harlem in the 1860s, to the Stonewall Inn and beyond, LGBTQ+ people have always found a way to meet up and have fun, even when to do so was illegal. Partying is in our queer DNA. It's where we found our people, our community and our sense of our true selves. It was a chance to shake off the shackles of oppression that may have once limited our day-to-day lives, to let loose and feel joy.

I'm actually convincing myself I need to go out more here, because it matters. There's a place for me on the queer scene, there's a place for you and there's a place for Stu (if only he'd be confident enough to find it). Because if there's one thing we queers know how to do, it's throw a good party, whether it was the Roman

Empire or Berghain, Sappho's soirees or Studio 54, you best believe there was a homosexual of one kind or another behind the bash.

On a rainy afternoon in April, I meet up with Amin Ghaziani, who is a Professor of Sociology and Canada Research Chair in Urban Sexualities. He's a neat and precise man, with a short crop of grey hair and an uncanny ability to speak in intellectually complete and coherent sentences (by comparison I 'um' and 'errr' and muddle my way through most conversations). He's also written a brilliant book called *Long Live Queer Nightlife: How the Closing of Gay Bars Sparked a Revolution.*

I start by asking him why queers love partying.

'I feel like so much of queer culture has incubated in, expressed itself in, revised itself in, and revolutionized itself through partying. Queer partying in many ways has been life-saving for a number of people in the absence of places where we can comfortably and safely be together. It created these alternate pockets where we have formed kinship connections with each other.

'Nightlife is also a place that incubates a political consciousness or a political ethos where we can think about what it means to be queer, what it means to be a sexual minority, what it means to be LGBTQ+, how we can think about, formulate, alternative worldviews and consciousness apart from the heteronormative socialization in which we all grow up.'

I wonder if Professor Ghaziani has ever been to GAY in Soho at eleven on a Saturday night as B*Witched plays on the video monitors and some random buys you an Archers and lemonade and tells you they love you . . .

One of the other very clever things Amin says that really resonates for me and makes me feel even keener to get Stu into his heels and out to a club is that 'none of us can overstate how important it is to find yourself in the centre of a dancefloor that centres you in return'.

When Amin really comes to life is when I ask him about when and where he has felt the euphoria of belonging on a dancefloor. He says, 'Some of my best memories have taken place in gay bars. But so have some of my most complicated memories. I frequently have been sexually fetishized in these places where people will ask me, *well, where are you from*? I would say I'm from Chicago. And then the follow-up question that most people of colour will have heard to that response is, *no, no, no, where are you really from*? And that, that's a difficult question to answer. Because it forces you to be different. It's exoticizing you or fetishizing you or marginalizing you.'

He continues: 'In London I met another South Asian queer man who took me to a night, about an hour's train ride from my flat. I walked into this cavernous room and projected on a bare white wall across from the DJ booth were clips of iconic Bollywood videos and Indian films and there are songs from those films that I recognized from my childhood. Every Sunday morning, they would come on. My mum would be cooking or cleaning, singing along to these songs, and here's a remixed version of it.

'I'm looking around me, and everyone at this place looks like me, and I have never been at an event, at a queer event, where I was surrounded by everyone that looked like me, where no one's going to ask me, "where are you *really from*" in this place.

'And those are some of the most memorable nights for me because it enables me as a child growing up listening to a set of music with my parents to dance in an adult body that knows how to do it a little bit better around people who are like me in ways that really helped to heal some of the scars of loneliness or difference from my childhood.'

How does a nice boy like you end up in a place like this?

Cain, the sex worker we met in Chapter 13, was eighteen when he first took the train from Nuneaton, a small village in the Midlands, to London to experience the gay nightlife. He hopped from afterparty to hookup to club and one night soon turned into a week, then a month and another. He never moved back to his family home. He shares the story of his descent into the darker side of queer partying with me, and explains how he pulled himself out of it to become one of a growing number of young, sober scene-queens.

I ask Cain if that life he describes, of hopping between parties as an eighteen-/nineteen-year-old, felt safe to him at the time?

'It was all very glamorous and fun and I didn't really see any negatives in it. I'm four years sober now, and it was only up until like halfway through that sobriety – so almost a full eight years later, that I realized, *it was not fun*. In fact, it was incredibly dangerous and I'm lucky to have gotten away with that situation like I did.'

Cain, who it should be reiterated is gorgeous-looking, with a soft boyish face and a body that stuns in a leather gimp suit, tells me his first gig was as a nightclub host. I ask what this actually involves and learn that it's basically just rocking up in a pair of sexy pants and bringing a guest list of a couple of other young, hot people. 'I was grateful to do it. It probably paid for my drugs that evening.'

His use of alcohol and drugs started as a confidence boost. It served a purpose – when he was exhausted it simply helped him to get to the next gig. But after he lost a job running a night at Heaven during lockdown, there was no purpose to his drug and alcohol abuse and he was confronted with his addictions.

Cain tells me: 'There were loads of times when I was drinking and using that people would say to me, *you need to go sober, I'm either going to move out, or I don't want to go to this thing with you, I don't want to date you any more*, and I lost so many people from it, but none of it got through to me. There were so many instances where I lost my keys and I had to break into my own house. I've been arrested, I've had stints in hospital, I've been assaulted, but it was never those things that made me go sober.'

There was no single dramatic moment that helped Cain realize his partying was out of control, but instead a gentle awareness that if he was to achieve his ambitions as a performer he'd have to sort his life out first. 'I was trying to do a drag version of the Seven Deadly Sins – a different look a day in the run-up to Halloween in 2020. I was on day three, and I was just so miserable. I was drinking and using so much to even just get through the day, I had lost all passion in myself. I remember saying, *I'm going to give sobriety a proper run now*, because I used to do months here and there to remind myself that I could.

But it would always come up to day twenty-eight and I'd be like, *Oh, that's basically a month. I'm done.* But yeah, this time it stuck for a month and then for two. Then it came up to about six months. And I remember thinking, *I'm attracting good people. I'm attracting good opportunities. I'm feeling better about myself.*

Once lockdown lifted Cain was back in the queer nightlife world as a sober person and, he tells me, it was hard to navigate those same spaces without the crutches he was used to. He would pretend he was drinking alcohol to avoid questions from people and to allay his biggest fear – that club promoters would think he was boring and not book him.

Why do queer partiers go so hard with drugs and alcohol?

We've been speaking for about an hour on Zoom, and I'm so touched by Cain's openness and vulnerability. He tells me about a sexual assault that happened during one drug- and alcohol-fuelled night. He tells me about how making porn videos as a teen helped pay for a new oven for his mum when he was still living at home. He tells me about the open relationship he has with his boyfriend, who is also insanely good-looking, a nightclub performer and – inconceivably – a dentist.

What I haven't quite got a handle on yet is why Cain and so many other queer people become addicted to drugs and alcohol in the first place? Is it a panacea to the kind of social anxiety Stu and many other queer people suffer from?

'Maybe subconsciously my addictions stemmed from gay shame, but I think it was just gay culture,' he muses. 'I did not know any other places or ways to be on the scene without drugs or alcohol. It meant when I went sober, I just completely was lost in London in terms of how to socialize. It's really hard to rewire how you celebrate, how you express yourself. So much of gay culture is contingent on getting fucked up.'

According to the Crime Survey for England & Wales, drug use among gay and bisexual men is three times higher than use among heterosexual men. For lesbian and bisexual women, use is more than four times as high than for heterosexual women. Unsurprisingly, the largest difference is in the use of amyl nitrite (poppers), the second most commonly used drug by gay and bi men, and twenty-five times more common than among straight men. When this drug is sniffed, it can relax muscle tissue, including the muscles found in the anus, making anal sex easier and, for some, more pleasurable. We also see large differences in 'club' drugs such as ecstasy (almost five times higher in LGBTQ+ people) and ketamine (seven and a half times more common).

According to London Friend, an organization that supports the health and mental wellbeing of the LGBTQ+ community in and around London, reasons for this difference in drug-taking between straight and queer people probably stem from a mix of factors;

'our primary association by identity as LGBTQ+ people is done in bars and clubs, and we can usually stay at play longer than our heterosexual counterparts with responsibility for childcare still less common. Certainly we normalize longer partying behaviour, and more recently drugs have crept increasingly into our bedrooms, with chemsex noticeably on the rise among some gay and bi men. When drugs are used less for fun but to self-medicate, we know all too well that the reasons – depression, anxiety, prejudice – are more prevalent in our populations too.

When he first went sober, Cain wondered if he actually liked nightlife or if it was a means to an end. 'Do I feel egotistical with my free entry and my drink tokens? Is it an enabler to something else or do I actually love it? And I realized I do love it and I really want to stay in it.'

Then Cain says something about the queer nightlife scene that really gets me thinking. He says, 'It's a bit of a playground.'

Obviously as a parent this is a very triggering word that makes me instantly think of the hours I've lost to standing in cold, concrete yards with someone shouting, 'Look at me, Mama, look at me, look at meeee!'

But putting that to one side for a minute, lots of the LGBTQIA+ people I've spoken to reference a sense of lost youth. Maybe when we're children we're too worried about being perceived as weird or different to play the games we want to, or dress up in the clothes that make us happy. Then as a teenager we go to house parties where our best friend snogs someone in the year above while we hide in the garden talking about our favourite pop songs with the other definitely not gay kid.

We aren't ever really able to relax into ourselves and let our guard down, and be silly and messy like our straight peers. Whether you're out as gay or not, there's too much at stake. So maybe this is why, once you're a gay adult surrounded by other gay adults, there's a hedonistic drive to reclaim some of that lost youth and make up for the time when we were most likely the only or one of the few LGBTQ+ people in our friendship group.

So nightclubs and after-parties become our playground. Finally we can choose the fancy dress costumes we want, and maybe drugs, alcohol, sex are our toys. We deserve to have some childish, irresponsible fun and this could be true, we do. But when we're still going out and getting fucked up every weekend at thirty, at forty, at fifty even . . . maybe it's not fun any more. Maybe it's serious.

WHAT IS CHEMSEX?

Chemsex refers to the use of drugs (such as crystal methamphetamine, mephedrone or GHB 'G') to enhance sexual activity, often in the context of gay and bisexual men's communities. It is sometimes associated with prolonged and uninhibited sexual encounters, often occurring in group settings like sex parties, which commonly happen after a night out, once the clubs have closed, to keep the party going. Chemsex can pose serious health risks, including addiction, mental health issues and the transmission of sexually transmitted infections such as HIV.

I've always had an aversion to drugs. I don't like how they change people, how unpredictable and off-kilter they become. Plus, if you've ever been trapped chatting to someone on cocaine at a party, you'll know how self-absorbed and boring the interaction is. I have wondered if I've closed myself off to some queer euphoria by never fully letting go or getting swept up in the hedonism of the moment. But honestly, I'm just so happy and at peace with who I am, I've never felt the need to lose myself. I guess I worry I might never come back!

Partying has been pivotal to some people's journeys to becoming their fully actualized, best queer selves. And I'm keen to learn more about this, so I speak with Glyn Fussell again, the man behind Sink The Pink, who we spoke to about the difference between being a gay man and queer in Chapter 3. I ask Glyn to tell me why queer partying has been so important to him.

Glyn says: 'I had always felt deeply threatened, deeply insecure about gay clubbing. I totally understand Stu's fears. Growing up I would feel more akin to my lesbian friends, because I'm someone that needs to emotionally connect with people. I used to go out on the gay scene and I would either feel very judged, I felt like I wasn't butch enough, or I wasn't femme enough, or I wasn't *fashion* enough. It was really only in discovering the queer world, which is full of all kinds of social misfits and broken biscuits, when I went, *fuck me, we finally found this place.* It's church. It's like the church for queerness. We're the raggedy dolls, the ones that didn't quite fit in. The great thing about queerness is that you find solidarity in your difference. With Sink The Pink there was a childlike quality to it, with us doing poppers and being wild and chucking things around the room.'

There's that word again: childlike.

Parties like Glyn's Mighty Hoopla – a pop festival 'with freedom and expression at its heart' – aim to bring our community together and are a place where all manner of LGBTQIA+ identities mingle. And it works and it's fabulous because maybe there's less time for analyzing and deconstructing and comparing ourselves to each other when we're all just dancing.

Why are there no lesbian bars?

When I first came out there were about five or six lesbian bars that I would frequent. But over the past twenty years each one has closed down. I ask Glyn why he thinks this is. 'In the same way that white straight men come in and they absolutely bulldoze, gaslight and take over everything, they claim it's their own, they say they invented it – the gay white male has done the same thing. When I arrived in London in 1999, there were lesbian clubs. And there was a way bigger lesbian presence. And, slowly but surely, I felt like lesbians waved their white flag and went, *Fuck this. This is too frenzied. We can't keep up.'*

There might not be many bricks-and-mortar lesbian venues any more, but there are thriving club nights. These events feel more about fun and community than fucking.

I spoke to the lesbian DJ Michelle Manetti about the comparative lack of lesbian nightlife and its less pivotal role in our queer culture compared to our gay male friends.

We're a similar age, and we lament the loss of places like Vesper Lounge where you could play pool all night or The Oak Bar, a dykey pub in north London. But Michelle is excited by what's on offer for queer women now. She says, 'The wonderful thing about the clubbing scene at the moment is that we do have these beautiful pockets of really niche parties where you can go to something that fits you.'

I ask her why partying is so important for the queer community. She muses for a second, then says, 'I think it is very much a way for people to escape from themselves and find themselves. I know for myself, like when I first started going clubbing and when I first started experimenting with drugs, which was quite early, sort of like fourteen, fifteen. It was a way, weirdly, for me to actually connect with myself, even though I was disconnecting. The euphoria that I felt when I was taking these drugs in these spaces made me feel like a real person and made me feel like I understood where I fit in and belonged.'

Can we find a sense of belonging on a dancefloor?

Cassie Leon helps run The Cocoa Butter Club, a cabaret collective that platforms queer performers of colour, redressing the UK performing art scene's lack of representation among BIPOC and LGBTQIA+ individuals, and those of marginalized genders.

We talk over Zoom about all the brilliantly specific nights for different queer cultures around the UK, and she tells me, 'I don't think it's a problem until those spaces become exclusionary. So there's definitely space for people who want to go out and wear leather. Then there's G-A-Y, where you go to sing Ariana Grande all night. Great. And then you have Black-centred parties that are not saying nobody else can come. They're saying, *we actually don't want to sing Britney all night.* It's a much more Caribbean vibe that's happening there. It's music we were brought up on. Those spaces are really necessary.'

Cassie tells me that when she's running nights aimed at queer Black people, she will often have to go out into the crowd to make sure that she can move the Black and brown people who are trying to get into their specific night to the front, 'because otherwise the crowd becomes taken over by white bodies. And then they do things like they'll be listening to our music and our DJs for a while, but then they'll come up to the DJ and say, *Oh, could I request some Britney or some Shakira?* And no, sorry, but you can't, because this night is specifically about The Cocoa Butter Club and what we listen to. So if you want to request Dua Lipa, that's fine, but it's not going to happen on this night.'

On the subject of belonging, let's pick up the chat I was having with Flora, the trans woman I met at the FLINTA night in Dalston. I ask her how she feels being out and proud on the dancefloor at a night like Fèmmme Fraîche, or Queer House Party, which are, I think, such fun safe spaces for all of us. She says, 'The euphoria I feel in the rave is deliciously sweet. Unhinged, deranged joy that's tricky to reduce to words. Best simply to experience it and ascend.'

God, I love that. It makes me want to go out immediately, and it's a rainy Monday night.

I understand better now why partying is so important for queer people. I see the appeal of feeling part of something bigger than yourself and the freedom that clubbing offers. Drugs help some people lose themselves, others find themselves, but there's a point at which it becomes a dangerous panacea for shame and social anxiety. I've loved staying up past my bedtime and pushing myself to have more fun. I've certainly broadened my friendship group by doing so.

Being a parent to a young child dominates so much of my life at the moment, and if I didn't make the effort to embrace queer nightlife, my day-to-day and cultural life would be very hetero! I hope to go *out* out on the queer scene with Stu one day soon, as I'd love to bear witness to his nightlife epiphany, and the euphoria that comes from finding your people, your music, your playground.

Chapter 16

Is That All There Is?

Lotte and Stu

How can we possibly sum up the wild ride into queerness we've just been on? As we've discovered, sometimes there just aren't the words to express the expansiveness of an experience or idea. It's been messy, challenging, triggering, joyful, tragic, mind-opening and a whole lot of chaotic fun. We started this book at one kind of party, and we've ended up at a very different one, where we have expanded our guest list beyond our cis gay mate Andrew, who is still very much welcome with his twunky friends, of course.

Something we've both really taken away from this experience is that there is no 'us' and 'them' when it comes to our community. No one person's queerness is more or less valid than another's. There's no rulebook or criteria you have to meet to be officially 'One of Us'. But to be truly open-minded and empathetic as allies within our own ranks we must accept that there is something beyond the specificity of our identity that unites us. The eighteen-year-old otters (keep up!), lesbian mums, eighty-year-old queens, Christian non-binary bods, the single bisexual from Hebden Bridge, the non-monogamous trans women, different races, different classes and backgrounds – there is a magical thread that connects us all. Unravelling this is heart-expanding and beautiful. We contain multitudes and understanding this is the only way that we will survive the challenges of the next decade and beyond.

In our evolution of queerness we are now reaching out beyond the bars and clubs we have historically frequented to form book clubs, sporting teams, knitting circles, religious get-togethers and cultural gatherings. Hopefully these multi-generational, multi-background, multi-faith, multi-everything groups will take our community to the next level of unification over the coming years, and we can better strengthen our relationships with each other. Perhaps it is time to rethink our definition of a queer space beyond a venue that serves vodka sodas in plastic cups with a drag queen sparkling in the corner? As important and fun as that is, our community is so much more.

MJ Barker, who we spoke to in Chapter 1, gave us some wonderful final thoughts about queerness that we have been saving up to share here, in our last chapter. MJ says:

> *If we take queer to mean being in any way outside of the cishet norm, then my sense is that everyone is eventually queered by life. However hard we try we cannot maintain the kind of gendered appearance, happy romantic relationship and hot sex, required by the cishet norm, nor can everyone meet every stage of the successful cishet life (e.g., meeting someone at the 'right time', buying property together, having children, doing well at work, retiring, etc.). We might think of moments like discovering we can't, or don't want to, have children, of relationship break-down or divorce, or of menopause or becoming disabled, as moments of being queered by life.*
>
> *I find this useful because, again, it reminds us that the narrow idea of what it is to be normal is bad for everybody: those who can't (or don't want to) fit within it, and those who do attempt to fit within it. Instead of pitching straight against queer, or cis*

against trans, we might all turn towards these rigid cultural ideas that hurt everyone, and try to shift them for the betterment of all.

We've realized over the last fifteen chapters that maybe we've worked so hard to prove that we are just like straight people, we can get married, have children and be upstanding members of society. that we're in danger of creating a new kind of homonormativity and, yikes – that's the last thing we need. Some of us want this kind of life and some of us are running as far from it as we can get, and that's a good thing. It's so important that we continue to challenge and defy the traditions and expectations that our cishet friends are up against when it comes to what makes a good, a happy or a successful life.

For this book it was always going to be impossible for us to cover everything about queer life, love and culture today, but believe us, we've tried. Early drafts of *Don't Ask, Don't Tell* ran at hundreds of thousands of words, much to our editor's dismay. We've had to cut a lot, and as much as it pained us to do so, every person we've met and every place we've been have informed our understanding – and we're so grateful for that.

Are we queerer than we were when we started this endeavour? Maybe. We've certainly opened our eyes to the diverse intersections within the LGBTQIA+ community. And yes, we have been changed by what we discovered.

I, Lotte, have really gained the confidence to explore my gender and sexuality in a way I haven't dared over the last twenty years. Meeting so many trans and non-binary people has helped me recognize that I don't need permission to think about myself differently. I don't need to pass a test or prove myself, I can just keep quietly evolving in my selfhood, and isn't that cool?! One of the quotes that I encountered during writing this book that has stayed with me most is from the queer theorist Juan Carlos Pérez Jiménez. Maybe it stood out for you too. It was, and I paraphrase, 'Queerness is always the horizon, never the shore.' To me this means we are constantly seeking, travelling, becoming. We move. We don't need to arrive. That for me has been hugely freeing in my own thinking and understanding of myself as queer.

I've also rediscovered the joy of queer partying and realized that there are nights out there for me, places where I can look and feel myself and experience the thrill of belonging. Thankfully we've found a great new babysitter – a queer non-binary person no less! So I can bring my wife along on these nightlife extravaganzas, though the 6am wake-ups the next day mean we're certainly not partying as much as our child-free queer friends.

I, Stu, am asking myself if I still feel like a basic vanilla gay after throwing myself so deeply into more facets of queer life. Maybe I do (now with a dash of sprinkles), but what I've also discovered is that's OK. There is no one way to be a gay man. Just because I've never sucked someone off in a dark room, or found myself on a ketamine high on the dancefloor, or even laid around on a beach with a gaggle of fellow bestie gays, does not make me less part of the community. I define *my* gayness in the same way anyone can define how they want to identify. We are so varied in so many ways, and that's what makes us us. I've faced a few fears, learned new things and potentially started a journey of faith beyond Kylie. I've enjoyed listening to other people's experiences, leaned into stereotypes and smashed down a few preconceptions that I may have had. I've always been proud to be queer, but that pride has started to glow just a little bit brighter.

There is a long way to go before we can all better understand other people's lived experiences, and it takes more than a book to do that – it's a lifetime of learning. But for us, writing *Do Ask, Do Tell* has been a start and we hope you have felt the same.

We've heard from people who in their own way feel 'othered' from the atypical gay experience and we're excited to continue these conversations. Perhaps you feel we've not represented you in this book, and if so, we want to hear from you. This is us asking, do tell us your story.

When we think of the world that our own children, who at the time of writing are all under the age of ten, will grow up in, we can't help but feel hopeful. Despite the many steps backwards we are seeing, particularly in terms of trans rights and the growing paranoia about LGBTQ+ people's influence, ideologically Gen Alpha (our kids) are so much more evolved than we ever were. Words like trans and non-binary are normalized for them, they're going to read books about different kinds of people, families and life experiences and will see these reflected on TV and in films, too, in a way that we never did. Having queer parents might not make children gay, but surely it'll make them great friends to, and supporters of, the community. This will hopefully create a ripple effect where every person they connect with throughout their lives will learn from their LGBTQ+ understanding until the ripple becomes a deluge of love, acceptance and understanding among swathes of the population. Wishful thinking? Maybe, but if being queer has taught us anything, it's that our fabulous fantasies have a power to create real change.

If we are all queered by life, then us queers sure know how to live.

Glossary

AFAB (Assigned Female at Birth): A person who was categorized as female when born, based on biological characteristics. However, their gender identity may not necessarily align with this assignment.

AIDS (Acquired Immunodeficiency Syndrome): A chronic, potentially life-threatening condition caused by the HIV virus. It severely weakens the immune system, making it harder for the body to fight infections and diseases.

AIDS epidemic: Refers to the period during the late twentieth century when AIDS became widespread, particularly among the gay male population, which was associated with immense fear, stigma and loss for the LGBTQ+ community.

AMAB (Assigned Male at Birth): A person who was categorized as male when born, based on biological characteristics. However, their gender identity may not necessarily align with this assignment.

Amyl nitrate (poppers): A chemical inhalant used recreationally, especially within LGBTQ+ communities, to enhance sexual pleasure by relaxing muscles, often during anal sex. Poppers can also cause short-lived feelings of euphoria or dizziness.

Autosexuality: Finding oneself sexually attractive.

BDSM (Bondage, Discipline/Dominance, Sadism, Masochism): A variety of erotic practices involving consensual power exchanges, pain and control, ranging from playful activities to more intense experiences.

Bear: A term used in the gay community to describe a larger, often hairier man with a more rugged appearance; part of a subculture celebrating body diversity and masculinity.

Bisexual erasure: The tendency to ignore or dismiss bisexuality as a valid sexual orientation, often assuming that someone is either gay or straight.

Body dysmorphia: An obsessive focus on perceived flaws in appearance, leading to distress and impairment in daily life.

Bottom: The receptive partner in sexual acts.

Chemsex: The use of specific drugs (e.g., crystal meth, mephedrone, GHB) to facilitate extended sexual sessions, commonly associated with the LGBTQ+ community, particularly among gay and bisexual men.

Chosen family: Close, supportive relationships in LGBTQ+ communities with friends, mentors, or partners that often replace biological family ties.

Cisgender (cis): A person whose gender identity aligns with the sex they were assigned at birth.

Cishet norm: The cultural expectation that people are both cisgender and heterosexual, marginalizing those who don't fit into it.

Cottaging: British slang for anonymous sexual activity between men in public restrooms, often conducted in secret due to legal or societal prohibitions.

Dark room: A space, usually in a nightclub or gay bar, where people engage in anonymous sexual encounters in the dark.

Deadname: The birth name of a transgender person who has chosen a new name after transitioning. Referring to someone by their deadname is considered disrespectful.

Diesel dyke: A traditionally masculine-presenting butch lesbian who works in masculine professions like construction or trucking.

Drag king: A performer, often female or non-binary, who dresses in exaggerated masculine attire for entertainment, parody or art.

Drag queen: A performer, often male or non-binary, who dresses in exaggerated feminine attire for entertainment, parody or art.

Elite controllers: Rare individuals who are HIV-positive but naturally suppress their viral load without needing antiretroviral therapy.

Facial Feminization Surgery (FFS): A set of surgical procedures to alter typically masculine facial features to make them more feminine.

Fem/Femme: A person who identifies with or embodies traits traditionally associated with femininity.

FLINTA: An acronym for female, lesbian, intersex, non-binary, trans and agender individuals, used to describe inclusive and safe spaces for marginalized gender identities.

Gender dysphoria: The psychological distress experienced when a person's gender identity does not align with their assigned sex at birth.

Glory hole: A hole in a partition used for anonymous sexual acts, typically in public spaces.

Golden Retriever lesbian: A masc-leaning, friendly and cheerful lesbian who is often eager to please.

Grindr: A location-based dating app primarily used by gay, bisexual and queer men for casual meetups and hookups.

Heteronormativity: The societal assumption or belief that heterosexuality is the default, normal or preferred sexual orientation. Heteronormativity can be present in cultural practices, media representations, legal systems and everyday interactions, shaping the way people think about sexuality and relationships, often to the exclusion or detriment of LGBTQ+ identities.

HIV (Human Immunodeficiency Virus): A virus that attacks the immune system, which, if untreated, can lead to AIDS.

Homonormativity: The assimilation of LGBTQ+ individuals into heterosexual norms, particularly around marriage and family life, often at the expense of queer diversity.

Internalized homophobia/transphobia: When LGBTQ+ individuals internalize negative societal attitudes, leading to self-hatred or shame.

Intersectionality: A framework for understanding how different aspects of a person's identity, such as race, gender and sexuality, intersect and create overlapping systems of oppression or privilege.

Lithsexuality: Experiencing sexual attraction but not desiring reciprocation or a relationship.

Minority stress: Chronic stress experienced by members of stigmatized minority groups due to prejudice, discrimination or social exclusion.

Molly houses: Underground meeting places for gay men in eighteenth- and nineteenth-century England, providing community and sexual freedom despite persecution.

Monogamy: A relationship structure in which two partners are romantically and sexually exclusive to one another.

Neurotypical: Describes people whose neurological development and functioning are considered 'typical'.

Non-binary (NB or enby): A gender identity that doesn't fit within the traditional categories of male or female.

Otters: A gay slang term for a man who is thinner than a bear but still has body hair, typically younger and smaller than bears.

Passing: The ability of a transgender person to be perceived by others as their affirmed gender.

Pillow princess: A lesbian who prefers to receive rather than give during sexual encounters.

Polyamory: The practice of engaging in multiple romantic (and sometimes sexual) relationships with the consent and knowledge of everyone involved.

Poppers: See amyl nitrate.

Power bottom: A receptive partner in sexual acts, who is active and assertive during the encounter.

PrEP (Pre-Exposure Prophylaxis): A medication taken by HIV-negative individuals to prevent HIV infection.

RuPaul's Drag Race: A reality TV competition where drag queens from around the world compete to become the next drag superstar.

Scissoring: A sexual position where two partners interlock their legs and rub their vulvas together.

Sexual fluidity: The idea that an individual's sexual orientation or attraction may change over time.

Sides: Gay men who prefer not to engage in penetrative anal sex but enjoy other forms of sexual intimacy.

Soft butch: A butch lesbian who presents masculinely but embraces some traditionally feminine traits.

Stone butch: A butch lesbian who does not prefer to receive sexual touch but enjoys giving and often presents masculinely.

TERF (Trans-Exclusionary Radical Feminist): A feminist who excludes transgender women from their understanding of womanhood and feminism.

They/them: The most common gender-neutral pronouns used by non-binary or genderqueer individuals.

Top: The active or dominant partner during sex.

Touch me not (TMN): A term used by Black lesbians or studs to describe someone who enjoys giving sexual pleasure but does not want to receive it.

Tribbing: The sexual act of two women rubbing their genitals together, also known as scissoring.

Twunk: A muscular version of a twink (a young, slim gay man).

Undetectable Equals Untransmittable (U=U): A public health campaign spreading awareness that people living with HIV who are on effective treatment and have an undetectable viral load cannot transmit the virus.

Vanilla: A term to describe conventional or traditional sexual preferences, without elements of kink or BDSM.

Vers (Versatile): Someone who switches between being the top and bottom during sex.

Resources

General LGBTQ+ Support

- **LGBT Foundation**: Offers advice, support and information for LGBTQ+ individuals.
  https://lgbt.foundation

- **Switchboard LGBTQIA+ Helpline**: Provides a listening service offering support and information.
  https://switchboard.lgbt

Mental Health Support

- **MindOut**: A mental health service run by and for LGBTQ+ people, offering support, advice and information.
  https://mindout.org.uk

- **MindLine Trans+**: A confidential emotional and mental health support helpline for people identifying as transgender, agender, gender fluid or non-binary.
  https://www.consortium.lgbt/member-directory/mindline-
      trans

Sexual Health

- **LGBT HERO**: Provides information and support on sexual health, including resources on HIV and sexually transmitted infections (STIs).
  lgbthero.org.uk

Gender Support

- **Mermaids**: Supports gender-diverse young people aged 19 and under, along with their families and carers. Offers a helpline and webchat services.
  https://mermaidsuk.org.uk

- **Gendered Intelligence**: Runs youth groups in London and Leeds for trans, non-binary and questioning young people, as well as a peer-led support group in London for individuals aged 18 to 30.
  https://genderedintelligence.co.uk

Eating Disorders

- **Beat**: The UK's leading charity supporting those affected by eating disorders. They offer resources specifically addressing the unique challenges faced by LGBTQ+ individuals.
  beateatingdisorders.org.uk

Drug and Alcohol Misuse

- **Antidote at London Friend**: Provides information and support exclusively to LGBTQ+ individuals around drugs and alcohol.
  https://londonfriend.org.uk

- **LGBTQ+ Rehab at UK Addiction Treatment Centres**: Provides information and support exclusively to LGBTQ+ individuals around drugs and alcohol.
  https://www.ukat.co.uk/rehab-treatment/lgbt

Muslim LGBTQ+ Support

- **Hidayah**: A nationwide organization supporting LGBTQI+ Muslims. They run social and support groups in various UK cities, including Manchester, London, Newcastle, Glasgow and Leeds.
  consortium.lgbt

- **Imaan**: Established in 1999, Imaan is a social support group for LGBTQ+ Muslims, their families, friends and supporters. They offer monthly meetings in London, providing a safe environment for discussions and support. imaanlondon.wordpress.com

- **Naz and Matt Foundation**: This foundation works to tackle homophobia triggered by religious and cultural beliefs. They offer support to LGBTQ+ individuals seeking acceptance within their communities and families. nazandmattfoundation.org

Catholic LGBTQ+ Support

- **Quest**: A group for LGBT+ Catholics offering support and resources.
  https://questlgbti.uk

Jewish LGBTQ+ Support

- **KeshetUK**: An education and training charity supporting Jewish LGBT+ individuals and their families, promoting inclusion within Jewish life.
  https://www.keshetuk.org

Christian LGBTQ+ Support

- **OneBodyOneFaith**: A dynamic grassroots charity that enables LGBT+ Christians and advocates for change within the church, working ecumenically and in partnership with like-minded organizations.
  onebodyonefaith.org.uk

- **House of Rainbow**: A fellowship for LGBTIQ+ individuals, particularly those from Black, Asian, and Minority Ethnic (BAME) backgrounds, offering Christian support and community.
  https://www.houseofrainbow.org

Acknowledgements

Huge thanks to all of our contributors for sharing their stories with us. Particular thanks to those we spoke to for research whose quotes may not be in the final text but whose input has helped shape the book you hold in your hands now. Thank you Luke Day, Finnbar Love, Kabir Khurana, Charley Beal from the Gilbert Baker Foundation, Mark Fletcher and James Alison. Thank you to Sheldon Larry and the team at the Tom of Finland Foundation in LA. Thanks to all our queer friends and family for discussing these themes with us. Lotte would also like to thank the students and tutors at Regent's University for their enlightening discussions and input into the themes explored in this book.

Jodie Lancet-Grant, you've been an incredible supporter from the very start and we are so grateful that you gave us this opportunity and that you are committed to publishing a powerful portfolio of LGBTQ+ authors at Bluebird.

Thanks to Sian Gardiner, Maya Conway, Amy Winchester, Katy Denny and the entire Bluebird staff. You are a dream team.

Abigail Bergrstom, big love to you for your gentle steering of us through the ups and downs of writing this book and your support throughout.

Where to even begin when it comes to thanking our respective partners? Jenny and John have been by our sides throughout – and to our children who we hope will one day read this book and think how things have changed for the better. Thank you all – we love you.

And thanks to every ally who may have picked this book up at a library or bookshop and decided to take a leap into queerness with us.

Finally, I, Stu, want to thank Lotte. I've had some serious ups and downs while writing this book including self-doubt and a fair dose of self-loathing. You put up with a lot from me and thank you for being a good friend and helping me get back on track. I love you and I'm proud of the book we've created together.

Thank you Stu for being my work wife and dear friend. We've learned so much on this big queer rollercoaster together and I love having you by my side.

Endnotes

Chapter 1

1   https://www.stonewall.org.uk/system/files/lgbt_in_britain_
bi.pdf

Chapter 3

1   https://www.urbandictionary.com/define.php?term=collective%20
noun%20for%20lesbians

2   https://www.thepinknews.com/2024/05/20/what-is-a-black-cat-
lesbian-everything-you-need-to-know/#

3   https://www.them.us/story/what-does-sapphic-mean

4   https://www.thebody.com/article/jacquie-bishop-black-lesbian-
health-care-worker-early-aids-epidemic

5   'Why Don't Gays and Lesbians Get Along Better: https://www.
out.com/entertainment/michael-musto/2014/06/30/
why-don%E2%80%99t-gays-and-lesbians-get-along-better
https://www.nbcnews.com/feature/nbc-out/lesbians-more-
accepted-gay-men-around-world-study-finds-n1118121
https://www.bowiecreators.com/article/lesbians-and-gays-a-one-
way-alliance

Chapter 4

1   https://www.theguardian.com/commentisfree/2021/jun/27/
the-observer-view-on-the-right-to-free-expression

Chapter 5

1   www.them.us/story/living-stealth-as-trans-visibility-passing-essay

2   https://www.bps.org.uk/research-digest/eating-disorder-rates-vary-among-different-groups-transgender-and-gender-diverse

Chapter 9

1   2018 Stonewall Mental Health Report https://www.stonewall.org.uk/resources/lgbt-britain-health-2018

2   2012 Stonewall Mental Health Report

3   https://www.justlikeus.org/blog/2021/11/25/lgbt-young-people-twice-likely-suicide/

4   www.thebraincharity.org.uk/lgbtqia-neurodiversity-neurodivergent-lgbtq/

Mental Health Issues:

https://www.nhs.uk/mental-health/advice-for-life-situations-and-events/mental-health-support-if-you-are-gay-lesbian-bisexual-lgbtq/

https://www.mentalhealth.org.uk/explore-mental-health/statistics/lgbtiq-people-statistics

https://www.mind.org.uk/information-support/tips-for-everyday-living/lgbtqia-mental-health/trans-and-non-binary-mental-health/

https://bmcpsychiatry.biomedcentral.com/articles/10.1186/s12888-023-05202-z#:~:text=Minority%20stress%20theory&text=This%20theory%20posits%20that%20sexual,concealment%20%5B4%2C%205%5D.

Chapter 11

1   The CDC (the US Center for Disease Control) reports

2   https://www.aidsmap.com/news/jul-2022/nationwide-australian-data-shows-prep-has-largely-neutral-effect-sti-incidence

3   www.tht.org.uk/news/heterosexual-hiv-diagnoses-overtake-those-gay-men-first-time-decade

4   HIV Sperm Donation Laws – www.gov.uk/government/news/people-with-hiv-can-now-donate-eggs-or-sperm-to-start-a-family#:~:text=Under%20current%20rules%20on%20in,(shared%20motherhood)%20IVF%20treatment

5   https://www.gov.uk/government/news/people-with-hiv-can-now-donate-eggs-or-sperm-to-start-a-family

Chapter 12

1   'Shaping Attitudes about Homosexuality: The role of religion and cultural context', Amy Adamcysk – https://www.sciencedirect.com/science/article/abs/pii/S0049089X09000039

2   https://assets.publishing.service.gov.uk/government/uploads/system/uploads/attachment_data/file/721704/LGBT-survey-research-report.pdf

3   www.gov.uk/government/speeches/the-kings-speech-2024

4   www.christian.org.uk/news/conversion-therapy-ban-included-in-kings-speech/

5   www.bacp.co.uk/events-and-resources/ethics-and-standards/mou/;
     https://5pillarsuk.com/2022/02/23/over-250-muslim-leaders-express-concern-over-lgbtq-conversion-therapy-ban/

6   https://metro.co.uk/2022/06/06/i-wont-ever-be-able-to-come-out-ive-made-peace-with-that-16741855/

Chapter 14

1   www.vanityfair.com/style/2023/07/love-liberty-and-the-pursuit-of-polyamory

https://www.theguardian.com/lifeandstyle/2022/may/22/what-if-he-finds-someone-better-the-agony-and-the-ecstacy-of-an-open-relationship